W9-BFG-149

THE BURNING OF WASHINGTON

THE

BURNING OF

THE BRITISH INVASION OF 1814

Anthony S. Pitch

BLUEJACKET BOOKS

Naval Institute Press
Annapolis, Maryland

Naval Institute Press
291 Wood Road
Annapolis, MD 21402

© 1998 by Anthony S. Pitch
All rights reserved. No part of this book may be reproduced or uti-
lized in any form or by any means, electronic or mechanical, including photocopying and recording, or by any information storage and
retrieval system, without permission in writing from the publisher.

First Bluejacket Books printing, 2000
ISBN 1-55750-425-3
ISBN-13: 978-1-55750-425-8
The Library of Congress has cataloged the hardcover edition as follows:
Pitch, Anthony.
    The burning of Washington : the British invasion of 1814 /
Anthony S. Pitch.
      p.   cm.
    Includes bibliographical references (p. 273) and index.
    ISBN 1-55750-692-2 (acid-free paper)
    1. Washington (D.C.)—History—Capture by the British, 1814.
I. Title.
E356.W3P49   1998
973.5'23—dc21   98-13805

Printed in the United States of America on acid-free paper ♾

16 15 14 13 12   16 15 14 13 12

For Marion, Michael, and Nomi

Contents

Preface

I slipped naturally into an early feel for history by growing up in the precincts of Canterbury Cathedral while boarding at the oldest school in England, The King's School, Canterbury. History's embrace was always snug and warm and has offered much understanding of the human odyssey. But it was never so full of delights and surprises until I began researching this book. Every rare document brought to light matched the thrill of discovering ancient coins from a millennium and a half earlier when I used to explore the Mediterranean shore at Caesarea. This book has been a treasure hunt from beginning to end, and many were the times when I wanted to shatter the silence of research libraries and shout for the joy of discovery.

For the last two decades I have lived just twenty miles north of the White House and often wondered what it must have been like to witness the burning of Washington by the British in 1814. Seizing the nation's capital and burning the President's House, the Capitol, and most of the public buildings seemed so bold and wanton, but also savage and unforgivable. It had to rank among the most dramatic events in American history. Perhaps the story is not well known because it is a painful reminder of a humiliating episode. But I kept wondering how the residents felt at the loss of landmarks that had taken years to erect and beautify. And I wanted to know how they had conducted themselves, and whether they fled in terror, just as history's streams of refugees have tried to escape other cities about to be overrun.

Halfhearted attempts to locate nineteenth-century literature on the subject petered out as there were so few books available. Naively, I assumed this had to be because so little information had survived. But by the summer of 1992 I was yearning to write another book and I began to feel my way around the archival treasure houses almost at my doorstep. For a researcher and writer, it is sheer paradise living within commuting distance of the Library of Congress, the National Archives, the U.S. Senate Library, and the Washingtoniana Division of the District of Columbia Library. I was in and out of these repositories so often over a period of five years, often between appointments or during lunch hours, that each of them became a home away from home.

It was breathtaking to touch letters and journals dating back to the early years of the nineteenth century. They were the visible link to the past and the tangible proof of its happenings. One day, in the Rare Book and Special Collections Division of the Library of Congress, I remember feeling boyishly excited as I wore the mandatory white gloves to handle the very book stolen from the U.S. Capitol as a souvenir by Adm. George Cockburn, at the moment that British troops set fire to the building. The sheepskin-bound book, inscribed in his hand as a memento of his presence in Washington on that fateful day, was donated to the Library of Congress in 1940 by Dr. A. S. W. Rosenbach, noted collector and dealer in rare books and manuscripts. A few years later I was gleefully impatient as Rex Scouten, White House Curator, led me to the Map Room to see and touch the small wooden medicine chest taken as a souvenir by a British sailor just before the mansion burned, and returned by his Canadian grandson in 1939.

My research on both sides of the Atlantic yielded much that is new and unpublished. What had begun with a few queries became a joyful obsession, and my tale is enlarged to cover not only events surrounding the burning of Washington but also a campaign that evolved into the bombardment of Fort McHenry and the final clash at New Orleans.

In chapter 16 the word *shell* is used to describe explosive British metal cannonballs fired at Fort McHenry. It was the term used in British ships' logs and in the official report by the American commander of Fort McHenry. By contrast, the defenders used nonexplosive, solid shot balls.

Acknowledgments

My wife, Marion, and my children, Michael and Nomi, endured long
stretches of neglect during the five years it took to research and write this
book. My hope is that the quality of the work may be found somewhat
deserving of their limitless understanding and patience.

Dr. Donald Ritchie, Associate Historian, U.S. Senate, gave help and
encouragement from the moment I told him I was thinking of writing this
book. I benefited in countless ways on multiple occasions from his long
experience, fine scholarship, and wise judgment in suggestions for improv-
ing the manuscript.

Rex Scouten, White House Curator, honored me with a private tour of
rooms off-limits to the general public, especially to see the scorch marks
still visible from the fire of 24 August 1814 on the stone archway leading
into the kitchens below the north portico. I cherish acquaintance with this
gentleman of the old school, since retired, described by one White House
correspondent as "a prince of a man." He also read through the manuscript, offering sound advice and encouragement. His successor, Betty C.
Monkman, was marvelously quick in responding to requests for articles
on the early furnishings of the President's House and for the typescript
copy of Lord Francis Jeffrey's Diary.

A chance meeting with Austin Kiplinger, president of Tudor Place
Foundation, which is charged with preserving the ancestral Georgetown
estate of Martha Washington's granddaughter, Martha Custis Peter, led to
his invitation to view the Kiplinger Washington Collection of more than
six thousand works of art relating to Washington, D.C., and was followed

by his kind permission to select and reproduce some of the illustrations for this book, including the front cover. Cindy Janke, curator, was warmly enthusiastic in guiding me through parts of this astonishing collection that is nothing short of a national treasure.

Scott S. Sheads, one of the nation's leading authorities on the Fort McHenry National Monument and Historic Shrine, where he is a Ranger/Historian, offered insightful comments after reading the manuscript and gave unstintingly of his time in providing copies of documents requested, or which he believed might be useful. My thanks also to John W. Tyler, Superintendent of the fort.

Research was made quicker and easier through the frequent personal attention of Greg Harness, head Reference Librarian, U.S. Senate Library, and Matthew B. Gilmore, Reference Librarian, Washingtoniana Division, District of Columbia Public Library. I am filled with admiration for their rare familiarity with obscure resources. I spent countless hours in the Washingtoniana Division scrolling microfilm of the nation's first daily newspaper, the *National Intelligencer*, its vigorous editorial opponent, the *Federal Republican*, the indispensable *Niles' Weekly Register*, and the library's microcopies of the National Archives' Record Group 42 relating to proceedings and correspondence of the District of Columbia's earliest commissioners. Roxanna Deane, chief of this invaluable division, was unfailingly helpful over the years.

This book relies heavily on primary sources, and the bulk of research was done in the Manuscripts Division of the Library of Congress, where staff also helped decipher nineteenth-century handwritten scrawl. My grateful thanks to Mary Wolfskill, head of the manuscript reading room, and to Reference Librarians Fred Bauman, Ernest Emrich, Jeff Flannery, Mike Klein, and Katie McDonough. John J. McDonough, Manuscript Historian, even loaned me his personal copy of the doctoral dissertation by Dr. Marilyn Parr, with its anthology of hilarious letters by the British diplomat Augustus John Foster. Clark Evans, Senior Reference Librarian, Rare Book and Special Collections Division, Library of Congress, was most helpful whenever called upon.

I am deeply indebted to staff at the National Archives, particularly Rebecca Livingston, Archivist, and Rod Ross, the latter an Archivist with the Center for Legislative Archives, for plucking dusty files from sheltered safekeeping. Hon. Donnald K. Anderson, then Clerk, House of Representatives, kindly permitted access to papers in the National Archives relating to the Thirteenth Congress and the congressional inquiry into the burning of Washington.

My talented multilingual wife, Marion, translated correspondence of French Minister Louis Serurier in Washington to Prince Talleyrand in Paris. Professor Roberto Severino of the Italian Department, School of Languages and Linguistics, Georgetown University, translated passages from the Diary of Giovanni Grassi, President of Georgetown College.

Though I pride myself on having found documentary proof for The National Society of The Colonial Dames of America that Dolley Madison sought sanctuary at the Georgetown building they now occupy as their national headquarters, they more than returned the favor by making available unpublished correspondence of the Morris and Nourse families from their Dumbarton House Collection. Special thanks are due to Nancy Edelman, Curator of Education, History and Research, Jeannette Markell Harper, Manuscript Librarian, Laura Belman, a descendant of Commodore Joshua Barney, and Judy Frank, the last of whom alerted me to the Pulteney Malcolm Papers at the William L. Clements Library, University of Michigan.

Early in my research I was given an extraordinary private tour to the oldest parts of the U.S. Capitol by William C. Allen, preeminent architectural historian at the Office of the Architect of the Capitol. Later, with the gracious permission of then House Speaker, Hon. Tom Foley, I was taken by Edward Fogle, Architectural Draftsman, Office of the Architect of the Capitol, through a trapdoor in an area closed to the public, to see a staircase which survived the fire of 1814.

Mayor Ann Ferguson of Riverdale, Maryland, guided me around Riversdale, the restored plantation home of George and Rosalie Calvert, close to the battlefield at Bladensburg.

Diane K. Skvarla, Curator, and Scott M. Strong, Administrator, Office of the U.S. Senate Curator, made available the unedited Papers of Isaac Bassett, and steered me to research material relating to the building of the U.S. Capitol.

Officials at all state, county, and local libraries were highly efficient and readily available. Special thanks go to Jennifer A. Bryan, Curator of Manuscripts, and Jessica M. Pigza, then Assistant Curator of Manuscripts, Maryland Historical Society Library; Susan Helmann, historian at The Maryland–National Capital Park and Planning Commission, for the loan of a copy of the diary of Col. Arthur Brooke, for which formal permission to quote extracts was later obtained from Dr. Patrick Fitzgerald, Assistant Curator, Ulster-American Folk Park, Omagh, Northern Ireland; Susan G. Pearl, research/architectural historian, also with MNCPPC, for helping define Bladensburg's geography; Nicholas Scheetz, Manuscripts Librarian, Special Collections, Georgetown University Library; Cheryl A. Chouiniere, Manuscripts Librarian, Special Collections, Gelman Library, George Washington University; Gail R. Redmann, Reference Librarian, Historical Society of Washington, D.C.; Marie Washburn, Librarian, The Historical Society of Frederick County, Maryland; John Dann, Director, Robert Cox and Rachel K. Onuf, Curators, and Catherine A. Price, Curatorial Assistant, William L. Clements Library, University of Michigan; Margaret Heilbrun, Director of the Library, Curator of Manuscripts, New York Historical Society; Peter Drummey, Librarian, Virginia Smith, Research Librarian, and Celeste Walker, Associate Editor, the Adams Papers, Massachusetts Historical Society; Michael F. Plunkett, Director of Special Collections, University of Virginia Library; Richard A. Shrader, Reference Archivist, Manuscripts Department, University of North Carolina at Chapel Hill; Linda Stanley, Manuscripts and Archives Curator, Historical Society of Pennsylvania; William R. Erwin Jr., Senior Reference Librarian, Special Collections, Duke University; Ann Toplovich, Executive Director, Tennessee Historical Society; Julia Rather, Archivist, Tennessee State Library and Archives; Joyce McMullin, Manager, Lloyd House, Alexandria; Officials at the Marine Corps History and Museums Division, Washington, D.C.; Barbara A. McMillan, Librarian, Mount Vernon Ladies Association; Lynn Bassanes, Archives Specialist, and Alycia Vivona, Museum Specialist, Franklin D. Roosevelt Library, Hyde Park, New York; Amy Begg, Reference Librarian, National Museum of American History, Washington, D.C.; The History Factory, Chantilly, Virginia; Suzanne Rosenblum, then Curator of Education, The Octagon, Washington, D.C.; Anne C. Webb, Registrar/Archivist, and Leni Preston, Curator, Tudor Place Foundation; and Suzanne Levy, Virginia Room Librarian, Fairfax County, Virginia, Public Library.

My thanks are also due to Barbara Dodge, Dodge Family Association,

Lakewood, Colorado; Dr. William S. Dudley, Director, Naval Historical Center, for providing a condensed bibliography of 1814 material; Christopher T. George, Editor, *Journal of the War of 1812*, for volunteering a lead on research collections at Fort McHenry Monument and Historic Shrine; James A. Greenberg, for invaluable guidance and technical assistance on computer use; Darren Kapelus, for reading the manuscript for a possible screenplay; Eric Morsicato, Town Manager, Bladensburg, Maryland; Andrea Murphy, cultural officer, Embassy of Belgium, Washington, D.C., for papers on historic buildings in the city of Ghent; officials at the Navy Department Library, Washington, D.C.; Margaret Shannon, author/researcher, for documents and guidance on location of various church archives; Edward J. Stark, Corporate Secretary, American Security Bank, for directing me to the 1814–15 Minutes of the Bank of the Metropolis; John Washington, of Chevy Chase, Maryland, for help in tracing his fellow descendants of the extended George Washington family; and John H. Wren, Salt Lake City, Utah, for leads on the Wren family in Virginia.

Abroad, the following helped immeasurably in pinpointing, transmitting, or advising on research material: Michelle Cale, Curatorial Officer, The Royal Commission on Historical Manuscripts, London; Judithe M. Blacklaw and Timothy J. Eldridge, Ministry of Defence Whitehall Library, London; John Montgomery, Librarian, Royal United Services Institute for Defence Studies, Whitehall, London; Ian Hook, Keeper, Essex Regiment Museum, Chelmsford, England; Dr. Peter B. Boyden, Head, Department of Archives, National Army Museum, London; G. Archer Parfitt, Curator, The Shropshire Regimental Museum, Shrewsbury, England, particularly for permission to quote from the letter of Capt. John Knox in the book *The 85th King's Light Infantry*, edited by C. R. B. Barrett; Chris Weir, Senior Archivist, Nottinghamshire Archives Office; Mrs. M. M. Rowe, County Archivist, Devon, Exeter; John V. Howard, Librarian, Special Collections, Edinburgh University Library, Scotland; Mrs. Sheila Mackenzie, Manuscripts Division, National Library of Scotland, Edinburgh; Robert Parker, Music Library, The British Library, London; Officials at the British Museum's newspaper library at Colindale, London; Col. P. S. Walton, Secretary, Army Museums Ogilby Trust, Feltham, Middlesex; staff at the Public Record Office, Kew, Richmond; and Broeder Overste Georges Pieters and W. De Smet, Ghent, Belgium, for documents on the Treaty of Ghent, some of which were translated by Martine Reynders.

The Burning of Washington

1. War

A whirlwind of hate and violence spun through Baltimore with America's declaration of war against Great Britain on Thursday, 18 June 1812. Until then Baltimoreans had scornfully tolerated the antigovernment froth of newspaper publisher Alexander Contee Hanson. Now they wanted him silenced, and many wished him dead.

The final straw was Hanson's vow, forty-eight hours into war, to pound the government in print until he had won over public opinion. "Silence would be treason," he wrote bluntly in his *Federal Republican and Commercial Gazette*. Believing the war to be neither necessary nor wise, he promised to undermine the administration of James Madison with every legal means. The war had been declared rashly, "without funds, without an army, navy or adequate fortifications." It would bring destruction and iron rule, with "the prostration of civil rights and the establishment of a system of terror." Sensing himself surrounded by whooping jingoists, Hanson took on the mantle of beleaguered patriot, duty-bound by his profession to "cling to the rights of a freeman, both in act and opinion, till we sink with the liberty of our country, or sink alone."[1]

The twenty-six-year-old Hanson had all but opened a new front, positioning himself to fight a war within a war. Instantly, he ceased to be a mere nuisance or even a mouthpiece for the antiwar Federalist Party. He had become much more than a loathsome enemy. The feisty Marylander had set himself up as an open target. It was a perilous move in a city so blinded by war fever that few cared much about freedom of the press.

Other city editorialists ganged up on the outcast, helping to incite an already outraged citizenry. Inevitably, ruffians took to the streets, and at sundown on Monday, 22 June, they headed rowdily toward the offices of the *Federal Republican* at the corner of Gay and Second Streets. Hanson, a resident of Georgetown, some fifty miles southwest, happened to be out of town, and his coeditor, Jacob Wagner, had been forewarned and already slipped away. Undeterred, the rioters broke into the newspaper building, shattered the windows, threw out the paper and type, and smashed the presses by hurling them onto the street below. Then, using grappling hooks, ropes, and axes, they pulled down the frame building until nothing remained but rubble.

The vigilantes menaced anyone daring to hold them in check, indiscriminately roughed up blacks, and vandalized shipping mistakenly linked to Britain.[2] The wreckage and lawlessness were a foretaste of much worse to come. Hanson retreated to his Georgetown home, adjacent to Washington. There he smoldered and plotted a defiant comeback.

Baltimore shrugged off the incident as Hanson's comeuppance. None of the authorities seemed to care, and most bade good riddance. He was lucky to be out of town when the mob struck; otherwise he might have been clubbed to death or axed to pieces. In the eyes of many he was nothing less than poison, a traitor no less, for coming out so publicly and energetically against the war.

The city was, after all, home to entrepreneurs, boisterous immigrant artisans, and solid civic elders who could no longer stomach the threat to their livelihoods by marauding British ships. Like many around the country, they had reached a breaking point over Britain's humiliating practice of boarding U.S. ships to haul off British-born, naturalized American sailors. Most Baltimoreans spoiled for a fight, and the declaration of war stoked their eagerness just as Hanson's outburst filled them with revulsion. He had scandalized the Maryland port city, more so as other Federalists had begun to rally around the flag.

Five weeks later, Hanson sneaked back into Baltimore with some friends and a new edition of the *Federal Republican*, printed in Georgetown. He settled in at the paper's new offices in a house at 45 Charles Street and the following day distributed the paper. The young editor made no attempt to lie low or to conceal his office address, which appeared on the masthead.

The latest broadsheet was just as incendiary as the previous edition. In it he accused public officials, and the mayor in particular, of fomenting and encouraging the riots and disorders and then turning a blind eye to the terrible consequences. Far from feeling chastened by the demolition of his property and the frenzy of the masses, Hanson let it be known that the martyred *Federal Republican* had risen from its tomb and would "steadily pursue the course."[3] He would neither hide nor be chased out of town. Clearly, he had come to stay.

Like-minded intellectuals and sympathizers arrived at the Charles Street office to boost the numbers of Hanson's supporters, until later that day they totaled about three dozen, including Henry "Light-Horse Harry" Lee, a cavalry hero from the distant Revolutionary War. Hanson did not intend to let the mob have its way again, and would brook no attempt to shut down his paper or muffle his voice. He braced for an imminent face-off, whether from public officials or again from the mindless riffraff. This time he and his armed cadre would give as good as they got.

It did not take long for word to get around that the despised publisher was back in Baltimore. By twilight four hundred ruffians and street toughs had found their way to Hanson's three-story building. For the moment they milled around, taunting and jeering at the men barricaded inside. Only a surrounding brick wall "of good height," twelve paces from the building, kept the two sides apart.[4] But when a carriage pulled up and men swept out of the house to offload muskets and ammunition, the crowd came unhinged. Screaming abuse and roaring for blood, they hurled rocks and stones until they had shattered every front window and all the wooden shutters.

As the rioters closed in to tighten the siege, Hanson appeared at a top-floor window, shouting an ultimatum that they would be gunned down if they tried to break in. They answered with jibes and profanities. Light-Horse Harry tried to calm the young publisher. "They are in the wrong," said Lee. "We must be sure to keep them in the wrong." On no account, he warned, should they open fire unless absolutely necessary for self-defense.[5]

But Hanson was in no mood to delay the showdown he craved. As the mob heaved and swayed toward the building, Light-Horse Harry gave in to Hanson, but only on condition that they aim high in an effort to scare off the rabble. The blast banged far into the night that Monday, 27 July 1812. It briefly stunned the crowd, but they stood their ground. Then they became even more aroused and suddenly very much louder.

Nobody would ever know how Lee came to be among Hanson's tight band of allies, most of whom were out-of-town, die-hard antiwar zealots. The retired general had been a close friend of Hanson's father, but he had not been passionate about the war, even though he had warned of the "possibility of disastrous defeat."[6] Baltimore's mayor would later state absurdly that Lee told him he was at Hanson's office "to play a game of whist."[7] Whatever the reason, the former cavalry officer took charge of the defenses. No one had been more artful in warfare than the youthful Lee, especially in daredevil hit-and-run raids against British supply wagons.[8] Like many other Americans, Hanson knew of Lee's heroic rout of two hundred enemy cavalry when in command of only seven men near Valley Forge, Pennsylvania. Hanson had even recalled it for his supporters to raise expectations of a successful armed stand in the Charles Street house. But the difference this time was significant. The enemy outside was growing by the hour and closing in for the kill.

Light-Horse Harry covered every possible point of entry. Ten of his stoutest men guarded the entrance, the front room, and the backyard. Hanson and about a dozen others watched over the second story. The rest waited above. Piles of logs lay next to the windows, ready to be rolled onto anyone trying to vault inside. Lee demanded silence and absolute obedience not to shoot. Not everyone agreed with him, but nobody squeezed a trigger.[9]

When the attack came it was sudden as the thugs charged and battered down the front door. They were about to swarm into the hallway when a blast of musket shot stopped them short. The fusillade cut down those in front and stalled the rest. In an instant they backed off, dragging away their wounded as they scuttled out of the line of fire and back into the darkened street. The old warhorse had once again held off the enemy. He had always survived because he planned so minutely and struck like a rattler, but this time he was fifty-six and very much slower in mind and body.

The sound of gunfire and the persistent drumroll rallying citizens to join the mob alerted officials throughout Baltimore. But they seemed powerless against the crush of insurgents. When criminal court chief justice

John Scott tried to get the raucous mass to back off at about 10 P.M., they ignored him. Another prominent Baltimorean, Brig. Gen. John Stricker, who lived a few houses down the same street and commanded the five-thousand-man Maryland militia, at first turned a deaf ear to the clamor.

Around midnight, however, the face-off worsened. One of the loudest ringleaders, Dr. Thaddeus Gales, motioned the others to advance with him. Cursing and hollering how he had fought for his country and was a true heir of George Washington, he got as far as the front entrance when shots rang out. The physician slumped to the pavement with a fatal wound. More gunshots wounded others and the crowd fell back again, pulling the bodies with them. Just as suddenly, the drumbeat stopped. All was quiet for about twenty minutes.[10]

But then some firebrands hauled a cannon out of an alley in full view of the house. Light-Horse Harry armed three of his men with muskets and told them to scale the wall at the back, then raise eight or ten citizens "obedient to the rule of law."[11] However, as soon as the trio dropped over the other side of the wall they were pounced upon, disarmed, and roughed up.[12]

Lee had already made up his mind to lead a bayonet charge if anyone tried to fire the cannon when, unexpectedly, Maj. William Barney rode up with about two dozen mounted horsemen. Men and boys scattered down the street and into the alleys yelling, "The troop is coming!"

Barney was a prowar Republican, and he, too, had to weigh the consequences of falling afoul of the masses. He knew only too well where the sympathies of the military lay. Almost a thousand other militiamen had stayed home or out of sight because, many told him later, "they never would turn out to protect traitors or disorganizers."[13]

The major dismounted, shook hands with rioters, and said in a soft, almost conciliatory tone, "I am your friend and you are all my friends."[14] He told them he would take everyone in the house into custody, adding, "I am of the same political sentiments with yourselves."[15] But when he saw people dragging a cannon and someone holding a match just inches from its touchhole, he dashed toward it. As he clutched the muzzle and pressed his chest against it, he was driven backwards. Those who had heard him speak massed around the fieldpiece. Voices rose above the din. "Hear him! Hear what he has got to say!" Barney jumped up on the cannon, repeating that he would not let anyone flee from the house. The mob responded with three cheers, promising not to open fire if he kept his part of the bargain. But when one unappeased rioter handed him a lighted match, Barney deliberately let it fall into water in the gutter. Some in the mob continued to threaten. "Never mind, major," said a voice from the crowd, "we have got cigars enough and we'll make matches of them."[16]

Lee had watched Barney put his life on the line and was impressed. He had been waiting for someone to stand up to the wild men surrounding the house. Though he would not surrender any of the men inside, he allowed Barney to station dragoons by the front door, lower windows, and along the backyard wall, where they remained until dawn. But Barney made no effort to disperse the crowd, and ominously, the drummer continued to parade up and down the street.[17]

The city's most prominent political and military leaders were either unable or unwilling to step in and enforce the rule of law. They all knew that Baltimore faced catastrophe if the British squeezed shut its seafaring income. And no one had the stomach to protect pariahs like Hanson, whose politics they detested. Besides, they all knew the fate awaiting anyone who would dare order shots fired against the rioters. The city's most senior general, Tobias Stansbury, despised Hanson's kind. When Sheriff William Merryman asked for his help the general fumed, "The house in Charles Street ought to have been blown down over their heads."[18] Had he been on the spot, Stansbury said, he would have defied civilian orders and blasted the house with cannon fire.[19] Mayor Edward Johnson seethed at Lee and other "foreigners" who came to Baltimore to meddle in the city's politics.[20] In such a volatile climate it was safer to stay clear of the polarized majority.

When word got out that the military would go into action if authorized by two magistrates, one of the judicial figures stuck his head out of a second-story window, begged out because he was a Federalist, and told them to go and find a magistrate of another political stripe.[21] The mayor and General Stricker just as prudently withheld cartridges from militiamen so they could not injure anyone.[22]

Early that morning, Stricker and Johnson entered the house to offer safe conduct to the jail, the mayor expressing fear of a civil war. "To jail! For what!" fumed Hanson. "For protecting my house and property against a mob!" And then, prophetically, "You cannot protect us to jail, or after we are in jail!" The newspaper editor said he knew of Stricker's personal animosity toward him and had no faith in the general's promise that he would "never quit them while there was danger, and if they were attacked he would rescue or fall with them."[23] But Hanson now stood alone. Everyone else agreed with Lee that they could not hold out indefinitely. They had gathered in the house a day before the mob's arrival and had now been awake for two days. There was no one to relieve them, and they would soon run out of provisions.

Some had escaped in the darkness, leaving twenty-three who now, at about 7 A.M., surrendered their swords and larger weapons. Several held onto their pistols as they left the house bunched together inside the moving, protective square of militia and cavalrymen. The boisterous mob quickly encircled the bodyguards. They hurled paving stones with such ferocity that one almost blinded the fifty-three-year-old Stricker as he walked with an arm protectively over Hanson.[24] One of the ringleaders, the editor of the *Baltimore Sun*, repeatedly screamed, "We must have blood for blood! We will not be satisfied till we put them to death!"[25] Time and again Barney deliberately jabbed the sharp tip of his sword at those pressing too close. At one point he recognized a Dr. Lewis rushing toward him in obvious fury. Shouting in French so that few would understand, Barney told Lewis that the prisoners would stand trial, but if the law did not hang them the time would come for Lewis and his friends to take over. Seemingly satisfied, the doctor called out to his friends, "They will all be hung. Never mind, let the law have its chance."[26] The ordeal dragged on as the custodians and their charges inched through the profane and tumultuous crowd. It took two hours to cover the single mile from the Charles Street house to the double-story jail, where, kicked and punched, they staggered up the steps.

The iron door of a single cell slammed shut behind Hanson and his loyalists that Tuesday morning. Outside, the crowd dispersed and the militia stood down. But Judge Scott refused bail, even as visitors warned the detainees of rumors that the mob planned to storm the jail that night. By midday the mayor urged Stricker to call out the military again, and when this was done both men went to the jail to assure the regrouped throngs that none of the incarcerated would be allowed out during the night. Inside the jail they renewed their promises of protection. According to one prisoner, the mayor even pledged "he would lose his own life before we should be hurt."[27]

At that moment a man edged up to the civic leader and whispered a warning to be careful what he said because he was being closely watched. The mayor looked around and saw two men standing against the wall, their faces almost obscured by their hats. He did not know them, but they looked threatening.[28] One was John Mumma, a butcher who had been making mental notes of the identities of prisoners from out of town.[29]

Apparently satisfied that the captives would be held at least overnight, remnants of the thinned-out mob went away. Yet again, the few dozen militiamen were stood down. But at nightfall the terror returned. Packs of predatory toughs idled around the jail. One of them leaped into the yard and shouted, "We must have them out! Blood cries for blood!"

The mayor learned his identity and called out, "George Wooleslager!"

"Who are you?" Wooleslager asked.

"A friend," said the mayor.

"What do you want with me?"

"I wish to speak with you," Johnson said as he walked forward.

"Who are you, Sir?"

"My name is Johnson. I am the mayor of your city."

"What do you want with me?"

"Those persons in jail are my prisoners. That jail, which is their punishment, must be their protection. It is my duty to protect them, and I am here for that purpose. I call on you to assist me in doing so."

They huddled for a few moments when the mayor promised to look into Wooleslager's complaints of his own unfair detention, and invited him to visit the mayoral office the following day.

"Mr. Mayor, you talk very reasonably. My boys, we will support the mayor! Three cheers for the mayor!"

For a moment it seemed Johnson had won over the crowd, but others pulled Wooleslager by the coat and led him off. Johnson, worried that they were talking him out of the pact, stepped forward and said he depended on his support.

"It was only my brother that I wanted to speak to me," the mob leader replied. "I will support you."

But some in the crowd were murmuring how simple it would be to break into the jail and snatch the inmates. One of them lifted a log and boasted how easy it would be to bash down the door.

Putting his hand on the man's shoulder, Johnson cautioned, "My friend, you must not talk so. I am the mayor of your city. They are my prisoners and I must and will protect them."

"*You* protect them!" a voice challenged.

"You damned scoundrel," thundered another. "Don't we feed you! Is it not your duty to lead us on to take vengeance for the murders!"

Wooleslager and two others headed off a confrontation by stepping between the mayor and his antagonists. "We will protect the mayor," he declared.

But four or five men ignored the comment, climbed the steps, and struck at the jail door with an ax.

"It is not yet too late!" the mayor pleaded with Wooleslager. "Support me and we may prevent the horrid scene."

"I will support you, Sir," he replied as he led Johnson up the steps. But then, placing both hands on the mayor, he conceded, "We are only risking our own lives, without any prospect of success."

Losing his balance, the mayor jumped down to prevent a fall. Again the crowd was massing. A colonel grabbed the mayor's arm, yanked him away from the crowd, and told him he had done all he could and should not now risk his life. The mayor could do nothing but look on helplessly as the vigilantes broke into the jail, and he did not resist when an acquaintance pulled him away.[30]

A passing horseman galloped on to Stricker's home to plead for help, but was told he could not be seen and that anyhow, "he had already done all he could or would do."[31]

As the would-be assassins closed in with a sledgehammer and ax, Lee and Hanson again debated in their cell whether to fire on the crowd. Killing one or two, Lee believed, would not help and would only "exasperate" the mob.[32] They agreed instead to snuff out the lights and dash for their lives at the moment the attackers broke in. It was their only hope of escaping certain death.

As soon as the jailbreakers stormed through the last door, nine or ten inmates bolted to safety. An oil lamp was knocked over and extinguished. Above the screams and grunts in the darkened cell someone yelled out,

"More lights!"[33] With no hope of flight, the trapped men were punched, kicked, and knifed in the flickering light of more candles brought in from the jailer's room and passed overhead. Clubs swung and beat against heads, opening deep gashes and splashing blood over capes, coats, and hats. One wounded man smeared a bloodied handprint on the wall. Most victims were dragged out and clubbed at the jail's entrance by Mumma the butcher. Others were savaged by rogues waiting their turn in the street.

Hanson, Lee, Gen. James McCubbin Lingan, and half a dozen others were knocked down the prison steps and tortured as they lay in a heap of unconscious and semiconscious bodies. Their assailants used penknives to slash and poke at faces and hands. Hoodlums forced open the eyes of other victims to let burning candle-grease drip in. As the victims shrieked and cried out, the town's fire-alarm bell tolled more urgently than usual.

In his death groans, the sixty-year-old Lingan cried out for mercy, pleading that he was old and weak. Pitifully, he reminded them how he had fought for their freedom during the Revolutionary War. His tormentors did not care at all. It made no difference that the aging general had survived a British prison-ship before being appointed collector of the port of Georgetown. His cries for mercy were met with more kicks and punches. One thug, stomping on the general's torso and landing a series of blows, complained, "The damned old rascal is hardest dying of all of them." Lingan feebly extended his hand to a companion and uttered his last words, "Farewell, I am a dying man."[34]

As Light-Horse Harry Lee lay battered upon the ground, someone tried to slice off his nose but succeeded only in bloodying his face. A knife aimed at Lee's eye missed its mark and nicked open his cheek. His glorious past was of no consequence now. No one cared that Congress had turned to him to deliver the funeral oration for his friend, George Washington, whom Lee had eulogized as "First in war, first in peace, and first in the hearts of his countrymen."[35] Light-Horse Harry, father of Robert E. Lee, then five, was beaten into a limp and bloody casualty for the first time in his long life as a soldier, patriot, and elected public figure.

One of the physically strongest of Hanson's friends, John Thompson, had been clubbed almost senseless, then hauled away in a cart, his clothing ripped off and scalding tar smeared over his bleeding body. Shrieking "traitor" and obscenities, the rabble beat him with an iron bar, cut him with rusty swords, and failed to gouge out his eyes only because they were protected by congealed tar. Thompson made out he was dead until they set fire to his tarred flesh, forcing him to roll over convulsively. "For God's sake," he begged, "if you want my life, take it by shooting or stabbing!"[36] They spared his life, but only after he agreed to name everyone who had been at Hanson's house and to tell what they had been up to. Thompson was taken to a tavern and plied with whiskey. Then he gave them the names but said they were there only to defend Hanson and his house. Thompson's ordeal was not over. They told him he would be hanged in the morning unless he signed his confession before a magistrate. The following day, after his signed statement was read aloud, Thompson was taken to a hospital by the mayor, though the mob insisted he be ferried in an open cart rather than in a carriage summoned by the civic leader.

Outside the jail, meanwhile, Hanson pretended to be dead, as did a physician, Dr. Peregrine Warfield, and John Hall, a lawyer and professor of rhetoric and belles lettres at the University of Maryland. Defenseless, they heard some in the mob arguing whether to bury them or toss them into the nearby stream. Others were for castration, slitting their throats, or tarring and feathering. The victims were spared further harm only because a doctor talked the murderers into leaving the apparently dead and dying bodies in his custody until the morning. One by one, the supposed corpses, bruised and bloodied, were carried back into the jail and into the tender care of several physicians. The long night of terror seemed to have come to an end. Even Mumma the butcher had had his fill, telling the remaining doctor that "they had been beat enough to satisfy the devil."[37]

Hanson, barely conscious and unable to walk alone, was brought to with raw rum. He brooded over the pulped corpse of General Lingan. The old man had survived a full-fledged war with Britain only to be savagely cut down by his own people. But there was no time to lose. A few lingering rioters said that in the morning they would kill Hanson and tar and feather the eight other wounded. The newspaper proprietor was piggybacked out of the building into the dark, where he hid under a sewer bank while his assailants were temporarily distracted. The last of the tired rioters eventually left after looking over the survivors and agreeing with Mumma that enough was enough.[38] By late morning all of the casualties had slipped out of Baltimore by cart or carriage.

Light-Horse Harry, groaning and barely recognizable, was taken to a hospital. He was among the most severely injured. A visitor who saw him after he had been spirited out by carriage to Pennsylvania the following day reported a gruesome sight: "Lee was as black as a negro, his head cut to pieces [and] without a hat or any shirt but a flannel one which was covered with blood. One eye [was] apparently out, his clothes torn and covered with blood from tip to toe, and when he attempts to stir he tottered like an infant just commencing to walk."[39] The once-revered cavalry officer would never recover from internal injuries, and his face would be scarred for the remainder of his life. He died half a dozen years later a feeble wreck, incapable of restoring his health in the warmer climate of the Caribbean islands.[40]

The war with Great Britain was only forty-one days old, and the bloodletting on the soil of the United States had just begun. But all the victims and every assassin and their accomplices were Americans. Such were the savage passions in a deeply divided country that even noble Light-Horse Harry had become fair game.

The threat of war with Britain had loomed ever larger since the turn of the century. Swaggering upon the world stage like a mighty overlord, the English time and again boarded American ships to snatch away, or, in the language of the day, impress, British-born sailors. Begun even before the U.S. government moved down to Washington, impressment had become so common that during a six-year period through 1810, almost 5,000 sailors had been hauled off American ships, including 1,361 whom the British later freed after acknowledging they were Americans.[41]

Unable to find sufficient numbers of sailors to man their growing merchant fleet, Americans had looked abroad, and British seamen, attracted by the higher pay and better conditions, had deserted and signed up in droves. Alarmed by the drain on its own manpower, the British Admiralty reacted with the blunt instrument of its fearsome navy. British politicians trumpeted the country's lifelong claim to the services of anyone born a British subject. The reach extended so far that Britain did not even accept the right of its people to renounce citizenship. Under such laws, the Royal Navy was free to roam the seas and grab even those Britons who had become naturalized Americans. But as citizenship was so difficult to prove, especially at sea, American-born sailors were often dragged off their own ships.[42] To many Americans, these were broadsides on a nation's sovereignty, indignities that could not be endured.

American fury came closest to war when the British frigate *Leopard* fired on the American frigate *Chesapeake* off Norfolk, Virginia, in 1807, killing three U.S. crewmen. Americans clamored for war on learning that a boarding party had seized three of their countrymen and a lone British sailor. Passions subsided while diplomats quietly searched for a solution. But the mightiest maritime power saw no good reason to give way to the weaker American challenge. It was a time to flex imperial muscle, as the young British diplomat, Augustus John Foster, wrote to his mother from Washington: "While we are aiming blows at the French marine we want elbow room, and these good neutrals won't give it to us, and therefore they get a few side pushes which make them grumble. However, I hope they will see their interests better than to seriously quarrel with us."[43]

Americans had been caught in the Anglo-French cross fire for more than a decade. Determined to weaken each other, the belligerents across the Atlantic tried to cut off their enemy's maritime trade with neutral countries. It was naked interference with America's right to free trade. The more restrictions the Europeans imposed, the more hackles they raised in the New World. Napoleon's Berlin and Milan decrees of 1806 and 1807 targeted British cargo. The French proclaimed they would seize it if found aboard American or other foreign ships. The new laws also placed European ports off limits to ships which had called earlier at British harbors. London matched these burdens with equal severity. Her Orders in Council of 1807 announced blockades against any harbor excluding British vessels, and the interdiction of all ships from entering French-controlled ports unless they had earlier anchored at British harbors. Unwilling to go to war, Jefferson slapped a blanket embargo on trade with foreign countries, but the shortsighted policy backfired as exports shriveled.

In 1811 a defiant mood swept through Washington when new youngbloods took their seats in Congress. Henry Clay of Kentucky and John Calhoun of South Carolina would dominate Capitol Hill with their oratory, but they also excited a new sense of bold and impetuous nationalism. They had been born after the Declaration of Independence and reared in a free and sovereign nation. What was tolerable for older Americans would be insufferable for the young war hawks. Their election would put an end to the insults Americans had suffered for so long at the hands of foreign powers. Diplomacy would yield to confrontation. War was no longer merely an option. It was the only honorable course for a people claiming to be free and independent.

Clay and Calhoun gave clear and resonant voice to the call for war. But aristocratic Rep. John Randolph of Roanoke, Virginia, convinced others that warmongering was madness. The great debates on war or peace raged in the crimson-draped chamber of the House of Representatives from the closing month of 1811 into the dramatic summer of 1812 when the votes were counted.

Henry Clay cut a memorable figure in the halls of Congress, giving dramatic passion to the force of his eloquence by gesturing with long arms as his hair waved wildly.[44] Isaac Bassett, a Senate page and assistant doorkeeper for sixty-four years, had often seen Clay stay up all night playing cards, then take the Senate floor for another virtuoso performance.[45] His relationship with Randolph was immediately adversarial after Clay's unprecedented election as Speaker on his first day in the House of Representatives, when he put an end to Randolph's habit of bringing hunting dogs onto the floor of the House.[46]

No one cut a more drably striking figure than the sickly Randolph, who described much of his life as "a long disease."[47] Many thought the spindly anglophile was close to insane. When addressing Congress he often appeared with a handkerchief wrapped around his head as he drank several bottles of ale.[48] His hairless skin and soprano's voice gave the impression that he had never passed through puberty.[49] But what he lacked in overt manliness he more than made up for with intellect, swaying many in Congress with formidable arguments against the drift to war. Deeply under the spell of British culture, Randolph reminded congressmen of how much they owed the English, with whom they shared the same blood, language, religion, legal system, representative government, and even Shakespeare and Newton.[50]

John Calhoun, whose iron-gray hair "hung down in thick masses like a lion's mane," sneered at Randolph's emotional ties to England.[51] "He asks how we can hate . . . a country having the same language and customs. . . . If we have so much to attach us to that country, powerful indeed must be the cause which has overpowered it."[52] Calhoun shared none of Randolph's feelings for the mother country, and he would later fight hard to reject an Englishman's half-million-dollar bequest to create the Smithsonian Institution in Washington, thinking it beneath the dignity of the United States to receive such a gift.[53] Calhoun preferred "war with all its accompanying evils to abject submission."[54] He wanted to swoop down on colonial Canada, evict the British, and end their arms sales to and influence over hostile Indians along the northern border. The hawks knew that war on the high seas was unthinkable against Britain's armada of more than a thousand ships. But robbing the British of their valuable colony, on which they were even more dependent since being blocked from Europe by the French, would be a telling blow.

Randolph mocked such talk, saying the barren rocks of Bermuda were worth more than Canada. But his sentiments were clearly not shared by most congressmen seeking a showdown. Rep. Richard Johnson of Kentucky declared he would "never die contented until I see her expulsion from North America."[55]

The wound that festered in Henry Clay more than any other was the ease with which Britain hauled sailors off American ships. The Kentuckian argued that the real cause of British aggression "was not to distress an enemy but to destroy a rival. . . . She sickens at your prosperity, and beholds in your growth . . . the foundations of a Power which, at no very distant day, is to make her tremble for naval superiority."[56]

In June 1812, Randolph heard rumors that a declaration of war was only days away. He feared a calamity. No one could deny his charge that the states doing most of the foreign trade—New York and those in New England—wanted nothing to do with war.[57] Others took up the cry, predicting ruin and defeat. Congressmen from Massachusetts to Maryland presented resolutions and citizens' petitions against the war. In the Senate, James Bayard of Delaware forecast self-destruction and disaster. Cities and even ships at sea would be at the mercy of the British. "What can you expect but to add new distresses, defeat and disgrace?" he asked. "You have twenty vessels of war—Britain upwards of a thousand. . . . We can lose nothing by delay; much will be certainly saved."[58]

But there was no stopping the momentum of the war hawks, even though they had been unable to put the matter to a vote in the House of Representatives. For weeks they had been blocked by antiwar Federalists mounting a determined filibuster through days and nights of endless waffle. Frustrated beyond endurance, the hawks pounced one night during a commotion when one of them claimed the floor and finessed his opponents by moving "the previous question."[59] The procedural ploy halted the filibuster and opened the way to a vote on war. When the count was taken on 4 June, the hawks had won by 79 to 49. But the geographic split showed the depth of antiwar sentiment in the Northeast. The Senate was even more bitterly divided when two weeks later it voted 19 to 13 to go to war.

Prophetically, Randolph told a clutch of war hawks, "Gentlemen, you have made war. You have finished the ruin of our country. And before you conquer Canada your idol [Napoleon] will cease to distract the world and the Capitol will be a ruin."[60]

On 18 June 1812 a document was set before President Madison. With his signature he locked America into its second war of independence: "Be it enacted, That war be and the same is hereby declared to exist between the United Kingdom of Great Britain and Ireland and the dependencies thereof, and the United States of America and their Territories; and that the President of the United States is hereby authorized to use the whole land and naval force of the United States to carry the same into effect."

Across the country, partisan passions burst into the open. Alexander Contee Hanson and the Baltimore mobs represented the dark and violent extremes, but in some remoter settlements the news was welcomed festively. Four neighboring communities in rural western Pennsylvania competed with one another to see who could fly the Stars and Stripes the highest. Sunbury, Danville, and Milton erected towering poles, but when rivals in Northumberland tried to raise a "liberty pole" forty feet higher, it fell down on the market square and broke into pieces. A Northumberlander reported how neighboring villagers "now laugh us to scorn." Americans could afford to giggle and play the fool. The war was new and the guns still cold. But many were deeply disturbed. "Our hapless citizens cannot raise their flag to scare away the British lion," sighed the same Northumberland chronicler.[61]

2. Target Washington

*A*t noon on 1 July 1814, James Madison presided over an emergency meeting of his cabinet in the President's House. For weeks he had secretly told his most trusted aides that the war might soon escalate. News had begun to trickle in of the fall of Napoleon, a dramatic event that would free thousands of British troops for the war across the Atlantic. The president expected them to lunge at Washington. Seizing the capital would give an enormous boost to British morale.

Fresh dispatches from American officials in Europe at the end of June forced the president to act quickly. One by one, the top five men in government arrived at the chief executive's mansion.[1] Secretary of State James Monroe was the most senior as head of the oldest government department. Attorney General Richard Rush and Secretary of the Navy William Jones were among the president's closest friends and confidants. Ailing Secretary of the Treasury George Campbell entered with the odd man out, Secretary of War John Armstrong, who held powerful sway even though so disliked by his colleagues that one of them thought his "nature and habits forbid him to speak well of any man."[2]

Until now the war had been a distant rumble on the Canadian frontier. Americans had suffered humiliating setbacks as the British repulsed attacks and captured Detroit. By the close of 1813 the British had also taken Fort Niagara and torched Buffalo. American glory was confined to a spectacular victory on Lake Erie, where Commodore Oliver Hazard Perry abandoned his sinking flagship, rowed through gunfire, and penciled a message on the back of a letter: "We have met the enemy and they are ours."[3] The only other area touched by the war lay fifty miles east of Washington, where a small British naval force continued to plunder and terrorize the small, isolated settlements along the shores of the two-hundred-mile-long Chesapeake Bay. Until now, no one in Washington had been alarmed by the proximity of these sailors, knowing they could never take the role of infantry and march inland.

The president told his cabinet he wanted two or three thousand armed men placed between Washington and the Chesapeake. And he suggested that another ten to twelve thousand militiamen and volunteers be put on standby in the District of Columbia and neighboring states. Not much help could be expected from the regulars, then numbering only twenty-seven thousand and spread thinly from the Canadian frontier down to New Orleans.[4] There was little discussion and no formal vote. No one objected before the officials departed.[5]

The following day the 10th Military District came into being, covering the District of Columbia, Maryland, and parts of Virginia. But the man placed in charge, thirty-nine-year-old Brig. Gen. William Winder, was a transparent political appointee. Cooperation was expected from his uncle, Levin Winder, the Federalist governor of Maryland, whose territory lay between Washington and the Chesapeake Bay. The new commanding general was far better known as an eminent Baltimore lawyer. His military experience was scant and undistinguished. The year before he had even been captured at the battle of Stoney Creek near Niagara, then released to serve as intermediary during short-lived armistice probes.[6]

For weeks General Winder rode across his vast new compound, cramming a feel for the lay of the land. Communications were poor, his staff pathetically thin. Significantly, the promised force never materialized. In Pennsylvania a law regarding the militia expired which effectively disbanded that force and halted five thousand from rushing down to Washington. Winder was fast becoming frantic, but the biggest obstacle proved to be the secretary of war, his superior, who had effective day-to-day control over the military. John Armstrong, officious, stubborn, and cocksure, refused to concede any dire threat to Washington. He would not even let available militia take the field unless a serious assault looked imminent.[7] Nothing could change his mind, not even Winder's argument that British reinforcements would be just a day and a half's march from Washington. Armstrong was so convinced of his own clear judgment that Secretary of State Monroe would much later charge him with being "infatuated," never able to believe there was any danger to Washington.[8]

Armstrong's inaction went unchallenged, even as lonely critics grew restless. He was, after all, a general and former U.S. minister to France. Few cared to question the man at the helm of the War Department, whose access to military intelligence would be expected to give him deeper insight. Like Winder, the discontented had to hope that the enemy would strike elsewhere. Exasperated, one colonel asked a well-connected military acquaintance, "How long are we to be the laughing stock of the world? The enemy can with a small force destroy Washington in its present situation."[9]

Worried observers were as powerless as Winder, even as the vanguard of enemy reinforcements arrived, sailing past Point Look Out and up into the Chesapeake Bay before sundown on 14 July.

But even then Armstrong berated his critics. "By God," he ranted at the uneasy chief of Washington's militia, "they would not come with such a fleet without meaning to strike somewhere. But they certainly will not come here! What the devil will they do here? No! No! Baltimore is the place, Sir. That is of so much more consequence."[10]

The British commander in chief of the North American station, fifty-six-year-old Vice Adm. Sir Alexander Cochrane, made no secret of his yearning to capture Washington. In a letter to the British government in mid-July 1814, this younger son of an earl seemed assured that Washington could be "either destroyed or laid under contribution."[11] As soon as he got wind of reinforcements for his American command, he forecast, "Mr. Madison will be hurled from his throne."[12] He outlined possible invasion routes to Washington, Baltimore, and Philadelphia, then waited impatiently for reaction from Rear Adm. George Cockburn, his zealous subordinate. Cockburn was so hated for burning and pillaging settlements along the banks of the Chesapeake that an American had offered a reward of $1,000 for the admiral's head and $500 for each of his ears.[13]

Cockburn was eager to sign on. His spies and captives had deepened his already intimate knowledge of the area, and he was confident of a quick conquest. He predicted the capital could be taken without difficulty within forty-eight hours of landing troops at the village port of Benedict on the banks of the Patuxent River, about forty-five miles southeast of Washington. Intelligence reported good quarters available for the troops at Benedict and a fruitful countryside to feed them. The locals also had more than enough horses to haul heavy British armament over the hilly road to Washington. Cockburn recommended seizing Washington before Annapolis and Baltimore, as the latter would be more vulnerable if attacked in their rears via roads leading in from Washington. Targeting the ports of Annapolis and Baltimore first would pit the English against armed cities with shallow watery approaches into which large ships could not sail, giving Washingtonians valuable time in which to sneak state treasures and precious documents out of the nation's capital.

Cockburn pushed hard for his daring plan, arguing that the fall of a capital was "always so great a blow to the government of a country." He even touted the idea of sending a diversionary force of bomb ships up the Potomac River "to distract and divide the enemy" as it approached Washington from the south while the land army closed in from the east. He was quick to add that he had no fear of getting lost on land or water, as renegade guides were easy to hire. "I have already one who has been ill-treated in his own country and seems extremely anxious to be revenged. I have employed him on all occasions . . . he being both a pilot for the rivers and a guide for the roads."[14]

A day later, Cochrane, a former governor of the Caribbean island of Guadeloupe, gave orders "to destroy and lay waste such towns and districts upon the coast as you may find assailable." Only the lives of unarmed Americans would be spared.[15] It was to be retaliation for American excesses in Canada, where U.S. forces were charged with a series of "disgraceful outrages" after destroying public and private buildings, most recently along the Niagara frontier.[16]

Capt. Joseph Nourse, conducting fleeting raids along the western shore of the Chesapeake from his frigate, the *Severn*, reported to Cockburn in July that "in one of our expeditions an American told us he guessed we were the advanced guard of a considerable force intended to land at Benedict and march to Washington."[17] Nearby settlers panicked and fled.

Nourse retained a few of the countless runaway slaves as guides, but one of his most valuable intelligence sources was an American named Hopewell, married with children, who was prepared to betray his country because he thought the war "most unjust and most unnatural."[18] He filtered across details of U.S. troop strength in the area and reported on events in the capital. More importantly, as soon as he received copies of current newspapers he slipped them to Nourse. Hopewell's treachery enabled Nourse to advise Cockburn that the Americans were so disorganized and unprepared that "it would require but little force to burn Washington, and I hope soon to put the first torch to it myself."[19]

But the British needed a cover to mask their real intentions. The hunt for Commodore Joshua Barney's needling flotilla provided the perfect feint. Seven weeks earlier this veteran American seafarer had led his lightweight craft with oars and flimsy sails in hit-and-run attacks on British warships in the Chesapeake Bay. Barney's flotilla had fled into the Patuxent River, from where there was no escape. They could only move upriver to the shallows and a marshy dead end. The British would stalk the Revolutionary War hero and destroy his gallant but inferior squadron. It would eradicate the only American opposition in the mighty Chesapeake Bay. More significantly, the chase would bring the foreigners to a number of roads within a day or two's march of Washington.

When Cochrane anchored in mid-August near the mouths of the Patuxent and Potomac Rivers to finalize plans for the twin targets, he had with him the two subordinates who would lead the invasion by land and water. Cockburn and the newly arrived land commander, Maj. Gen. Robert Ross, were polar opposites. The Irish-born Ross, forty-eight years of age, was a decorated leader beloved by his men as much for his courage in combat as for his courteous manner. He had been singled out to lead the American expeditionary land forces by none other than the "Iron" Duke of Wellington, the man who would at last bring Napoleon to heel.[20] Warm and deferential, Ross had neither the need nor the inclination to project rank or pedigree to command respect.

Ross's more cautionary style would contrast sharply with the headstrong drive of George Cockburn. Even though the general would outrank the admiral as soon as their joint forces stepped off the ships onto American soil, Cockburn would be a formidable presence, ill-suited to the constraints imposed on a man playing second fiddle. Descended from titled medieval Scottish landowners, Cockburn had been at sea even before his teens, and as a young man he had caught the eye of England's foremost hero, Adm. Horatio Nelson, for his "zeal, ability and courage."[21] Such was Cockburn's standing in the highest reaches of the British military that he would be chosen to haul Napoleon into exile on the island of St. Helena. It would be a chastening experience for the captive emperor, who learned while walking the decks and playing card games with Cockburn that the admiral could be overbearing, no matter that the prisoner had been the most feared man in Europe.[22] "It is clear he is still inclined to act the sovereign occasionally, but I cannot allow it," Cockburn would scratch in his diary.[23] Such was the fiber of the man about to march on Washington.

With Cockburn and Ross primed to stalk Barney's flotilla, attention focused on Capt. James Gordon, a naval warrior who hobbled on one leg. He would lead a squadron of bomb vessels and other warships up the Potomac with the twofold task of destroying Fort Warburton at the southern approaches to the capital, then covering the British army once it had conquered and begun to withdraw from Washington. Gordon's task was even more daunting because he would have to navigate unknown waters. But he, too, had already proved himself with conspicuous bravery. Three years earlier, during a much-heralded victory over French warships, a 36-pound enemy shot had hurtled through a porthole of his frigate, grazed a gun carriage, and sliced off a sailor's leg before crashing into Gordon's knee joint. His shattered limb had dangled uselessly by tendons before being amputated. But the bloodied captain had been an inspiration in his pain, continuing to give orders calmly before being carried below deck.[24] Admiral Cochrane could not have wished for a more dependable trio than Ross, Cockburn, and Gordon as he prepared to plow deep into his enemy's soft underbelly.

The die was cast when more than four thousand warriors set sail up the broad Patuxent River. If all went well, they would strike a blow for Britain that would resound around the world. It would be the most dramatic action of the war between the supreme imperial power and the snippety transatlantic upstart. A conquered capital would humiliate the Americans more than any battlefield loss. It would be so demoralizing that it might even sunder the Union. The prospect of imminent action sent a wave of patriotism surging through the warships. These were men who thrived on glory and valor with their tableaux of bloody battle and victors' laurels. Unfurled admirals' flags streamed from the mastheads, uniting the troops and signaling, as in centuries past, the resolve and pride of a truly invincible people. British muscle had toppled Napoleon and was now flexed to strike at the far weaker Americans. A fifteen-year-old on the main deck of one frigate grew heady with expectation. The troops looked to Robert Barrett like "eager souls, panting for fame and opportunity to sustain the laurels they had gained in many a bloody field of Spain and Portugal."[25]

3. A Village for a Capital

*W*ashington, the capital the British hoped to storm, was a gawky village, a mere embryo of the city it aspired to be. Only fourteen years earlier, in 1800, First Lady Abigail Adams had lost her way in dense woods en route from Baltimore to join the president in the raw new capital. "Woods are all you see from Baltimore until you reach *the city*, which is only so in name," she wailed in a letter to her daughter.[1] Forests covered much of the area set aside for Washington. There were just over three thousand residents, of whom one-fifth were slaves.[2] The tangle of protruding roots of sycamores and other trees hampered residents walking the banks of Tiber Creek in search of turtle nests.[3] Pennsylvania Avenue, conceived as the city's grandest thoroughfare and linking the unfinished, single-winged Capitol with the incomplete President's House one mile west, was, in the sad opinion of a newly arrived congressman, "a deep morass covered with alder bushes."[4] The few, potholed roads were muddy quagmires when it rained and dusty passageways when dry. An attempt to cover a sidewalk with chips from blocks of stone hewn for the Capitol failed because it cut pedestrians' shoes in dry weather and smeared their footwear white when it rained.

The city planner, Pierre L'Enfant, was an arrogant French-born engineer whose weakness for designing extravagantly grand projects was as infamous as his habit of running roughshod over others. L'Enfant's inevitable fall from grace came swiftly after he demolished the home of a Washington notable to make way for a street. But by then the talented Frenchman had drawn up a characteristically grandiose plan for the new capital, flanked by the confluence of the Potomac River and its Eastern Branch (today called the Anacostia River). Lesser rivals might have glanced over the wooded hills and settled for a standard commercial center tightly surrounded by residences. L'Enfant's vision, however, was splendidly expansive. He lined up landmark buildings, monuments, and walkways far from each other, confident that the vacuum between them would be filled in good time with majestic additions. Having blueprinted the focal points of the city, he crisscrossed the gentle rise and fall of pastoral land with a grid of right-angled streets, cut diagonally by broad avenues, whose circular intersections would highlight fountains and heroic statuary. An oak-covered hill rising seventy-eight feet above the mosquito-infested swamps appeared to him as "a pedestal waiting for a monument." Atop this commanding summit, known to later generations as Capitol Hill, L'Enfant positioned the proposed legislature. A little more than a mile west, down Pennsylvania Avenue, he marked a site for the President's House.

But it would be decades before the city took form. Secretary of the Treasury Oliver Wolcott, writing to his wife in 1800, the year the government moved down from Philadelphia to Washington, observed mournfully that "there is one good tavern about forty rods [220 yards] from the Capitol, and several other houses are built and erecting; but I do not perceive how the members of Congress can possibly secure lodgings, unless they will consent to live like scholars in a college, or monks in a monastery, crowded ten or twenty in one house, and utterly secluded from society. The only resource for such as wish to live comfortably will, I think, be found in Georgetown, three miles distant."[5] Many congressmen from the South opted to live in Georgetown, the flourishing settlement built on the hilly swoop down to the Potomac River, even though it meant running up expenses for hackney coach rides back and forth to the Capitol. Senators and representatives roughing it out in the Federal City paired off to share rooms in the sprinkling of isolated boardinghouses, though, in deference to status, the Speaker of the House had a room to himself.[6]

Two of the more prominent property speculators, James Greenleaf and Thomas Law, suffered huge losses because they miscalculated the direction in which the city would grow. The blocks of buildings and rows of brick houses they put up south and east of the Capitol, near the arsenal and the navy yard, remained empty for years while the city rose up in the opposite direction, closer to the President's House, government offices, and bustling Georgetown.

The capital grew so slowly that even those developers who profited saw how foolish George Washington had been to forecast that the area would become a metropolis by 1800. The first president constantly linked public confidence in the designated new capital with visible advances in the public buildings. With only twenty-two months remaining before Congress was scheduled to assemble in the federal capital, an impatient Washington deplored the possibility of "limping progress."[7] The two neighboring port cities of Alexandria and Georgetown continued to overshadow it.

Residents who stayed put in Washington could enjoy local theater, though horse racing, begun in Georgetown in 1769, was the most festive entertainment, with Congress often adjourning early to give time to those who had to walk the four miles to the enclosure.[8] However, visiting Britons were unimpressed. Charles William Janson, crossing the Atlantic in search of speculative business ventures, found the city "grotesque," its avenues "pompous," and his hotel another failed private adventure housing "the lowest order of Irish."[9]

The young secretary of the British legation, Augustus John Foster, despaired of his sanity in "this melancholy capital."[10] In a stream of letters to his mother, who was living in a ménage à trois with the Duke and Duchess of Devonshire, the bachelor diplomat grieved for himself. "It is an absolute sepulchre this hole."[11] Having lobbied for the post to advance his career, he now confessed he would "rather lie on the shelf in England waiting an opportunity than to waste away the best years of my life in so fruitless a place as Washington."[12] With surpassing horror he saw how President Thomas Jefferson received the British minister, Anthony Merry. "He [Jefferson] is dressed and looks extremely like a very plain farmer, and wears his slippers down to the heels. Only think what must have been poor [Merry's] embarrassment when at his first audience he went all bespeckled with the spangles of our gaudiest court dress. The doors opened suddenly too. He thrust out his hand to me as he does to everybody and desired me to sit down. Luckily for me I have been in Turkey, and am quite at home in this primeval simplicity of manners."[13]

Foster allowed to pass without comment the calamitous arrival of Tunisian diplomats, who had to be rowed to Washington after their frigate grounded on a Potomac River sandbar.[14] However, he could not overlook what followed. "My dearest Ma . . . there is an ambassador from Tunis arrived here with the most splendid dress on I ever saw, and the President receives him in yarn stockings and torn slippers as he does us all."[15]

The presence of the diplomatic corps and Congress gave to the humid capital a sense of refinement and culture, but it was no more than a veneer. Their romantic frolics and domestic quarrels amused and scandalized fellow transients. In 1805 the French minister, Baron Louis-Marie Turreau de Garambourville, had a violent falling out with his wife, leaving both of them disgraced in the eyes of their American hosts after she reportedly burst in and found him dancing with ladies of scant virtue. Far from being silenced by the beating he gave her, the baroness discredited him with such vengeance that the baron's valet intervened in the spousal contretemps, telling her she was *une canaille* (scum).[16]

Many foreign observers rated congressmen little more than a scurvy lot of undistinguished men, an opinion reinforced by later arrivals from European waters. To the jaundiced eye of Augustus John Foster, who frequently attended sessions of Congress, there were "about five persons who look like gentlemen. All the rest come in the filthiest dress and are well indeed if they look like farmers—but most seem apothecaries and attorneys."[17] Floor fights had broken out, even before the lawmakers moved down to Washington. Occasionally they fought in their common lodgings, as when House Republican leader John Randolph tangled with Rep. Willis Alston Jr. in 1804, though they graciously waited for female diners to leave the room before hurling tableware at each other.[18] In the following decade, Henry Fearon gave mixed reviews to thirty-nine English families waiting to hear whether he would recommend immigration. Though silent about the legislators' grooming, he was dismayed to discover as many as three-quarters were lawyers, which he dutifully reported as "a great and crying evil."[19]

The very proper Mrs. Trollope, visiting in the twilight years of James Madison, was stricken by the sight of congressmen "sitting in the most unseemly attitudes, a large majority with their hats on, and nearly all spitting to an excess that decency forbids me to describe."[20] At about the same time, another British traveler, Thomas Hamilton, was disgusted by many who appeared "vulgar and uncouth, in a degree which nothing in my previous experience had prepared me to expect. It is impossible to look on these men without at once receiving the conviction that they are not gentlemen by habit or education."[21]

A new sense of sophistication swept the bare settlement after Madison's inauguration in 1809. Guests invited to the executive mansion fawned over the irrepressible cause of it all—First Lady Dolley Madison. Her charm was so magical that she singlehandedly seemed to lift Washington out of its coarse beginnings. Her effortless style and dignity would make her the most beloved First Lady ever to occupy the historic home. She drew hyperbolic praise, whether resplendent in one of her fabled ostrich-plumed turbans or dressed in a plain gown with bonnet. "She is admired and esteemed by the rich and beloved by the poor," wrote one female devotee.[22] Another young admirer gushed, "She may have worn jewels, but if she did they were so eclipsed by her inherent charms as to be unnoticed."[23]

Her presence was even more striking beside the delicately boned president, five feet, four inches tall, who powdered his hair and dressed only in black, from his coat and breeches down to his silk stockings and buckled shoes.[24] While she was outgoing and gregarious, her husband was thoughtful and retiring. When Francis Jeffrey, the eminent Scottish barrister and essayist, met him at the President's House in 1813, he thought Madison had "the air of a country schoolmaster in mourning for one of his pupils whom he had whipped to death." Though the president was cordial, Jeffrey viewed him as "a little, mean-looking, yellow, cunning, sour, awkward personage, attired in proper black with a profusion of powder on his lank scanty locks and the wrinkles of his orange colored forehead."[25]

The President's House, which some were already calling the White House by early 1812, was an impressive landmark.[26] However, its roof and gutters leaked "like a riddle," and, despite multiple repairs, rain had continued to cause damage to the ceilings and furniture since the tenancy of John and Abigail Adams.[27] More recently, lead ripped off the roof during a violent summer storm had been replaced and painted over. Workmen had laid new timber floors and partitions after throwing out the original green and unseasoned wood, rotted by the constant seepage of rainwater.[28] The mansion was now surrounded by a high stone wall and flanked by brick buildings housing government agencies run by the secretaries of the navy, war, and state on the west and by the secretary of the treasury on the east. Inside, the executive mansion was, in the words of Elbridge Gerry Jr., son of the vice president, "a perfect palace."[29] Guests invited to receptions would walk through the pillared entrance hall, handsomely furnished and lit by large lamps down its entire length. They would see Gilbert Stuart's full-length portrait of George Washington in the magnificent East Room, and a portrait of Dolley Madison in her adjacent sitting room. The public would also get to see a grand view of the Potomac from an oval drawing room, whose red velvet curtains framed windows almost as high as the ceiling.[30]

But the city was still, according to Attorney General Richard Rush, "a meagre village, a place with a few bad houses and extensive swamps."[31] By 1810, halfway through Madison's first term, there were only 8,208 residents in the capital, of whom 5,904 were white, 867 free blacks, and 1,437 slaves. Though sparsely inhabited, Washington had overtaken Georgetown's population of 4,948, including 1,162 slaves.[32] However, with so little sophistication, a rare flash of elegance brought activity to a gawking halt. Once, as guests prepared to leave a presidential reception, they were silenced by the sight of what appeared to be "a rolling ball of burnished gold, carried with swiftness through the air by two gilt wings." When the apparition stopped outside the mansion, the French minister and his entourage stepped out of a glittering carriage, attended by footmen with *chapeaux bras*, gilt-braided skirts, and splendid swords. "Nothing ever was witnessed in Washington so brilliant and dazzling," an onlooker remembered. "You may well imagine how the natives stared and rubbed their eyes to be convinced 'twas no fairy dream."[33]

4. Invasion

*A*lthough Captain Nourse had conducted darting raids along the shore, the invading fleet bunched together protectively because of scant navigational knowledge. No one had taken soundings of the Patuxent River, flowing south into the western edge of the Chesapeake Bay, and none of the pilots were familiar with the dangers below water. Vessels that grounded on the shoals were hauled clear with minimum delay so as not to stall the rest of the armada. Unused to the broiling August sun, the British sweltered on deck. One of the flag officers cursed "this oven of a river." Officers and crew made good use of the cooler hours, generally rising at 3:30 or 4:00 A.M. and bunking down before 9:00 P.M.[1] Beyond the sandy shoreline they saw small fields of corn, green meadows, and a few white-painted wooden houses with orchards and gardens. Cultivated patches were hemmed in by thick masses of forests.

While the heavier line-of-battle ships dropped anchor many miles south of Benedict, two frigates, one commanded by Nourse, sailed close to the village's shoreline. With just enough water to keep them afloat above the shoals, the frigates turned broadside, their guns loaded and ready to fire at the slightest provocation from shore. They would stand sentinel while rowboats shuttled thousands of troops off the vessels and onto the American mainland. Even though British intelligence pointed to weak American defenses, they had not expected to get this far without some show of force, especially since the occasional heights seemed to be logical positions for gunposts.

The invasion began in the thick of night. Boats were lowered off the *Albion*, Cockburn's flagship, at 2:00 A.M. The sunburned admiral, in a rusty, gold-laced hat, followed two hours later.[2] Lighter now, the vessel sailed upriver and at 7:30 A.M. anchored again about ten miles south of Benedict.[3] When they had rowed several miles, the troops would hoist themselves aboard lighter ships anchored higher up. Decks, cabins, and even holds filled with exhausted men resting as if in halfway houses, until about sunrise when a cannon boomed aboard a frigate. It was the signal for everyone to get back in the boats and head for land. As a substitute for horses, two hundred seamen prepared to drag the ammunition, rockets, the lone 9-pounder, a 5½-inch howitzer, and two 3-pounders.

Benedict was one of the oldest settlements in America, beginning with wharves and warehouses to export tobacco and lumber from nearby plantations to the other colonies and Britain. Shipbuilding followed in the late seventeenth century, when it became one of the first official ports along the commercial water route. By the time the British landed it had grown into the Patuxent River's main port.[4] But now it was quiet, still, and abandoned.

As the soldiers and marines washed ashore, they inhaled the scent of bales of tobacco and the fragrance of peaches, apples, and apricots. Cooped up aboard ship for so long, they relished the chance to walk and run about, or even just to loll on the grass. Many quickly set about stealing sheep, poultry, and pigs in violation of standing orders to pay for anything taken. Lt. George Gleig and some men of lower ranks guzzled milk and cream in abandoned homes. It was not long before they were hunting partridges, quail, wild turkeys, and hares.[5] The few sailors who had to stay put to service the ships would soon make a sport of hunting wild boar.

Before the day was out, a grotesquely disfigured American came into the enemy camp volunteering treasonable information. He was taken to Capt. Harry Smith, the deputy adjutant general also in charge of secret intelligence. The traitor gave his name as Calder and proved to be a shrewd and intelligent man. Smith thought he had leprosy and had crossed over in the hope of receiving medical treatment. Later Calder was joined by another turncoat, a healthy-looking young man named Brown, who was put to work as a well-informed guide and scout.[6]

As night fell, three cannons pointed westward on the crown of a hill above the drowsy brigades. Pickets stationed two and a half miles inland set off a rash of rumors that the entire British expeditionary force had advanced to that point.[7] In Washington, meanwhile, there was consternation over a credible report of Admiral Cockburn boasting that he would be in the capital within two days. A courier had sped from Joshua Barney's flotilla anchored off Nottingham with the commodore's message for Navy Secretary Jones: "One of my officers has this moment arrived from the mouth of the Patuxent and brings the enclosed account. I haste[n] to forward it to you; the Admiral said he would dine in Washington on Sunday, after having destroyed the flotilla."[8]

Barney's spy reported forty-five large craft and many more small boats forging up the Patuxent. The anonymous agent did not record how he came by his information, but its detail lent authenticity. The troops aboard were quoted as saying they had "a determination to go to the city of Washington."

As the British landed at Benedict, the navy secretary dictated a flurry of communications to three of the spunkiest commanders in the American navy. He confided to Barney that he was not sure Washington was the real target. "Appearances indicate a design on this place but it may be a feint to mask a real design on Baltimore. If, however, the enemy's force is strong in troops, he may make a vigorous push for this place. In that case he probably would not waste much time with the flotilla." To gain time, whatever the enemy's goal, Jones ordered Barney to burn the flotilla if the British approached "with an overwhelming force," and then retreat to Washington.[9] Barney could not communicate as quickly as he wished because there was no horse available for the courier.[10] But another note from Jones directed Barney to sabotage the British advance on Washington by destroying bridges and felling trees across the roads. The secretary also promised to provide two horsemen to speed up communications.[11]

There was no ambivalence about the British target in Jones's letter to Capt. David Porter in New York City. "The enemy has entered the Patuxent with a very strong force indicating a rapid movement upon this city," he wrote. Porter was told to rush to Washington without delay, bringing with him those crewmen who had survived the recent destruction of their ship off the Chilean coast by British warships.[12]

The navy secretary ordered Commodore John Rodgers, then anchored on the Delaware River at Philadelphia, to take three hundred men and go "with the least possible delay" to Baltimore.[13] But this last letter took three days to arrive because it was sent a day later through the regular mail and arrived in Philadelphia on a Sunday, when all deliveries were suspended.[14]

At Benedict, the restless British army had stirred before dawn but did not break camp until late that afternoon, Saturday, 20 August. As the invaders milled around roasting under the blazing sun, Secretary of State Monroe spied on their shipping from a rise in the land three miles away. They were too far off for his naked eye, and, having left his telescope behind in Washington, he could not get a reliable fix on their strength. Though Monroe was the most senior cabinet secretary, he was still a hands-on man of action and fervid patriot. Even now he had a bullet wound in his shoulder from Revolutionary War combat, a condition which made him look as though he walked with his left side foremost.[15] Characteristically, Monroe had volunteered to scout the invaders' movements immediately after the president told him of their landing at Benedict. The situation had looked grave and Monroe had ridden hard for the village port, accompanied by more than two dozen cavalrymen. At 1 P.M. he dashed off a note to the president, promising to keep him updated: "We shall take better views in the course of the evening. . . . The general idea is that they are still debarking their troops. . . . The general idea also is that Washington is their object."[16]

Three hours after Monroe's courier galloped off to Washington, General Ross appeared on horseback among his expectant troops. A mighty cheer erupted from the ranks. They felt deep affection and respect for this brave and chivalrous man who had led them so well in Spain and Portugal. Ross doffed his hat, smiled, and dipped his head in acknowledgment. Then he gave the order to march north, and at the sound of a bugle they set off for Nottingham in strict formation.[17]

Simultaneously, Cockburn led a squadron of tenders, launches, barges, and cutters up the Patuxent parallel to the infantry. Their colors streamed gaily in the breeze as they cut through the water to trap Barney's flotilla. The light craft were manned by marines and sailors who would protect the army's right flank and rush in to help the instant they were signaled from shore.[18]

Ross's infantry brigades tramped for eight grueling hours in the baking heat, their discomfort made worse by the weight of weapons and ammunition carried by each man. Out of condition from so many weeks aboard ship, the men tired quickly. The toll was heavy as many straggled behind, slumping down from sheer exhaustion. Only Ross and the staff officers rode horses. But the army pressed on cautiously, keeping rigid distances between units and flanking patrols to guard against ambushes. When they finally halted near a couple of empty farmhouses, they had little cover and got soaked during a heavy downpour.[19] The violent winds knocked down piles of weapons and blew drums out of the camp. When the winds reached the Patuxent they turned several ships on their beam ends.[20]

While the British breakfasted the next morning, Monroe counted enemy ships anchored eight to ten miles south of Benedict. From a closer lookout post below the village he saw twenty-three square-rigged vessels but very few barges. It confirmed his suspicions that the invading force was moving on Barney before closing in on Washington in a pincer movement with Captain Gordon's fleet in the Potomac. Monroe turned his horse around and rode twelve miles inland along the main road to Washington. He could not find any enemy tracks. In a new note to the president, he said he was on the way to Nottingham. The shoreline, he noted, had been plundered of all stock for three or four miles.[21]

On land, the elite British infantry—refreshed, reinvigorated, and swelling with anticipation—bounded ahead for Nottingham. Full-throated buglers and synchronized drummers filled the air with stirring notes from Handel's much-loved opera *Judas Maccabeus*. The long lines of aroused soldiers needed no further prompting. A chorus of masculine voices took up the defiant words in lusty unison as they sang like a triumphant army:[22] "See the conquering hero comes / Sound the trumpet, beat the drums."

That same day in Baltimore, eighteen-year-old Pvt. John Pendleton Kennedy romped off to war with a pair of pumps packed in his knapsack. The young volunteer expected to wear them at a victory ball in the President's House after they had whipped the British and saved the capital. He had, he confessed in maturer years, been "lured by the romance of our enterprise."[23]

The teenager was among the youngest in a company of eighty men of the United Volunteers attached to Gen. Tobias Stansbury's 5th Regiment.

Most were comfortably off, at the top of their business and professional careers, but these accomplishments were irrelevant to the dangers ahead. Kennedy would soon look upon his unfit unit as "a class of men who are not generally supposed to be the best to endure fatigue." But the young man was euphoric as they marched south out of Baltimore to Washington "with all the glitter of a dress parade. . . . [T]he pavements were crowded with anxious spectators . . . handkerchiefs were waving from the fair hands at the windows . . . the populace were cheering and huzzahing at every corner, as we hurried along in a brisk step to familiar music, with banners fluttering in the wind and bayonets flashing in the sun. What a scene it was, and what a proud actor I was in it!"[24]

When they camped that night, Kennedy shared a tent with five gentlemen used to the luxuries of life. They giggled at the idea of supping on rations of fat pork and hard biscuit and had no horror of tasteless meals to come because they had filled a wagon with their own food. That first day they co-opted a black mess servant from among the many strangers following the troops. When it came time to bed down, Kennedy's coat was not warm enough in the chill night air, but his father, a mounted sentry in another unit, thoughtfully came by with a borrowed blanket.

The next day they marched twenty miles under the searing sun in their winter cloth uniforms. Each man was also burdened with a long fourteen-pound musket and a knapsack filled with clothing weighing at least another ten pounds. The raw and ragged column looked even comical decked out in heavy leather helmets sprouting plumes. Sweating in the swirl of dust kicked up by so many marching boots, they quenched their thirst whenever they crossed the muddy brooks. But, still new to the hardships of army life, they did not gripe, and even managed to laugh at each other and sing a few songs out of tune. When the column rested for the afternoon rations, Kennedy's gentlemanly unit disappeared into a tavern to pay for fine meals with service. They camped that night at a hilltop village notable only because the stagecoach stopped long enough to allow a change of horses.

Mounted sentries continually rode by with rumors which ruffled the rank and file. They knew the British were somewhere on the road to Washington, but everything else was vague. One report particularly unsettled the novices. A shaken sentry they knew from Baltimore said he had stumbled upon British cavalrymen while carrying orders to General Stansbury. The enemy riders had chased him several miles before he eluded them. Kennedy's colleagues later found out that the cavalrymen were in fact Georgetowners who had themselves mistaken the sentry for a British dragoon. But it did not lessen their anxiety. The sentry stuck to his story that he had seen enemy riders next to foreign troops.

Secretary of State Monroe reached Nottingham ahead of the British and spotted three enemy barges when Cockburn's squadron was still four hundred yards offshore. Scribbling a message to the president, he dismissed the force as "not considerable."

"If you send five or six hundred men, if you could not save the town, you may, perhaps, cut off their retreat or rear."

But a while later he knew better: "P.S. Ten or twelve more barges in view. There are but two muskets in town, and a few scattering militia."

"Five o'clock. Thirty or forty barges are in view."[25]

By the time he withdrew from Nottingham later that Sunday evening, Monroe could just make out the head of a column of enemy soldiers entering the settlement. He guessed they were the same force that had come up from Benedict. Some American cavalrymen took potshots at the boats but scampered away when they spotted the long columns of advancing infantry. That night the British set up headquarters in Nottingham while the tenders and other craft anchored offshore. Residents had fled the little community so quickly that some even left bread in the ovens.[26]

Monroe conferred with a colonel who had been watching from a more commanding height. They concluded there were between four thousand and five thousand infantry and perhaps another one thousand enemy in the barges. Riding hard toward General Winder's camp at the Woodyard, fourteen miles east of Washington, Monroe arrived exhausted after midnight to pass on his intelligence estimate. Before going off to lie down he learned that Winder's force totaled only about twenty-two hundred, including some first-rate marines. But it also numbered green cavalrymen and the sorry militia from Washington and Georgetown.[27]

A powerful squadron of British warships was meanwhile battling treacherous shoals in the Potomac River on its path up to the capital's southern defenses. If the vessels made it over the hidden sandbanks and other uncharted perils, they would still have to pass by the formidable guns at Fort Warburton on the east bank of the river, twelve miles south of Washington. Led by Captain Gordon in his 38-gun frigate *Seahorse*, the ships included a second frigate, the 36-gun *Euryalus*, the rocket ship *Erebus*, the bomb vessels *Aetna*, *Devastation*, and *Meteor*, and the dispatch boat *Anna Maria*.[28]

The most fearful of the unseen hazards a third of the way upriver were deadly shoals known as the Kettle Bottoms. These were notorious oyster banks of varying sizes, some no longer than a boat, and separated from one another by unequal distances. Though the ships would later be led by an Alexandrian renegade pilot, the British had to negotiate this stretch of water without help.[29] Working from poor charts, they hugged closer to the Virginia shore, but it was not long before they discovered that one ship could pass by undamaged while another, sailing a few feet wide of the wake, became grounded. To the surprise of everyone, the *Euryalus* stuck like glue in the trail of the *Seahorse*, even though there appeared to be water all around. Only when divers looked below did they see the bilge caught in the grip of an oyster bank the size of a rowboat. They floated it after much heaving, but then watched helplessly as the *Seahorse* grounded on a sandbank. Valuable time passed by as they waited for the tide to rise, and even then they wasted a night offloading guns and provisions to help raise the hull. The entire squadron grounded the next day. This was the frustrating pattern as each ship's hull was clasped tight at least twenty times during the ten-day passage upriver.[30]

Further north, in Alexandria, worry was turning to fear as reports spread of the naval advance. Depending on winds, the enemy warships could be only days away from the port city, whose population at the last census four years earlier had numbered 7,227, including 1,488 slaves.[31] The town's militia had crossed the Potomac to take up defenses between Piscataway and Fort Warburton the same day the British had marched out of Benedict. Militiamen had taken all of Alexandria's artillery with the exception of two 12-pounders, useless because they were without ammunition. Nearly all of the light weapons had also been removed. Only about a hundred armed men could have been mustered in the city, and these were of questionable usefulness because they were either overage, exempted for sickness and other reasons, or had simply ducked their civic duties.[32]

For almost two years Alexandrians had been prodding the federal government to take drastic measures for their wartime defense. Fort Warburton was all that stood between them and an enemy penetrating from the river. If the British arrived on the Potomac, Alexandrians would be at their mercy. But they met with bureaucratic slothfulness. Fifteen months earlier Alexandria's civic leaders had implored the president to do something for their protection. But, said Mayor Charles Simms, Madison's dull reaction was to tell them that "any respectable body of men was entitled to attention and that the subject should be taken under consideration."[33] Secretary Armstrong even refused to meet with Alexandria's committee of vigilance, aloofly saying he would only listen to messages relayed through General Winder.[34]

The Common Council of Alexandria Committee had nowhere to turn. Unanimously, it resolved that "in case the British vessels should pass the fort, or their forces approach the town by land, and there should be no sufficient force on our part to oppose them with any reasonable prospect of success, they should appoint a committee to carry a flag to the officer commanding the enemy's force, about to attack the town, and to procure the best terms for the safety of persons, houses and property in their power."[35]

The flourishing old city with cobblestoned streets, where George Washington had worshiped regularly, was about to raise a white flag.

5. Pandemonium

A showdown over leadership of the Washington militia had only just come to the boil with the gruff resignation of its head, Maj. Gen. John Van Ness. A for-
mer congressman from New York and immensely wealthy through marriage
to the only daughter and heiress of a landowning mogul, the forty-four-
year-old Van Ness was one of the capital's most respected citizens and
chairman of the Bank of the Metropolis. However, there had been bad
blood between him and Winder. That weekend, when the two met to dis-
cuss activation of the militia, they clashed over who would command the
men. Van Ness said the law favored him; Winder claimed command over
the entire military district and of men in the field. When Van Ness sought
a decision one way or the other from the secretary of war, Armstrong
ducked, calling it "an embarrassing case," and passed it up to the president.[1] Van Ness went to see Madison, who refused to intervene without
talking to his secretary of war. Van Ness bunkered up in his home in a state
of limbo and grew increasingly impatient. He began to sense he was being
stripped of command. Unable any longer to delay, he sent a messenger to
demand a decision. The courier was kept waiting two hours before Armstrong sent him back with a note. Van Ness read it and concluded he was
no longer in command. Instantly he wrote out a one-paragraph letter to
the secretary of war: "Give me leave hereby to resign the command which
I have for some time past had the honor to hold, as Major General of the
militia of the District of Columbia. My commission would have been
enclosed, had I been able to lay my hands upon it. A principal regret which

I feel upon this occasion is that my resignation occurs at a moment when I would have been happy to have been permitted to participate in the defense of my country, and particularly of the District."[2]

The war of the generals was over. Van Ness, however, was careful not to appear as a spoiler during the emergency. Telling Winder he had not acted out of personal grievance, he offered to serve in any capacity. But the more he saw of Winder the less he thought of his "apparent sluggishness or procrastination."[3] He was flabbergasted when Winder told him he was afraid troops coming down from Baltimore would arrive too soon because the enemy would probably do an about-turn and attack Baltimore.

Word of the British approach spread rapidly amid scenes of mounting pandemonium in Washington. Lax officials had left the city open to catastrophe. Most at fault was the secretary of war, who had made up his mind that the British would never march on the capital.[4] However, Armstrong's influence did not paralyze every bureaucrat of lesser importance. The chief of ordnance, Col. Decius Wadsworth, dashed off a letter to General Winder requesting immediate release from militia duty of men in essential services. His own office was near bedlam, and he needed his clerk back. Likewise, gun carriages at Greenleaf's Point on the city's southern boundary could not be readied until a blacksmith was stood down from the militia.[5]

Wadsworth also started rounding up horses to pull the ammunition carts and artillery carriages. Knowing nothing of the enemy's strength or equipment, he could only guess at the scope of the danger.[6] But, fearing the worst, he removed five hundred muskets and ammunition from the arsenal at Greenleaf's Point. The boxes were taken across the long bridge over the Potomac and left under guard at the foot of the drawbridge on the road to Alexandria. Here he fully expected they would be safe and out of the clutches of the British. As a precaution, Wadsworth arranged with the quartermaster to have six wagons on standby to take this shipment even further if need be. However, pledges and promises fell by the wayside in the swirling panic, and Wadsworth would later learn to his dismay that the same six wagons reserved by him were wheeled several miles away and used to carry off important paperwork in the War Office.[7]

In its edition of Monday, 22 August, the *National Intelligencer* carried a notice from Mayor James Blake ordering the militia to take all broken or faulty weapons for quick repair at municipal expense to designated shops on Pennsylvania Avenue and near the navy yard.[8] Few heeded the mayor's handbills urging them to defend their homes.[9] Flight into the countryside seemed more sensible, and citizens took to the streets in droves. Some of those who could afford slaves had sent them deep into the country into the temporary custody of others, to avoid losing ownership or possession to the invaders.[10] But many residents were trapped by financial hardship and had nowhere to go. Former hotelier Pontius Stelle, who had fallen on hard times, agonized to an acquaintance, "I know not where to take my little helpless family."[11] Flight from the capital was costly for those taking out bulky possessions. Joseph Nourse, longtime register of the U.S. Treasury, paid $222 to have his furniture removed, but when he totaled up other expenses, including the hire of a hack for a day and rental accommodation higher up on the banks of the Potomac River, his outlay exceeded $2,000.[12]

Georgetown lawyer Francis "Frank" Scott Key had ridden as far as Fredericktown, forty-five miles northwest of the capital, before managing to hire two wagons on Monday to go back to his home and transport personal papers and other possessions out of the reach of the British. He gave more files, together with a gun and documents belonging to his close friend John Randolph, to a third party for safekeeping. Key had already spirited his children out of Georgetown to stay with his parents near Fredericktown. His wife of twelve years, Mary "Polly" Key, lodged at Middlebrook Mills Pond, closer to Georgetown. On Monday night, as he prepared to return alone to Georgetown, he wrote to his parents, cautioning them about multiple rumors and suggesting they all rededicate themselves to God, "who never will forsake those who trust in him!"[13]

The dry and dusty roads were clogged with desperate people hurrying to get out with any belongings they could wheel or carry. A sizzling heat wave added to their travail. Washington's clamminess was so common to August and September that Thomas Jefferson had once labeled them "the two sickly months."[14] But this was the hottest summer in memory. It had not rained for three weeks.[15] Wagons and carts were now more precious than jewelry, and owners clung to them tenaciously. Government agents combing the streets and neighborhoods tried in vain to impound them for official use. Residents who would have buckled under to bureaucratic threats in normal times now bristled with the power of possessors, even chasing off officials with abuse and profanities.

Mordecai Booth, senior clerk at the navy yard, had never been more harried. He was detailed by Commodore Thomas Tingey, the yard's commandant, to seize carts to take more than a hundred barrels of gunpowder out of Washington. First he stopped at Long's Hotel on Capitol Hill to advertise the navy yard's need for four or five carts if anyone was interested in public employment. Then he galloped after a wagon pulled by a team of five horses on Pennsylvania Avenue. The driver, a free black, had a shipment of tea for Georgetown, boxes for Washington, and molasses for Alexandria. Booth ordered the tea dropped off at nearby McKeowin's Hotel and the other cargo delivered to their destinations. Then he issued a certificate mandating the driver into service at the navy yard. It was the only lucky break he would have that day because the driver honored his orders.

As Booth continued on to Georgetown he overtook Navy Secretary Jones, who told him to impress every cart he could find. But sanction from a cabinet member was of little help in the general turmoil. Booth stopped a wagoner who tried to escape impressment by pleading he was already engaged to cart public papers for Treasury register Joseph Nourse. When he failed to present documentary proof, Booth slapped him with a certificate of impressment. Just then Nourse's wife, Maria, ran up to verify the driver's story, and she pleaded with Secretary Jones as he passed by. In an abrupt reversal, Jones released the wagon and told Booth to bypass all transport already in use on public business.

Next Booth stopped a black driver moving furniture for a Dr. Sims who lived nearby. The navy yard clerk rode to the doctor's house, intending to have the cargo unloaded, but Sims was out. His wife was in such a fitful state that Booth returned to the cart. Only then did he notice a wheel about to break, and he passed it over.

When he was on the south side of the President's House, known as the President's Walk, Booth saw seven loaded carts just in from Baltimore. Two had already been impressed by another official. Booth hastily seized the remaining five and followed them to Georgetown to hasten their unloading. While a wagon was emptied, Booth left briefly to scout for more transport. On his return he would feel the full fury and frustration of residents driven to vulgarity and selfishness by the press of events. A black man sat in one of the driver's seats. A white man stood by the wagon while a man named Riggs, whose company goods were being loaded, looked on. Booth asked the white man his name, but Riggs stepped in and ordered him not to divulge it. When Booth announced he was impressing the wagon for the Navy Department, Riggs exploded, swearing he would fight to the death to keep it. "They went into the store," Booth reported later to his superior. "I dismounted and followed them in when they made use of such language as was degrading to gentlemen. I had no one with me to enforce detention of the wagon, and it was hurried off in opposition to my positive command to the contrary, and except I had used violence, could not have prevented it, in which I did not think myself justified."[16]

When he got outside again, Booth tried to find the driver of the second wagon, but as soon as he was out of sight the wagon was spirited away. On his return Booth impressed the third cart, even though it had no cover. The driver claimed he had only a few miles to go to deliver his load but promised to report to the navy yard by 10 A.M. the following day if only he could go home to nearby Montgomery County and collect a tent and some food. Reluctantly, Booth consented, but the driver never did show up as promised.

The sun was about to set when an exhausted Mordecai Booth rode into the navy yard with five wagons in tow. It had been a long and arduous day, but trifling compared to the ordeal that still awaited him. He was up before sunrise to see one of his wagons loaded with provisions for Commodore Barney. Then he supervised the loading of 124 barrels and two quarter casks of gunpowder. But before he could leave, he had to commandeer a saddled horse from a stable after the owner objected to his wife's lending it to Booth.

The navy clerk overtook the gunpowder wagons before they crossed the bridge over the Potomac River. Here he met Col. George Minor, commandant of the 60th Regiment of the Virginia militia, who detached a military guard for the caravan of explosives. Booth arrived at Falls Church, Virginia, late at night. He was still a mile distant from the farm of Commandant Tingey's daughter and son-in-law, Sarah and Daniel Dulany, where the gunpowder would be stored.[17]

Many government agencies remained staffed because the clerks were over forty-five years old and therefore exempt from militia service. But the basement offices in the House of Representatives were almost empty because nearly all of the clerks were young men. Only J. T. Frost, a new-comer over forty-five, remained at his desk.[18] In this moment of unparal-leled crisis, a man of scant experience and weak authority was burdened with the need to make rapid decisions of national importance. He was sorely in need of the guiding hand of the clerk of the House of Repre-sentatives, Patrick Magruder, a former congressman and custodian of the Library of Congress.[19] But Magruder had been ill for months and had acted on his doctor's advice to leave town and restore his health at min-eral springs. No one was around to advise Frost on how and when to pro-tect the volumes of House paperwork from enemy vandals. His colleagues, Samuel Hamilton and Brook Berry, had been plucked from their offices to serve in an artillery company.[20]

Another clerk, Samuel Burch, had tried hard to reason with his superi-ors into letting him remain at his post to save the House documents, but he, too, had been marched out of the city to meet the enemy. Not until late on Sunday was he allowed to leave his company of the 2nd Regiment and return to Washington.[21] This was done through the personal inter-vention of Col. George Magruder of the 1st Regiment, who was also chief clerk to his brother, Patrick Magruder.

But when Burch arrived back in the disorderly capital on Sunday night, he was hamstrung by Colonel Magruder's specific orders not to begin packing until he knew for a fact that clerks at the War Office had begun to pack their own papers. Burch learned only at noon on Monday that War Office clerks were already moving their documents out. Much later he found out that evacuation work at the War Office had really begun a day earlier.

By the time Burch went looking for wheeled transport, it was too late. The military had grabbed most of them, and the remainder were piled high with the goods of civilians in flight. First he tried to hire the wagons. When he was rebuffed he tried pulling rank, claiming he had a right to impound them. But again he was snubbed, especially when it was obvious he had no force to back him up. In desperation Burch ordered three mes-sengers to scour the countryside, but all they came up with was one cart and four oxen procured from a man living six miles outside of Washington. It did not arrive in the capital until after dark on Monday night, when it was frantically loaded with the most valuable papers. The oxen were then turned around and driven nine miles away to deposit the documents in a safe and secret location in the countryside. The cart returned to Washington, where harried clerks tried to remove as much as possible of the remaining horde of paper. They toiled until Wednesday morning, then joined the general exodus. Frustrated beyond measure, both Burch and Frost knew that everything could have been saved, even the vast contents of the Library of Congress, if only they had been able to seize more carriages.[22]

The archival material of the U.S. Senate was in equal jeopardy because no one with administrative seniority was available to take charge. Samuel Otis, secretary of the Senate since 1789, had died in April, and though senators had mourned his loss by wearing black crepe armbands for a month, no one had appointed his successor during the intervening four months. The principal clerk was out of town, leaving only two younger clerks, John McDonald and Lewis Machen, to decide whether to take matters into their own hands. Machen, twenty-four and married less than two years, should have been called into active service with the District of Columbia militia, in which he commanded a company with the rank of captain.[23] But seven weeks earlier he had bought a farm in Maryland, eight miles outside Washington, which disqualified him from holding a commission in the District militia, though he was allowed to serve there as a rank-and-file volunteer.[24] He had not yet been enrolled in the Maryland militia, so he decided instead to make himself available for civilian tasks at the Senate.

Machen waited in vain for an executive order or for someone higher up to tell him what to do with the Senate documents, but neither was forthcoming. By noon on Sunday 21 he could wait no longer. All around him were signs of "doubt, confusion and dismay."[25] He gave McDonald, his superior, an ultimatum: help get the documents out of Washington immediately, or he would act alone. Even though McDonald was of the same mind and readily concurred, they now had to find transport. When he had ridden into Washington, Machen had passed a wagon driver and sounded him out about the possibility of hiring the vehicle. But now, when he returned to conclude the deal, the owner was away from his home. The driver balked at letting the wagon go but relented when Machen threatened to impound it. By the time they got to the Senate, however, McDonald had gone, apparently to make arrangements for the safety of his own family.

According to Machen, he and the driver, assisted by Tobias, the black office messenger, loaded only the most valuable documents. They included confidential papers, "one of which I knew to contain the number and positions of the entire American military force."[26] He believed the documents stashed into the wagon constituted the only copy of the Senate's quarter century of executive history.

They loaded the wagon until it could hold no more, then drove off for Machen's farm as the sun was about to set. But they were still within the boundaries of the District of Columbia when a wheel gave way. Fortunately, they were close to a blacksmith's shop and stole a replacement. Then, when only two miles short of the sanctuary in Prince George's County, Maryland, the wagon overturned. It took them several hours during the night to lift it up again and reload the precious cargo. But when McDonald turned up at the farm at ten o'clock the following morning he took the loaded wagon on to Brookville, Maryland, a more secure refuge because Machen's farm lay in the same county crisscrossed by the invaders on their way to and from Washington. The salvaged documents remained at their new location until the following month.

John Gardiner, chief clerk of the General Land Office in the Treasury Department, also packed all his official records on Sunday, August 21, but could not find any wagons to take them out of the city. A day later he found some in the country and loaded them that evening for shipment out of the capital the same night.[27]

Navy Secretary Jones had the good sense to anticipate a run on transport and allowed his staff to ferry departmental archives in boats up the Potomac River. Three clerks worked feverishly all of Sunday filling boxes and trunks with books, papers, maps, charts, plans, stationery, trophies, instruments, and even prints and paintings. That night the crews of two riverboats were paid to haul the heavy load upriver. The next day two municipal carts carried everything else, leaving behind the heavy desks and other furniture. They quickly covered the short distance to the near-

est Potomac River wharf, and by late afternoon the cargo had been transferred to a boat heading for Georgetown.

Surprisingly, two drivers with large wagons arrived at the Navy Department on Monday morning offering their services. The accountant leaped
at the opportunity, and soon the contents of his office had been carted off
to the riverbank. A day later the personnel made good their escape, the
chief clerk and one of his underlings going by boat up the Potomac, then
through the locks and the canal to safety above the falls.[28]

Late that night a horseman banged on the door of the house of his
friend Samuel Harrison Smith, president of the Bank of Washington and
commissioner of revenue in the Treasury Department. When it opened,
the rider skipped the usual greetings. "The enemy are advancing!" Willie
Bradley shouted. "Our own troops are giving way on all sides and are
retreating to the city! Go, for God's sake go!"[29] Having sounded the alarm,
he was gone. Smith's wife, Margaret, calmly supervised the loading of a
wagon with some personal keepsakes. It was still inconceivable to her that
the enemy would occupy the city, yet they heeded the warning. By 3 A.M.
they had bundled their goods into a wagon and set off slowly through the
darkness, heading north to Maryland with their daughter and servants.
Now and then Mrs. Smith got out of the wagon to walk, and at dawn they
stopped for breakfast. Ten hours after leaving Washington they arrived at
their destination, the secluded Quaker village of Brookville, set in a small
valley with mills by a stream.

Georgetown librarian and bookshop owner Joseph Milligan fled far
across Virginia, finding temporary shelter at the Hackwood Park home of
Sarah Young, sister-in-law of Joseph Nourse. Milligan was so scared that
he had become irrational. "Poor Milligan the Georgetown librarian arrived
here yesterday exhausted and insane," Sarah wrote to her sister, Maria
Nourse. "He thinks he was pursued by the British, that they guarded the
passes of the mountains to watch for the President. He feared he should
be taken for him. And finally brooding over his country's woes and his
own, his reason was shaken from her throne. How terribly has he over-
rated his own consequence. He is harmless but knows of treasons and
whispers them to all he meets."[30]

At the State Department a vidette (mounted sentinel) arrived with a note scribbled by Secretary of State Monroe ordering his staff to secure as best they could the precious national documents and departmental records. Stephen Pleasonton, a senior clerk, hurried to buy quantities of coarse, durable linen which he ordered cut and made up into book bags. Together with other State Department employees, Pleasonton gingerly packed the rare manuscripts: the scrolled Declaration of Independence; the Constitution; George Washington's correspondence, including the historic letter in which he resigned his commission; international treaties; and even the secret, unpublished journals of Congress.

As Pleasonton handled the treasured documents in the passageway connecting the State and War Departments, the secretary of war walked by on the way to his own suite. Armstrong paused to rebuke Pleasonton for being unnecessarily alarmed. "He did not think the British were serious in their intentions of coming to Washington," the clerk recalled. "I replied that we were under a different belief, and let their intentions be what they might, it was the part of prudence to preserve the valuable papers of the Revolutionary Government."[31]

With the packing done, Pleasonton assembled a number of carts and had the valuable cargo whisked across the Potomac and two miles upstream of Georgetown to Edgar Patterson's abandoned gristmill. But the State Department clerk was troubled and uneasy. If the British invaded Washington, they would surely send out a search party to destroy Foxall's Foundry, the nation's first and largest manufacturer of cannons and other heavy armaments. Pleasonton reckoned the mill was too close to the foundry, and he worried that a traitor or someone merely sympathetic to the British might lead them from the foundry, just west of Georgetown, to the hiding place in the mill. Determined to avoid this hazard, he procured more wagons from Virginia farms, loaded them with his priceless charge, and accompanied the wheeled caravan thirty-five miles further inland to the little town of Leesburg. There the linen bags were carefully stored and sealed in an empty house, the keys entrusted to Rev. John Littlejohn, the sheriff of Leesburg and a former collector of internal revenue. The day's activities so exhausted the State Department clerk, who would much later be promoted to an auditor of the Treasury Department, that he fell asleep early in a tavern.[32]

James Mason, commissary general of prisoners, had also correctly sensed the danger and begun tightening security against aliens. About the time the British landed at Benedict, he ordered the marshal of the District of Columbia to find out the location and occupation of all enemy aliens and to detain and move further inland anyone of "suspicious character or irregular conduct."[33] Six prisoners were sent to Fredericktown to be so closely guarded that escape would be impossible. A seventh Briton, claiming to be a deserter but suspected of spying, was held apart from the others to prevent communication.[34]

The capital's civic leader was besieged by people asking what he would do if the British crossed the city limits. Mayor Blake, a physician, answered with the best patriotic posture: he would take up arms and die in the streets rather than surrender the capital. But, he was quick to add, if everyone else abandoned the city, and that included the military, he would of course have no choice but to do likewise. Caught up in the havoc, he was in and out of the city limits, rounding up some two hundred men to fortify the defenses at Bladensburg. On Tuesday night, around midnight, he visited encamped troops, whom he later joined on the battlefield. His wife and four small children had meanwhile skipped town with their servants, leaving their house in the care of a lone female domestic.[35]

On Tuesday the wife of the secretary of the navy wrote a polite regret at having to cancel a scheduled social call on Dolley Madison. "In the present state of alarm and bustle of preparation for the worst that may happen, I imagine it will be more convenient to dispense with the enjoyment of your hospitality today," Eleanor Jones wrote to the president's wife. She declared that even as her husband was busily engaged in dispatching marines, she and her niece were packing just in case they had to flee, although "in the event of necessity we know not where to go."[36] Worse still, their carriage horse was sick and the coachman was nowhere to be found.

In the President's House, Dolley Madison yearned for her husband. At their parting on Monday morning he had asked whether she had the courage to wait for his return in a day or two. Ever the comforter, she assured him she feared only for the well-being of himself and the troops. He told her to take good care of herself, and urged her to protect the public and private cabinet papers. During the next day, Madison wrote her two letters in pencil, and when she read them her apprehension turned to alarm. The president, never one to exaggerate, warned her to have her carriage ready to take her out of Washington at a moment's notice. The enemy was apparently stronger than reported and might even break through to Washington and destroy it.

Dolley wasted no time. She packed so many trunks with cabinet papers that they almost filled a carriage. But this meant sacrificing nearly all of her personal belongings, since her staff could not find any other transport. The ragged exodus on Tuesday had snared so many refugees from all walks of life that even a colonel and his one hundred men guarding the presidential mansion had made off.[37] Strangely, Dolley's own distress gave way to a feisty spiritedness, "so unfeminine," she wrote a close friend later, "as to be free from fear, and willing to remain in the *Castle*. If I could have had a cannon through every window, but alas! those who should have placed them there, fled."[38]

Amid the turmoil, the president's wife kept a cool head. She quickly vetoed a suggestion by French-born Jean Pierre Sioussat, her indispensable "faithful domestic" at the mansion, to spike the two 12-pounder cannons at the front gate and booby-trap the British with a train of explosive powder.[39] "French John," as he was known to all in Washington, would have been chief usher if such a title had existed then. Dolley often took the advice of this tall, patrician-looking expatriate, who had sailed the world under the French flag before jumping ship in New York harbor a decade before. He knew so much about foreign customs and protocol, and exuded an air of such polished tact and subtle diplomacy, that he had risen from lowly doorman to be her trusted right-hand man.[40] Yet when he came up with his uncharacteristically harebrained scheme to blow up the British, and with them perhaps the President's House, the First Lady pulled him up sharply, even though she could not make him understand "why all advantages in war may not be taken."

Dolley Madison was far more troubled about her husband's security, and with good cause. "I hear of much hostility towards him. Disaffection stalks around us," she confided Tuesday in a letter to her sister.[41]

6. The Juggernaut Rolls On

As dawn was breaking on Monday, Cockburn resumed his chase. Today he planned to corner Commodore Barney and do away with the nettlesome flotilla. But he could push forward only with his lightest boats in the narrowing channel and shallower waterway. Before reaching Pig Point, where Barney was thought to be sheltering, Cockburn landed marines to attack on a flank and draw off any American fire. There was no need for it. The flotilla lay in the stream just ahead, with the commodore's broad personal pendant fluttering from his flagship, the topsail sloop *Scorpion*. The flotilla's fourteen open rowboats, each large enough to hold between forty and sixty men with heavy weapons, were stretched out in a long line behind. The British admiral closed in on his gig, but before he could give any command smoke and fire rose from Barney's large armed sloop. Then it exploded. In that instant the British realized the entire flotilla had been abandoned and gunpowder trails lit to their magazines. Eager for a scrap, the tars looked on with dismay as their prey self-destructed. Explosions ripped through one after the other as the Chesapeake Bay's only naval defenses burned upon the waters. A thunderous bang reverberated from the last of the boats, which held the munitions, and thick black smoke hovered over the crackling timber. Only a single rowboat survived, its fires failing to take hold. Thirteen merchant schooners anchored behind the raging flotilla were captured intact, but Cockburn put the torch to some of those worse for wear. The remainder were loaded with massive quantities of captured tobacco.[1] The climactic end to the hunt stirred many emotions. Midshipman Samuel Decimus Davies wrote home about how "we had some fun here down by the seaside."[2]

Cockburn did not know that Barney, accompanied by four hundred men, had left the day before for Upper Marlborough, two miles inland, en route to link up with American marines at the Woodyard.[3] On the instructions of Navy Secretary Jones, only a skeleton crew of six to eight men in each barge had been left behind to sabotage the flotilla the moment the British advanced in force.[4] But the British naval commander wisely kept on the alert. He had no sooner landed his aide-de-camp, Lt. James Scott, to reconnoiter the high riverbanks when someone fired from behind a bush. The bullet whizzed past Scott's ear. "He is below you, Scott! He is below you!" Cockburn shouted from his gig. The aide-de-camp turned and found himself within arm's length of a sailor, whom he quickly subdued. "Do not hurt him, Scott!" the admiral called out. A coxswain who had jumped overboard to help Scott grabbed hold of the captive and flung him down the slope, roaring, "I'll learn you, you beggar, to fire at my officer!" At that moment several more of Barney's crew opened fire on the gig, but within a few minutes they had all been taken prisoner.[5] A few American horsemen who showed themselves on the ridges bolted in the face of a handful of British rockets.[6] Two of the captives were found to be English naval deserters.

The successive explosions were heard by Ross's army as it cut inland from Nottingham. Winder sent a light detachment of infantry, cavalry, artillery, and riflemen to check the advance. The rest of the force took up positions on high ground. Then Winder and Monroe peeled off to take personal note of the enemy lines. But the cavalry broke at the first shots.

The British were within only a few miles of the bulk of the Americans waiting in line of battle when the invaders came to a fork in the road. To the right was Upper Marlborough. To the left was the American encampment at the Woodyard. Winder expected them to swerve left en route to Washington, and his scouts watched expectantly from overlooks. But Ross's force veered right, and as the corps marched by it was clear they had no cavalry escort.[7] This should have given the defenders a needed edge, but Lt. Col. Jacint Lavall commanded about 140 untested light dragoons who had been rushed through training school on lame and sick horses, their new mounts bought just nine days earlier. The cavalry school at Carlisle, Pennsylvania, had been so poorly funded that the first recruits did not even have horses.[8]

The bulk of the dispersed American units were even now tired and testy from fretful orders to quick-march over long distances with little or defective equipment. General Stansbury's brigade had trekked down from Baltimore in dribs and drabs over two days because there were not enough wagons at the outset to cart all their tents and supplies.[9] Short of tents, Brig. Gen. Walter Smith's 1st Columbian Brigade of just over a thousand volunteers and militia had slept in the open. Only one-fifth of the force could fire their weapons due to a shortage of flints. Almost two hundred riflemen had been refused rifles and had to make do with inferior muskets. This weary contingent had been roused in the dead of night and held on immediate standby until dawn on Monday, when they were moved forward to challenge Ross.[10] Another eight hundred riflemen and artillerymen under the command of Lt. Col. Joseph Sterett had stopped on their way down from Baltimore hoping to get properly equipped. But before they could get a chance for supplies to catch up they were ordered to move on at the double.[11]

The Americans fell back from the Woodyard to Battalion Old Fields, where they pitched tents midway between the sixteen miles separating Washington from Upper Marlborough. Winder thought the new campsite was more accommodating. Cavalrymen meanwhile had seized a couple of British troops wandering beyond their picket lines. During interrogation they said their army would stay put overnight in Upper Marlborough. It was of small comfort to the American commander. The head of the enemy's column was a mere three miles away—five miles beyond Upper Marlborough.

Harried from all sides, Winder had little time to himself for calm reflection. Enemy movements dictated the pace and momentum of the developing drama. The commanding general had no time to meet with the president and cabinet secretaries a mile behind the camp, though he dispatched a guard unit for their safety. Then he made sure Lavall's horsemen would keep the enemy under surveillance even after dark. Winder's own night was made long by the unending streams of people wanting to see him. He had twenty-five hundred men "not three days from their homes, without organization or any practical knowledge of service on the part of their officers." It was a heavy burden having to put up with what he sensed was "the officious but well-intended information and advice of the crowd, who, at such a time, would be full of both."[12]

Deep into the night he managed to snatch some rest, though still uncertain about the size of his adversary and their eventual target. His doze was cut short when a sentinel awakened him and everyone else with a false alarm about 2 A.M. No one got much sleep because a state of alert held until daylight.[13] After sunrise Winder was buffeted by even more rumors, the most serious of which had the enemy on the road to Annapolis. He sent cavalry charging down the road in search of the British, but it was midday before they could scotch the rumor.

The British had meanwhile looked rapturously upon the village of Upper Marlborough, founded in 1695 by Scottish Presbyterians who named it in honor of the greatest military leader of the day, the Duke of Marlborough. Lieutenant Gleig could not recall seeing a more beautiful landscape. A stream wound through the hilly perimeter, foliated with trees and flower-beds around the sprinkling of cottages. The long lines of dusty troops dropped their gear with great relief. It had been, thought brigade commander Col. Arthur Brooke, "a dreadful hot day's march."[14]

The village was almost deserted. Gleig and his Portuguese boy-servant foraged in a number of empty cottages and carried away bread, flour, chickens, and a bottle of peach whiskey. They shared the feast with junior officers under the cooling shade of a clump of trees. Later they were offered generous hospitality by Dr. William Beanes, the only resident of the town who had not fled. A wealthy physician who also owned a neighboring farm, Beanes had emigrated from Scotland about two decades earlier and spoke with the distinctive clipped accent of his mother country. He claimed to be a Federalist opposed to the war with Britain. Though Beanes was prepared to give them anything they wanted, the intruders paid him in full for supplies and horses. Gleig, however, thought better of paying for a little tea, sugar, and milk, thinking that to do so might be insulting.[15]

Ross, meanwhile, had sent word to Cockburn of the army's safe arrival, and the admiral rode up on horseback early Tuesday morning, 23 August, staying, according to one hearsay account, at Dr. Beanes's home.[16] It did not take the two Britons long to agree to make a grab for Washington.

They had met weak and petty resistance and were now less than a day's march from the American capital. Cockburn immediately sent word to the marines and sailors near Pig Point to catch up. The marines, Ross decided, would secure Upper Marlborough while the marine artillery and the sailors joined the land forces at their nocturnal camp five miles closer to Washington.[17]

Cockburn's ever-present aide-de-camp, Lieutenant Scott, boarded the admiral's gig and was rowed as fast as possible downriver to the frigate flying the pennant of Admiral Cochrane. He was with fleet captain Rear Adm. Edward Codrington when Scott handed over Cockburn's hastily scrawled message announcing the decision to take Washington. Keeping quiet about his own impatience to storm the American capital, Cockburn made out that it was solely Ross's idea. "I came here this morning to consult with him and learn his future plans," wrote Cockburn, "and I find he is determined in consequence of the information he has received and what he has observed of the enemy, to push on towards Washington, which I have confident hopes he will give a good account of." Playing down his own role, Cockburn added, almost as an afterthought, "I shall accompany him and of course afford him every assistance in my power."[18]

But the news did not sit well with either admiral, even though it had been debated only days before. Codrington believed they should hold back, thinking it would be rash to do otherwise. They conferred at length before both Cochrane and Codrington decided to abort the attack. They agreed that Cockburn, with no cavalry and only a few pieces of artillery, had already achieved more than England could have expected with his small force. A much greater objective would be at risk if an attempt was made to storm Washington. It would jeopardize the top priority of keeping troop strength intact for a major assault on New Orleans, planned for the coming winter in the Gulf of Mexico.[19] Victory there would fulfill Cochrane's craving to give the Americans "a complete drubbing," drive them out of Louisiana, and wrest command of the Mississippi River.[20] Cockburn, therefore, was on no account to proceed one mile further inland. On the contrary, Cochrane insisted he turn around forthwith and reboard at Benedict.

The fresh orders were written down and handed to Scott. But before he was sent on his way, Cochrane, a veteran of naval wars stretching back thirty-four years, made him memorize the contents. If Scott was taken prisoner on the route back, he was told, he must swallow the paper to keep their plans from the enemy.

It was already late at night when the aide-de-camp rode into Upper Marlborough, now patrolled by a rear guard awaiting his arrival. On the ride ahead to the overnight bivouac he encountered a few American horsemen who quickly fled. But the ride took longer than expected, and Scott was beginning to think he was lost when suddenly, around 2 A.M., he saw campfires ahead.

Ross and Cockburn were asleep, stretched out on their cloaks in a shepherd's hut, when Scott walked in. After waking them, he handed over Cochrane's new orders to Cockburn. The admiral looked it over without comment, then passed it on to Ross, who agreed they had no alternative but to return.

"No," said Cockburn, "we cannot do that. We are too far advanced to think of a retreat. Let us take a turn outside and talk the matter over."[21]

They walked backwards and forwards in the night air as aides caught snatches of comment.

"If we proceed," Cockburn argued, "I'll pledge everything that is dear to me as an officer that we shall succeed. If we return without striking a blow, it will be worse than defeat. It will bring a stain upon our arms. I know their force. The militia, however great their numbers, will not, cannot stand against your disciplined troops. It is too late. We ought not to have advanced. There is now no choice left us. We must go on."

Even though Ross outranked Cockburn on land, he was not immune to the admiral's influence. He would well remember Cockburn's persistence and the seductive appeal of the admiral's logic. The naval commander even suggested moving ahead as if tiptoeing through darkened woods. "Let us now push on so far as to feel their strength, at any rate, and, if circumstances require it, we can fall back to our shipping."[22]

They went over the pros and cons until first light of Tuesday, 23 August, when Ross, apparently animated by a conclusion, struck his forehead and declared, "Well, be it so! We will proceed!"[23]

Demoralized by rumors they would retreat, the rank and file now gave three hearty cheers on being told to march forward. The word among the rank and file was that Cockburn had vowed either to conquer Washington or die.[24] Freshly inspired, the exultant force surged ahead to Washington.

Unknown to them, a small unit of American volunteer artillerymen and others armed with light weapons were waiting about three miles ahead, atop a high hill with an overview of the countryside. The occupant of a nearby house had tipped them off that British officers had stopped by earlier in the day and let slip that the army would march on Washington about midday. Maj. George Peter prepared to stall them with his company of volunteer artillerists attached to the District of Columbia militia. He stationed his battery of six artillery pieces on the road along which the enemy would have to march, and flanked each side by men armed with muskets. But his trap was sprung when a messenger arrived with orders from Winder to pull back immediately. They had barely descended to the bottom of the hill when Ross and other red-coated officers appeared on the same spot they had vacated. Peter shouted at his men to shoot, expecting a platoon to take aim. Even though an entire company opened fire, every musket ball strayed wide of the target and Ross and his aides slipped unscathed out of sight behind the hill. During a brief shoot-out a quick-thinking mounted British officer dug in his spurs, hurdled a fence, and charged, but before he reached their hiding place the Americans had dropped their weapons and disappeared into the brushwood. As Peter led his men away he was filled with festering regret for a historic opportunity lost. For decades he would steadfastly believe that if only his men had been armed with rifles instead of muskets they could have picked off the British commander, and by his death caused the collapse of the march on Washington.[25]

Winder sent word out for a massive dash back to Washington over the Eastern Branch bridge. He was vastly outnumbered. The American commanding general was also afraid that if they stayed where they were during the night, he would lose the advantage of superior artillery. Darkness would also imperil his green militiamen and volunteers. He knew their limitations, and calculated that at least half his army might be cut down in the wild panic of a battle fought only by the light of flashing explosives.

Weighing just as heavily was the certain knowledge that if he headed north toward Bladensburg, he would distance himself even further from very real alternative enemy targets: the road to Washington through the Eastern Branch bridge or Fort Washington. The fifteen-hundred-foot-long Eastern Branch bridge was vital to his own lifeline to Washington.[26] Even though he had made preparations for its destruction to stop the enemy if need be, he felt uneasy at leaving such a crucial decision in the hands of "raw, undisciplined, inexperienced and unknown officers and men" during such a chaotic time.[27] He still did not know whether Ross would go south or even northeast to Annapolis on the shores of the Chesapeake. Intelligence was so faulty that the inexorable foe was numbered at anything from four thousand to twelve thousand strong.

Meanwhile, Secretary of State Monroe, still the trusted eyes and ears of the president of the United States, scribbled another message: "The enemy are advanced six miles on the road to the Woodyard, and our troops retiring. Our troops were on the march to meet them, but in too small a body to engage. General Winder proposes to retire till he can collect them in a body. The enemy are in full march for Washington. Have the materials prepared to destroy the bridges."

And then, "Tuesday, nine o'clock. You had better remove the records."[28]

The scramble to reach Washington left the men drained and weary to the point of collapse. There was no time to load all the supplies. Flour and whiskey were destroyed where they lay on the ground.[29] Quick-marching militiamen were pushed even harder so that it became a run of eight miles.[30] Capt. Benjamin Burch of the Washington Artillery was given orders to stay put until all the troops had left and then retreat with his guns in three staggered fifteen-minute intervals. But Burch had just sent off his second set of guns when a courier arrived with fresh orders to quit immediately. By the time he reached the bridge, his men were so out of breath "they could scarcely stand by their guns."[31] Lavall's cavalry, constantly on the move scouting, escorting, and acting as couriers, crossed the bridge an hour before midnight. The men and their horses were not only bone-weary but famished.[32] Barney filed his men into the marine barracks, then went to the navy yard to sleep at Commandant Tingey's quarters.[33]

Command and control of American contingents further afield broke down. Rumor was rife. General Stansbury was resting more than eight hundred exhausted troops outside Bladensburg when a militia captain rode in under guard. He passed on the grim news that Winder was thought to have been taken prisoner because he had not returned from reconnoitering.[34]

Winder was at that very moment six miles away on the Eastern Branch bridge telling General Smith to position his men next to it on the Washington side of the river. Then he rode on to update the president on unfolding events. He had expected to brief other senior members of the government but discovered they had all gone home. He dropped off his frothing, borrowed horse at McKeowin's Hotel on Pennsylvania Avenue but had no luck in finding a replacement, as every other animal was in the same feeble state. The man in charge of holding the nation's capital was left with no choice: Winder set off on foot for the bridge, almost three miles northeast. There he found about thirty men armed only with axes ready to destroy the double- carriageway bridge, almost a third of a mile long.[35] No materials were in place to wreck the bridge by other means, though he was told that men from the navy yard had checked it over for that purpose.

Winder walked to the camp where his army had regrouped. With rapid orders he rushed infantry to positions a half mile over the bridge to prevent the enemy from taking it by surprise. It was past midnight when he got to Captain Burch's tent, called him outside, and appealed directly to his patriotism. Burch remembered how the general "knew my men were worn down with fatigue and from the loss of rest; but that, in all probability, one of the last good acts which it might ever be in my power to do for my country, would be that night."[36] Winder's solitary plea was for Burch to take thirty of his men with three pieces of artillery and defend the Washington end of the Eastern Branch bridge. It was a vital move because Winder had made up his mind that the enemy would storm the bridge that night.

The plan was for Burch to open fire as soon as the American infantry had raced back over the bridge. If the British managed to get a foothold, Burch would torch a boat filled with explosives below the bridge, blow it up, return to positions, and keep firing on the intruders. The boat had not yet arrived, but Winder vowed he himself would not bed down that night until it did.[37]

The commanding general, accompanied by a junior officer, then headed for the navy yard to requisition powder, combustibles, and boats to blow up the bridge. But on the darkened way the general, now drained of energy and yearning for rest, fell heavily in a ditch, severely injuring his right arm and ankle. In great pain, he arrived at the navy yard after midnight and woke up Tingey, who told him powder had already been placed in waiting boats. Winder told him to load more powder and to include combustibles to guarantee destruction.

Determined to check that his orders had been followed, Winder returned to the bridge, and only after satisfying himself that the men were on alert and understood what they were about did the sleepy general head for camp. There he found Major Peter's tent. The artillery commander craved sleep after his exhausting round-trip dash to the outskirts of Upper Marlborough, where he had the brief encounter with Ross himself. Winder shared the major's straw mattress as he began to lament the "inefficiency" of the troops under his command, but Peter was too tired to listen and fell asleep. "When I awoke the general was gone," he recalled.[38] Winder finally got to bed after 3 A.M. but nodded off for less than two hours before rising and gathering drowsy aides at headquarters in a doctor's house near the doomed bridge.[39]

The rest of the armed forces had also passed the night in fitful motion with snatches of sleep. Edgy sentinels had sounded false alarms in the dead of night. Entire encampments had shuffled into readiness and remained suspended between the instinct to slumber and the need to keep awake.

Ensign George Hoffman hungered for food and rest. He had walked from Baltimore at a faster, more grueling pace than the rest of his 1st Regiment of Maryland militia. There had been no wagons available when the regiment departed, and Hoffman was ordered to stay behind and bring up the rear. He left four hours later and caught up the next day after a twenty-mile pant. By 4 P.M., when they pitched tents on the fields of Bladensburg, Hoffman was groggy with exhaustion. As the tired troops relaxed their alert, they became dangerous to one another. Just as they were about to push on to Upper Marlborough the next day, a militiaman in the company next to Hoffman accidentally shot dead two colleagues.[40] Hoffman would have to keep his wits about him, now knowing that the deadly enemy did not have to come dressed up in a British uniform.

They had covered less than a mile when everyone was ordered to turn around and march back to Bladensburg. It was a typical blazing-hot August day, and again they yearned for something to eat. The midday mealtime passed by without anyone being stood down. Finally they were told to pitch tents again. Hoffman was starving, but all he got to eat was watermelon.

Meanwhile, Colonel Sterett's detachment of the 5th Regiment had also arrived at Bladensburg. His men slumped onto the slopes of Lowndes Hill by the side of the road leading to Upper Marlborough and overlooking the village's river boundary. The long march had left young John Pendleton Kennedy with painfully swollen feet. In the evening he had taken off his new boots, slipped on his pumps, and relaxed in the warm camaraderie of fellow volunteers puffing on cigars. Elijah the servant reappeared with stolen chickens, and they sat in their tent enjoying a convivial meal of chicken, ham, biscuits, and coffee. The close fellowship was made more intimate by the light of candles tied to the end of a bayonet stuck in the ground. Kennedy was so excited by talk of the battle to be fought that he was awake long after the order sounded throughout camp to extinguish lights and turn in.[41]

Around 1 A.M. the alarm sounded, waking Kennedy in one tent and Hoffman in another. The entire encampment braced for an attack. Nervous pickets on the road to Upper Marlborough, from where the British were expected, thought they had seen movement and opened fire. Lieutenant Colonel Frisby Tilghman's cavalry rode ahead to inspect but returned to report a false alarm. The pickets had fired at nothing but shadows. It was a miserable interlude for the hapless regiments, who swayed and dozed under arms for an hour before being stood down.

Sterett was not told whether any reserves would support his rear. He was acutely aware of his men's shortcomings. Essentially untrained and sluggish civilians, they had no hope of resisting the oncoming tide of superior professionals led by officers with battlefield experience and luminous reputations. Sterett and other officers pleaded with Stansbury to allow them to fall back and bolster other units between Bladensburg and Washington. Stansbury would not hear of it. He told them what he would soon tell the meddlesome James Monroe.[42] He had orders to obey and would make his stand where they were. Besides, he declared, the troops were physically incapable of slogging anymore that night.[43]

But while the troops fell into thankful sleep, a militia officer arrived from Washington. It was only then that General Stansbury learned of Winder's flight to Washington. All through the night he had assumed his flanks and rear were covered. To his horror, he knew now that he was exposed and vulnerable. Tired as the men were after only one hour of sleep, they would have to fold their tents and march to a better position closer to the capital and nearer to the rest of the army.

Every drummer in camp beat out the long and rapid drumroll. It was the signal for men to stir themselves into action. A colonel pushed aside Hoffman's tent flap, roused the inmates, and told them to strike their tent, load the baggage quietly, and prepare to retreat to Washington. The British were just half a mile away.

Awakened from deep sleep, many thought they were under attack and scrambled to dress and arm themselves. Someone in Kennedy's tent struck a light so they could see what they were doing, but in the chaos a neighbor filched it to light his own and did not return. Unable to tell one piece of clothing from another, the blurry-eyed volunteers dressed in whatever came to hand. By the time they lined up to march out, many were ill-fitted in each other's boots and coats. Kennedy managed to turn out in his own gear, but he walked in the stylish pumps meant for the victory ball.

At 3 A.M. Hoffman and his numbed regiment walked like shackled slaves through the dead of night. Half an hour later Kennedy's 5th Regiment crossed the bridge at Bladensburg and trudged toward Washington. The young private's energy waned. He tried hard to keep awake but felt he was sleepwalking as he lurched forward. When they were occasionally brought to a halt, entire platoons stretched out and slept deeply until told to press on again. Dragging their feet, the bedraggled knots of clumsy novices held on for a mile and a half. Then Kennedy's unit rested until dawn at the foot of a hill near a brickyard. The inert army was too slack from wandering to care about the moist and dewy earth. Puffy-eyed soldiers crumpled where they stood, and slept with the comfort of oblivion.[44] At first light they found water and cooked rations of poor-quality salt beef with old and musty flour. Hoffman's company struggled for five hours before resting in a field. Their stomachs cried out for food but there was none.

A messenger arrived from Winder as Stansbury surveyed the country-side from the top of a hill. He was told to make a stand against the British if they advanced on Washington from Bladensburg. Every one of Stansbury's senior staff officers found the orders intolerable. Their disheartened men had been pushed to the limits with barely any sustenance or sleep. Sterett called openly for defiance. He declared it would be nothing less than "a sacrifice" to send such weak and sleepless officers and men into battle so distant from reinforcements.[45] Stansbury agreed. He gave orders for the wagons to move ahead to Washington. The troops would follow. But at that very moment an officer rode in with fresh news from Winder. The order was now firm and fixed. Engage the enemy at Bladensburg. Winder's forces would link up without delay.[46]

Aching, sweating, and close to collapse, the columns of flagging men wheeled around in midmorning to retrace their steps. While they trekked they looked back now and then at the reddening sky. Soon they made out some flames. The decrepit, seldom-used more northerly bridge over the Eastern Branch was on fire. Kennedy and the others were too far off to know what was burning. The rumor mill soon had it that Winder had crossed the upper bridge, then set it alight to thwart the enemy.[47] When the debilitated columns got back to where they had started out from, some of the men broke ranks and ran ahead to the apple orchard on the left of the road near the river. Hoffman and others lunged at the fruit and ate ravenously. It was the first substantial food they had eaten since breakfast the day before.[48]

The flurry of contradictory orders had taken their toll on the men who would have to fight and die. Now, ominously, new signs appeared of friction at the highest level of command. That night Treasury Secretary Campbell asked War Secretary Armstrong whether he had advised or even approved of the troop deployments. The headstrong Armstrong would not give a straight answer. He had been wrong in downplaying the threat to Washington, but he was far from admitting fault or showing humility. Winder was in command of the District and Washington, he sniffed, and "it was to be presumed he had formed such plans for defending the city."

Elsewhere in Washington, tempers flared over delays and the insensitivity of bureaucratic dullards. Col. George Minor, commanding the 60th Regiment of the Virginia militia, had arrived in Washington at early candlelight on Tuesday with about six hundred infantry and one hundred cavalry. He reported to the president, who shunted him to Armstrong, from whom he learned that he would have to wait until the morning to draw arms and ammunition. Minor looked frantically for several hours from early morning for the officer charged with equipping the force, but could not find him. Frustrated and angry, he would later charge that when he finally met up at the armory with the officer, Col. Henry Carbery, the latter explained he had left Washington the evening before to ride out to his country home.[49] In a flurry of recriminations, Carbery would heatedly deny this and later provide witnesses to prove his presence at various locations in Washington and Georgetown while Minor was looking for him.[50]

Eventually, Minor found Winder near the Eastern Branch bridge on Wednesday morning and received authority to draw weapons from the armory. There, a young man issued the supplies with slavish obedience to regulations. Even though impatient officers had counted a quantity of flints, the clerk demanded and carried out a painstaking recount. Minor ordered his men to continue ahead of him to the Capitol while he lagged behind to sign receipts. By the time his force set off for the battlefield, it was all over. They had not even reached the turnpike gate within the city limits.[51]

A little before daybreak, a boat loaded with eight barrels of powder anchored under the arch next to the thirty-foot draw of the Eastern Branch bridge. More scows and boats stacked with explosives were positioned there in the early-morning hours. About sunrise, Colonel Wadsworth, in charge of general ordnance, ordered firewood brought onto the bridge to make sure it would burn when the time came. Troops broke down a nearby fence and dumped the rails on the bridge. Then they pulled down a tollhouse and an adjacent small shed and scattered the planks over the same area.[52]

The rickety and unsafe 822-foot-long upper bridge, with its small draw, was already burning when Dr. Hanson Catlett walked over the larger bridge before 8 A.M. Catlett, surgeon with the 1st Infantry Regiment, had slept overnight in the open only about a mile from Battalion Old Fields.

As soon as he arrived in the capital he sensed commotion and disarray. There seemed to be no reliable information. The enemy was said to be less than three miles away on a direct path to the Eastern Branch bridge. They were thought to number at least nine thousand, even though several new enemy prisoners spoke only of four regiments and could not name more than one general and an acting brigadier. After personally interrogating the captives, Catlett would have bet his life that the formidable foe was almost completely without artillery and cavalry.[53]

Dragoons streamed into the presidential headquarters every few minutes with new reconnaissance reports from the outskirts. Most of those huddled with the president thought the enemy would first snatch Fort Warburton, then move on Washington. Everyone was impatient for Armstrong to arrive, and there was surprise at his delay. When he entered the room, about an hour after the president, he predicted that if Ross moved against Washington it would be "a mere Cossack hurrah, a rapid march and hasty retreat," since the British general was totally unprepared for a siege. The secretary of war favored luring the invaders to the precincts of the Capitol, where they would be pounded by artillery, ambushed by five thousand infantry hiding inside the House of Representatives and adjacent buildings, and charged by three hundred cavalry.[54]

The president and senior cabinet members decided to rendezvous at Fredericktown, Maryland, about forty-five miles northwest, if the capital should fall to the enemy.[55] But all this talk changed when an express arrived. They were now certain that the British army was headed for Bladensburg. A flurry of orders followed. They realized that the booby-trapped bridge could be defended just as well by half a dozen men as by five hundred. Barney, who had taken over defense of the Eastern Branch bridge around 10 A.M. from Peter's and Burch's artillery, was told to dash to Bladensburg with his marines, sailors, and heavy guns. Capt. John Orde Creighton, placed in charge of a sergeant's guard of marines, dug in next to the bridge with orders to blast it apart "on the near approach of the enemy."[56] If this came about, Creighton had to rush to the navy yard and help prepare its destruction.[57]

Madison took the secretary of war aside. With hostilities imminent, he asked whether Armstrong had any advice to give or plan to offer. Armstrong replied negatively. But with brutal candor he predicted defeat because it would be a contest between regulars and militia.[58]

The officials were already on horseback when Treasury Secretary Campbell, visibly in poor health, told the president about his nighttime conversation with Armstrong.[59] Perhaps at this moment the sickly Campbell loaned his pair of dueling pistols to the president, which Madison promptly put in his holsters.[60] Then Madison turned his horse toward Armstrong and, out of earshot of anyone else, directed the secretary of war to ride to the battlefield and "give such directions as were required." Shortly afterwards Madison indicated to Campbell that there would be no problem with Armstrong giving orders. In the event of conflict over authority to do so, Armstrong would be considered as having executive approval, and in any case, Madison intended to be close by for quick adjudication.[61] But by the time the president met Armstrong again, shortly before the opening shots rang out at Bladensburg, Madison had changed his mind. Now he told the secretary of war to let the military handle their own duties and responsibilities. Armstrong, in his own words, had been relegated to "a mere spectator of the combat."[62]

The spurt to reach the battlefield caught many off guard and inflamed tempers. Men of Lavall's corps of cavalry were carrying bales of hay on their heads to famished horses when the order came to ride posthaste to Bladensburg. The horsemen were furious. Finding the hay had not been easy, and it was at that moment being paid for. They did not yield it up lightly. But when someone blew a trumpet they ran to their horses, and in a few minutes Lavall was in command again and off to Bladensburg. His corps, however, had been cut to about 125 men. More than a dozen had dropped out through sickness and wounds. A number of unfit horses were also sidelined. Lavall had never personally been to Bladensburg, and when he arrived at the unfamiliar turf the enemy was already in sight. All the horses were in desperate need of water, so he rode them up to the river that would momentarily separate the combatants. He could not find Stansbury, to whom he was told to report, so he asked Monroe for orders. The secretary of state directed him to a ravine, and as he entered it Stansbury passed by and agreed with the cavalry's deployment. Hostilities were only moments away.[63]

Captain Burch had also just arrived on the battleground. He had only half his artillery. Three of the guns and more than a dozen men had been detached by higher-ups at the Eastern Branch bridge and on the main road next to Bladensburg. Burch rode up and down the lines looking for Winder. While he was gone his men could clearly see a large body of British troops entering the outskirts of the village, about a mile away. Their arms glittered in the midday sun. Sgt. John Law, a member of Burch's company, spotted Winder and marched the men over to find out where they should deploy. They were told to position themselves on the left of the Baltimore infantry. Winder, already resigned to the outcome of a battle yet to start, then pointed to the road leading from Digges's mill into the country and told Law, "When you retreat, take notice you must retreat by the Georgetown road."[64] Burch returned just as the artillerymen had organized their guns. When he asked for instructions, Winder pointed across the river and said, "Captain, there is the enemy. Take charge of your pieces."[65]

Ragtag lines of physically spent troops spread over the slopes facing Bladensburg. It was already a scorching-hot day. Hordes of militiamen in civilian clothing looked out of place on the battlefield. Many were clothed in black coats, some in shooting jackets, and others in round frocks. Only those few battalions outfitted in blue jackets looked like regulars. The rest would appear to the British as if they were spectators watching the invaders march on Washington.[66]

Many in Barney's elite unit, who had marched backwards and forwards without shoes for the past few days, covered the six-mile dash wearing new and unbroken footwear. They lagged behind their commander, who, like others, arrived almost at the moment of battle. He detailed an officer to hurry back and whip the men into shape. They arrived on the battlefield at a trot and quickly prepared their artillery. The flotilla crew would act as infantry under the command of twenty-four-year-old sailing master John Webster, a trusted subordinate who had commanded one of Barney's barges in the Chesapeake.[67] Barney placed them on his right to support the heavy guns.[68] One hundred yards ahead of Barney, on the right, Capt. Samuel Miller stood ready with his 113 marines, the best-trained and toughest unit on the field.[69]

More than a thousand dusty, perspiring men of the 1st Columbian

Brigade, who had set a desperate pace from Washington, were still looking for their positions when the first shots rang out. Their ranks had been thinned along the way by men fainting from hunger and lack of sleep.[70] General Smith, their commander, had sped ahead with Georgetown lawyer Francis Scott Key to survey the fields and map deployments.

While Smith's men were crisscrossing the fields, Col. William Beall's regiment of over seven hundred limped in from Annapolis. They had covered about sixteen miles on foot that morning. As they appeared on a hill on the other side of the river, in Bladensburg, they were mistaken by George Hoffman and his Maryland militiamen for British troops. But they quickly sent word of their identity, saying they had run four miles with the enemy close at their heels. The British appearance ten minutes later on the same hill confirmed how close they had come to being cut off from their compatriots.[71] One of Winder's aides led the footsore regiment to a commanding height about 250 yards to the right of the road.[72]

Meanwhile, a lone armed horseman, William Simmons, had crossed the bridge and was scouting the British advance into the village of Bladensburg. An accountant at the War Department for almost twenty years, Simmons had been in the public limelight after President Madison fired him on 6 July for alleged "bitter hostility to the government" and "rudeness to his superiors."[73] Simmons had countercharged the secretary of war with engineering his dismissal after they clashed on accounting procedures.[74]

Though out of a job, Simmons was eager to be in the forefront of action and danger and had set out from Washington ahead of Winder's forces. When he arrived on the slopes facing Bladensburg, he found Monroe and others still guessing the whereabouts and strength of the enemy. Simmons volunteered to cross the river and bring back eyewitness intelligence. In Bladensburg he stopped briefly at Ross's Tavern, where a handful of militiamen told him the British were closing in along the river road. He rode up Lowndes Hill, where Stansbury had camped the night before, and from where he could look down on the river road at the base of the hill and follow its course for miles. His patience paid off. Presently he caught sight of a swirling cloud of dust kicked up by a huge army on the move. A while later a few horsemen came into view. They seemed to be on reconnaissance and were soon followed by slow-marching columns of troops at least two dozen abreast. As the front line neared the base of Lowndes' Hill, Simmons could see thick packs of British soldiers stretching back a mile.

He lost no time in turning around to report his sightings. Simmons descended the hill in front of the Lowndes' house and sped toward the bridge. When he looked back he saw that an advance party had reached the Annapolis road east of the Lowndes' home. About two dozen enemy riders rode up a lane toward the Baltimore road while half a dozen more seemed to block off the entrance to the alley.

In testimony later admitted by a congressional committee of inquiry but rejected as preposterous by critics, the aggrieved and possibly politically vengeful Simmons said he caught sight of President Madison, Secretaries Monroe and Armstrong, and Attorney General Rush ahead of all the troops and about to cross over into Bladensburg.

"Mr. Madison!" he called out, "the enemy are now in Bladensburg!"

"The enemy in Bladensburg!" Simmons quoted Madison replying incredulously.

According to Simmons, the president and his senior advisers immediately turned their horses around and galloped away.

"Mr. Madison!" Simmons cried out. "If you will stop I will show them to you! They are now in sight!"

But Madison and the cabinet members ignored him and continued in flight. Only the attorney general reined in his horse. Simmons pointed out the party of half a dozen enemy blocking off the alley on the other side of the river.

"That cannot be the enemy. They are not in uniform," Rush declared.

Simmons explained that they were part of an advance party. At that moment swarms of redcoats appeared, some in front of and others to the rear of the Lowndes' house on the hill. A few were on the Annapolis road.

"I am satisfied," Rush remarked.

Abruptly he turned his horse, and as he rode away his hat slipped off.

"Mr. Rush! Come back and take your hat!" Simmons shouted.

The attorney general slowed down, wheeled around, and picked up his hat, then gave his horse full rein for safer ground. Before Simmons got to his compatriots' lines, Americans opened up with small arms and artillery fire from bushes near the bridge. Simmons looked in vain for the presidential party. Instead, he found Winder in the rear and told him he had just come from the village and that there were very few invaders in Bladensburg. They had opened fire too early. It would be better to wait for more British coming down the hill to bunch up on the Annapolis road, when they would be easier targets. But Winder was not listening.[75] The opening shots had been fired, and he had the fate of an army on his hands. His men were all that stood between the enemy and the nation's capital.

7. The Battle of Bladensburg

*A*s the hordes of redcoated combatants were coming into focus on the other side of the river, they were in no better shape than Winder's tired army. At first light they had broken camp on the Melwood estate, three miles east of Winder's abandoned Battalion Old Fields. The more than seven hours' march to Bladensburg had taken a severe toll on men with rubbery legs from weeks at sea. They had started out in open fields, then cut their way for hours through dense woods closed in with tangled thickets and brush. The overgrown path was not wide enough for more than four men pushed closely together. Their only comfort came from interlocking branches above which shielded them from the blazing sun. Almost five hours after setting out, they cleared the woods and passed by green meadows and cornfields, groves, plantations, and a few farmhouses dotting the landscape. The scenery lifted their spirits. Men who had pressed on grimly and silently now chatted among themselves. Buglers filled the air with invigorating marching tunes. The pace picked up. But for many the ordeal was too strenuous. Some dropped dead in their tracks. Clusters of soldiers lagged behind and others dropped by the wayside, too cramped and weak to put one foot ahead of the other. They would have to catch up later. The great bulk continued on, persevering doggedly under the scorching sun.[1] Each man was driven by the unshakable belief in duty and discipline which had forged the mighty British army.

Lieutenant Gleig had struggled to keep up with the marching army in the morning. When buglers sounded the call to halt and rest at 10 A.M., he was so exhausted that he remembered "my eyes were closed before my head reached the ground." Ninety minutes later they were up and marching again. After an hour they got the first glimpse of their opponents on the slopes of the hill facing Bladensburg.

"Are those Yankees or are they our own seamen got somehow ahead of us?" asked an inexperienced young officer alongside Gleig.[2]

Gleig could not repress a smile.

At that moment the Americans outnumbered their foe. Winder's own estimate of those under his command totaled about 5,000, including 350 regulars and Barney's unit.[3] The entire British expeditionary force was believed to number about 4,500. No more than 1,200 would see combat at Bladensburg, including 150 sailors armed only with cutlasses. The English fieldpieces added up to one 6-pounder and two 3-pounders.[4]

The tranquil town of Bladensburg was solemn and all but deserted as the massed armies prepared for indiscriminate slaughter under the midday sun. Until now the little community of less than fifteen hundred people had prided itself on being carved out of sixty acres in 1742 and thriving with its busy harbor. Named after William Bladen, who served as Maryland's commissary general a century before, the town lay on the main Post Road between Maine and Georgia and enjoyed a moment of fame in 1784 when Peter Carnes launched the first American unmanned hot-air balloon in the wooded fields.[5] It was dotted in and around with the spacious homes of wealthy merchants and plantation owners. Outsiders passed through the regular stagecoach stop, and Washingtonians and Georgetowners rode six miles for brief social outings at the Bladensburg taverns.

In 1808, when Rep. Barent Gardenier of New York took aim with his pistol and severely wounded Rep. George Washington Campbell of Tennessee for charging him with "falsehood, meanness and baseness," it was the opening shot of more than fifty duels fought out at Bladensburg.[6] During the next half century many men would die on the notorious turf which came to be known as Bladensburg's "dark and bloody grounds."[7] The flat clearing in the ravine below the trees, just off the stagecoach road, was shielded from prying eyes by thick surrounding foliage. Word spread fast that this ideal landscape for settling personal scores existed just across the boundaries of the District of Columbia.

The killing would now move from a patch of the ravine to the fields and hills on the west bank of the seventy-two-year-old settlement. As the British looked down from the eastern heights of Lowndes Hill, Col. William Thornton strained to charge across the narrow bridge. Capt. Harry Smith was aghast. Light-division professionals always scanned the field first, looking for weak spots. He suggested to Ross that they should at least make a feint of flanking the Americans' left by crossing the fordable river above the bridge. But as he was pointing out American gun emplacements Thornton cut in again, almost demanding swift action. Smith laughed at the colonel's impatience, but this only goaded the brigade commander. Angrily, Thornton turned on the junior officer. Fortunately for Thornton the general backed him up, even though Ross would report to London that the colonel began the attack "with so much impetuosity."[8]

"Heavens!" Smith thought to himself, "if Colborne [an admired contemporary British field commander] were to see this!" It was foolhardy, and he could not contain himself. "General Ross," he exclaimed, "neither of the other brigades can be up in time to support this mad attack. And if the enemy fight, Thornton's brigade must be repulsed."[9]

But Thornton had the green light and his men, in two columns, ran down the slopes of Lowndes Hill and onto the road leading to the bridge. The bridge was so narrow that no more than three abreast could cross at once.[10] It should not even have been standing at that moment. Before the British arrived Stansbury had ordered forty cavalrymen to chop it down with axes. The order, however, had been ignored, and Stansbury never found out why.[11]

As the British ran toward the bridge, they were without their standard cover of sharpshooters, who normally would have unnerved an enemy with rapid volleys of firepower. However, their blue-jacketed marine artillerymen fired off a salvo of whooshing Congreve rockets. The generally inaccurate but terrifying incoming warheads attached to launching sticks arced over the heads of the first line of American defenders and the knot of cabinet members around President Madison.[12] The politicians moved back out of range while Winder rode along the lines exhorting his men to disregard the novel explosives. Though the rockets would rattle the defenders, their use should not have surprised the Americans. Four months earlier a Baltimore newspaper had reported that the British fleet would soon bring rockets to the American coast.[13] The deadly new weapon had been developed over the past decade by William Congreve and could now be launched from land or ship.[14]

But even under the cover of rockets, none of the British made it to the bridge on their first dash. They were forced to scatter amid the houses under a blast of artillery from the Baltimore battery ensconced on the American left. A number of British officers lay dead. Smith did not relish being proved right, but he allowed himself a sigh of regret as he thought to himself, "There is the art of war and all we have learned under the Duke [of Wellington] given in full to the enemy!"[15]

Exhilarated by their opening challenge, the Americans whooped and cheered. Across the river a Scotsman slumped on the steps of a building, one shattered arm dangling pathetically from its bloodied stump. "Dinna halloo, my fine lads," he mocked. "You're no' yet oot of the wood. Wait a wee bit, wait a wee, wie your skirling."[16]

Like others in the forward ranks who had found sanctuary among the houses and a warehouse, Lieutenant Gleig lay down and waited for reinforcements while the Baltimoreans continued to lob explosives across the river. One of the cannonballs hurtled down and sliced a leg off a young soldier lying between Gleig and another officer. The amputee looked up at Gleig with such an odd expression, as if puzzled by the way he ought to be acting, that Gleig could not hold back his laughter. There was no time for explanations, nor even for first aid.

At that moment Thornton rode up with his sword drawn and summoned his men to attack once more.[17] "Now, my lads, forward! You see the enemy! You know how to serve them!"[18] Having galvanized his forces, the colonel called on a bugler to sound the attack, then follow him across the bridge. He swept into action, riding his horse with such gusto that he lay almost full length along its back as he charged at the head of his men.[19] He crossed the narrow wooden bridge in the face of a fusillade of fire and reached the American side unscathed.

As Ross prepared to gallop down and charge across with Thornton's men, the general turned to Smith and ordered him to bring up the other two brigades as fast as possible.

"Upon what points, Sir?" Smith asked.

But Ross was gone, shouting to the troops, "Come on, my boys!"[20]

With cries of "Forward! Forward!" men of Thornton's 85th Foot Regiment stormed the bridge as round, grape, and small shot with heavy artillery fire fell in and around their bunched ranks. Seven men fell but the others kept going, propelled by sheer courage and a finesse that came from years of superior training and experience. Simultaneously, other troops crossed the shallow water higher up. The onrushing veterans, conspicuous in their shakos (stovepipe-shaped headgear topped with a dark green plume), pushed past the willow and larch trees, ignoring volleys of musket fire from riflemen camouflaged by their beige-colored clothing in high grass near the barn on the right of the British.[21] Capt. John Knox had never seen such heavy fire since enlisting in the British army. He had grave doubts about his own survival after seeing three field officers downed and eight or nine soldiers of the 85th Regiment sprawling on the ground. "Before we had been a quarter of an hour under fire, thinks I to myself, thinks I, by the time the action is over the devil is in it if I am not either a walking major or a dead captain," he recalled.[22] Reloading their muskets after each shot, the American riflemen would later guess they felled as many as thirty attackers during the brief but furious encounter.[23]

The British line pressed on indomitably. Pvt. Henry Fulford, a Baltimore volunteer militiaman, watched in wonder as the British appeared to ignore the hail of gunfire. It seemed to him that "their men moved like clock-work. The instant a part of a platoon was cut down it was filled up by the men in the rear without the least noise and confusion whatever, so as to present always a solid column to the mouths of our cannon."[24]

American riflemen broke first, ignoring an officer's rallying cries to remain put. Maj. William Pinkney's two companies now bore the full brunt of the attack and betrayed their faltering nerve by firing too soon, without pausing for careful aim. The closer the British advanced, the less difficult they were to target because the guns had been placed on half-formed embrasures on elevated ground and it was almost impossible to lower the barrels of the 6-pounders. With their right flank about to be turned and the left inadequately protected, Pinkney's force of just over a hundred men, only half of whom were armed with bayonets, did not even wait for orders to flee. At first they retreated twenty to thirty yards to the skirts of an orchard, but they were now visible. They seemed hesitant, as if wanting to return to their original position, but then they scattered across open fields to the protective body of the 5th Regiment. In an instant the British moved into their deserted emplacements. Pinkney, a former U.S. minister to the Court of St. James and onetime U.S. attorney general, had hoped they might fire more rounds at the British, now within point-blank range, but he could not condemn his men for running when their artillery support collapsed. Deep down, as he later recounted, he knew that if his men had remained much longer "they must have been taken prisoners or cut to pieces."[25] A musket ball had struck his right arm slightly above the elbow and splintered the bone as it passed through. Without any horses nearby to speed his own retreat, the severely wounded Pinkney had to hurry off to catch up with his unit.

The flight of Pinkney's men aborted Capt. William Doughty's attempt to rush his company of seventy-one District of Columbia volunteers to their aid. Armed only with muskets as poor substitutes for the rifles they had been unable to obtain, the volunteers were less than halfway to the barn when they turned tail in the mad melee. After scrambling back to previous positions at the base of a hill, each man fired six to eight rounds at the onrushing British. But within minutes one of Winder's aides rode up and ordered them to fall back as far as "the heights behind Georgetown."[26]

Shortly before, Winder had counterattacked, ordering Sterett's men to move forward from their location on the left of Stansbury's line. Initially, Sterett's firepower kept the enemy at bay. But the British now had good cover from the apple trees, and their barely visible riflemen returned sharp, accurate, and steady fire which Stansbury found "galling." Other units joined in, and for a short while whiffs of smoke trailed upwards and the hot air filled with the pungent smell of burnt gunpowder as hundreds of weapons fired in both directions.

Winder decided to try and lure the British out of their orchard cover by placing his artillery and infantry further back, out of range and on a hill close by woods. But he had quick second thoughts for fear that his raw troops would mistake a tactical move backwards for a general retreat.[27]

Burch's three pieces of artillery had already opened up on British troops forming behind the barn, about 350 yards ahead on the other side of the road to Georgetown, when Winder told them to aim directly at the building. However, they had fired only three rounds when the Baltimore militia on the right began to cave in. The heavy gunners fired only a few more rounds before Winder ordered them to withdraw. There was a feeling of dismay among Burch's artillerymen. They had suffered no casualties and at least one artilleryman, Sergeant Law, thought the battle was only just getting under way. They fired off another two or three rounds before Winder returned to demand they obey orders and quit. After moving only a few yards, the general flip-flopped again and told them to resume fire with a single gun. Burch was in the act of setting up the artillery piece when Winder caught sight of the quick movement of advancing British soldiers. He signaled the gunners to flee the field without delay. It was their final order at the battle of Bladensburg. Their guns would remain silent from that moment. Their combat was over. They backed away so fast for more than a mile that they did not notice Burch falling behind. Drawn and wasted from lack of sleep and nourishment, and feeble from pushing his weak body under the merciless sun, Burch fainted next to a fence. None of the men ahead saw him collapse. When he came to, the captain of the Washington artillery was hot and feverish, but he was able to snag a horse and ride south to the capital.[28] Not all his men were there. As they left the battlefield they had come to a fork in the road which split three ways: to Washington, to Georgetown, and to Tenleytown and Montgomery Court House in Maryland. The downcast troops had split three ways, each taking the road of personal choice.[29]

Colonel Lavall, newly married only six months earlier, had been waiting for orders in a low-lying ravine about five hundred yards west of the barn with a mere fifty-five cavalrymen under his command.[30] He had no confidence in his fresh recruits or in the untrained horses purchased barely two weeks back. Throwing them against such great numbers of seasoned soldiers would be nothing less than a sacrifice without hope of doing any good. He knew at that moment what he would declare publicly later: "There is a distinction between madness and bravery."[31] When he moved up to the lip of the ravine to see what was going on, he was met with a shower of cannonballs and Congreve rockets. In no time at all it seemed to Lavall that the defenses had burst and hordes of troops and heavy guns were headed his way. Lavall's right wing, stationed just outside the ravine, had been covering a gate through which the routed Americans now poured in a mindless stampede. An artillery company crashed through the gate before the cavalry had time to steer clear, and several startled riders and frenzied horses were knocked down and overrun. Lavall himself barely escaped serious injury as careening wheels came close to thumping his leg and unseating him. Lacking orders, he remained as long as he could until it was clear that a general retreat must have been sounded. He could not delay any longer once he saw seven or eight hundred British infantry closing in on his right. Lavall's pack of battered horses and raw riders yet to see combat turned tail and walked away. They had not gone far before they were joined by James Monroe, who walked with them for a mile before leaving to keep the British under observation. President Madison and his entourage were also slowly making their way back to Washington at this moment.[32]

Meanwhile, Stansbury rode along his lines with brusque orders to the officers: cut down those who attempt to flee; on no account should any man be allowed to leave the lines.[33] But he had not reckoned with the calamitous effect of the hissing Congreve rockets. At first the British fired them too high, but after making adjustments to the angle of launch the rockets streaked through the American ranks, cutting fiery trails close above the heads of Lt. Col. Jonathan Shutz's and Lt. Col. John Ragan's men on Sterett's right. The effect was instantaneous dread made worse by volleys of incoming cannonballs. Hundreds of shaken men tried to escape the battlefield. Smoke temporarily shrouded this section of the battlefield, but when it cleared, George Hoffman could not find his file leader. When he saw his militia colleagues tumbling over a fence twenty yards distant, he shouted for all he was worth: "Men! Form! Form! For God's sake halt!"[34] But no one paid any attention. Hoffman scaled the fence and about fifty yards further on joined up with Ragan, his regimental chief, who had been thrown from his dying horse at the first exchange of fire. Ragan tried to stem the rout. "Men, stand by me!" he bellowed. "The enemy are flying before us!"[35] A handful of militiamen heeded his call and began to form around the colonel, but just then the enemy advanced and opened fire again. Instantaneously, the militiamen took to their heels and fled.

Winder, visibly livid, rode hard into their midst, screaming at them to stop the shameful rout. Thinking he had stemmed the flight and that other officers would consolidate the hold, Winder left to check on other defenses. But when he looked back he could scarcely believe what he saw. Only about eighty of the more than thirteen hundred men in Shutz's and Ragan's regiments stood their ground. The rest had been gripped by terror and were bolting in all directions to stay alive. The horseless Ragan, still trying hard to halt his men, delayed too long and was taken prisoner.[36]

Ensign Hoffman was faint with fatigue and hunger. His mouth was uncomfortably dry from shouting so much. Disconsolate over the quick turn of events, he came close to throwing in the towel and surrendering to the British. But just as suddenly he smoldered for revenge. If, as he hoped, the Americans were to stand and fight at Washington, he wanted to be among them. He would have to flee Bladensburg immediately. Hoffman set off for the capital with a heavy heart, distancing himself from the battlefield where there could be no doubt that Americans had been disgraced.[37]

In the general melee, John Pendleton Kennedy gave his musket to a friend so he could carry off Cpl. James McCulloch, limping with a leg bone fractured by a bullet. But when the friend himself was wounded, he discarded both his own weapon and Kennedy's. The young volunteer and his militiamen had run at the sound of the first fire. "We made a fine scamper of it," Kennedy recalled.[38] Even though the volunteers dispersed like startled prey, the British still managed to pick off and wound eight of the sixty-six militiamen in Kennedy's company. Another volunteer, Henry Fulford, guessed that if the militiamen had stayed put only ten more minutes, the British "would have either killed or taken the whole of us."[39]

Advancing British flankers fired upon and harassed Sterett's forces into total disarray on their flight along the road to Washington, notwithstanding the attempt by American officers to try and calm the men.[40] Many of those in Stansbury's regiment fled toward Baltimore, in the opposite direction from Washington, because they had not been told before the battle where to rendezvous if defeated.[41]

About eight hundred men from Col. William Scott's 36th Regiment and Col. William Brent's 2nd Regiment of Columbia militiamen, in the second line of defenses, never squeezed a trigger before joining the wholesale exodus. Moments before the rout, Scott had moved his men further away from Barney's left so that he could blast the adversary pushing up on the Americans' extreme left flank. They were perfectly positioned to inflict enormous casualties, but the tactical gain was thwarted with the sudden breakthrough by the British on the far right American flank. As soon as he saw what was happening Winder sounded the general retreat, but he had to convey it to Smith by messenger because Winder's horse, having crisscrossed the battlefield so often, was too tired to move fast enough.[42]

Brent's forces, idle behind a gully and woods several hundred yards behind Scott, left the battlefield with metal barrels as cold as they were the day before.[43] A rapid succession of orders from Smith and Winder in reaction to the quick British gains had them racing to a cornfield on their left to check the early enemy breakthrough, then to a deep ravine in their rear and on to the road on their left leading to Washington before finally being told to regroup at the Capitol. Snatched from the conflict, the eager militiamen had become bitter and frustrated. Their commanding colonel, proud of their spirit, would not forget how they had vented "their chagrin and mortification" at missing out on so many opportunities to engage the enemy.[44]

Colonel Brooke's brigade had followed Thornton's onto the battlefield, the 44th moving to the right of the bridge where it turned the American flank, and the 4th advancing on the opposite side of the battle lines, up the more uneven ground on the far left. About a hundred men gained ground with dogged determination in their ascent to the first line of Americans, each file keeping precisely ten full paces apart from the other in contrast to the closely bunched defenders who made easier targets. So many cannonballs whistled down upon the British lines that Gleig compared it to a hailstorm in driving winds. The earth was instantly pockmarked by heavy ammunition pounding holes on impact.

When the British came to a railing dividing a copse from cultivated fields, a junior officer just ahead of Gleig leapt over, shouting above the blast and roar of weaponry for his men to follow. Swiveling round to Gleig, he teased, "Who will be first in the enemy's line!" Gleig was telling him to slow down and not put such a distance between himself and the men he was leading, when a musket ball passed through the young officer's neck. He was dead before he hit the ground at Gleig's feet. The surviving subaltern did not even pause in his onward rush to scale the slopes.[45]

Not every casualty fell to withering fire. At least eighteen attackers died without sustaining a scratch. They collapsed from heat exhaustion and the strain of punishing forced marches over the five days since landing at

Benedict. Three soldiers succumbed as they climbed uphill with the 4th.[46] Another six from the 85th and nine from the 21st toppled over dead on the uphill assault.[47]

Fire was so intense that the British briefly retreated almost to the point where Gleig's fellow officer had fallen. A lone musket ball struck the scabbard of Gleig's sword and broke it. Another ball nicked his arm, but he was almost oblivious to the sting because he was so intent on rallying his men. At that point General Ross appeared at the head of the 4th Regiment to lead a renewed assault. The rank and file cheered as one when they heard him cry out, "Charge! Charge!" He had a close escape when balls missed his flesh but ripped his clothes.[48]

Throughout the fray, Cockburn was conspicuous on a white horse and easily visible with his gold-laced hat and rear admiral's epaulettes. He was within 140 yards of the second American line of defense when an aide warned that the enemy would target him to make up for their losses. He pleaded with the admiral to take cover behind a small stone quarry just a few paces to the right. "Poh! Poh! Nonsense!" Cockburn scoffed as he watched forward units of marine artillery launch more rockets horizontally. When he saw how much confusion and hysteria they stirred among the Americans, Cockburn was gleeful. "Capital! Excellent!" he exclaimed.[49] At that moment a marine next to him fell wounded, and another bullet passed between Cockburn's leg and his saddle flap, slicing his stirrup leather in two. He dismounted, and while an aide and a marine tried to tie the severed leather together, another round shot zinged over the saddle, killing the marine.

As thick columns of the 4th gained the road crossing the ravine they came under fire from Lieutenant Colonel Kramer's battalion of Maryland militia spread out in facing woods. After a brief skirmish the unequal militiamen fell back. Even less resistance was offered further behind by Beall's seven hundred militiamen guarding Barney's right. Still reeling from their sixteen-mile march from Annapolis that morning, they fled the field after firing off only one or two ineffective rounds.[50] Barney and his men were outraged. One of the flotillamen was so full of contempt he thought the militia "ran like sheep chased by dogs."[51] The commodore had expected solid support from Beall, more so because his troops occupied a commanding height.[52]

Colonel Magruder's 1st Regiment of District of Columbia militiamen, on Barney's left, opened fire for a few minutes with muskets until an order came to withdraw. But, according to one of the regimental officers, Lt. Col. J. Thompson, they continued firing because there did not seem to be any need to retire, especially as the marine artillery on their right showed no signs of letting up. But the Columbia militiamen backtracked eighty paces when a second order came to withdraw. They were still regrouping when the American left flank gave way and Thompson's men were told to fall back again. This time they withdrew six hundred paces before being told to go all the way back to the heights of Washington. "From thence retreat on retreat was ordered," Thompson recalled. "Such of the men as were not exhausted by fatigue, or had dropped from the ranks as they passed their homes—to afford personal protection to their wives and families—were halted for the night about fourteen miles from the battle ground."[53]

Barney had little time to regret Beall's lack of backbone. British sharpshooters let loose volleys of shot, though they met heroically stiff resistance from Captain Miller's marines. Only here was the battle fought ferociously. Together with cross fire from Barney's long 18-pounders, the marines pushed the British back in one of the most furious exchanges of fire.[54] Every time the British tried to gain footage up the main road, they were driven back by Barney's artillery. When Thornton rallied the British, they came within fifty yards of Miller's marines before the tide turned again. Suddenly Thornton's horse caught a bullet and crumpled. The brigade commander struggled to his feet, sword in hand, and continued to lead the charge but was severely wounded in the thigh while grape shot shredded his jacket. He was so close to his foe when wounded that he rolled down the slope to avoid capture.[55] His men ran for cover in the wooded ravine, hotly pursued by American sailors shouting to each other to "board them!"[56]

The marines gave ground only as their numbers thinned from mounting casualties. Out of the total of 114 marines, 11 were killed and 16 wounded. The bullet that pierced Captain Miller's arm left him hospitalized for ten months, and even then he never regained its full movement.[57]

As the British regained ground, the firing intensified. Charles Ball, a flotilla seaman and former slave who had run away from a Georgia plantation, was manning a cannon on Barney's immediate left when he saw Ross. The general's appearance was so striking that years later Ball remembered Ross as "one of the finest looking men that I ever saw on horseback."[58] Then, suddenly, Ross was thrown to the ground close to Barney's guns when a bullet struck and killed the favorite Arabian horse he had ridden so often in the Peninsula campaign.[59]

At about the same time, a British bullet thudded into Barney's horse and it slumped dead between two guns. The five hundred flotillamen were down to their last rounds, but they could not reload because the drivers of ammunition wagons had run for their lives.[60] The commodore was standing near one of his guns when a bullet slammed deep into his thigh, leaving him severely wounded and unable to walk. He was bleeding profusely when he realized the British had gone around his rear, leaving his position defenseless. The fifty-five-year-old Barney told his men to go while there was time. Three sailing masters tried to take him with them, but after supporting him a few paces the weak and bleeding commodore could go no further and they laid him down.

At that moment a man named Wilson rode close by. Barney called out to him but Wilson rode on, even though he was the commodore's temporary aide, had seen him collapse, and heard the summons. The sailing masters protecting Barney ran after Wilson, but he gave them the slip and rode off. It was a fleeting incident in a day of momentous events, but it left such a shameful impression on the lame commodore that he branded Wilson a "wretch" who had "behaved like a villain." Barney was convinced that if Wilson had reined in his horse, all five of them—Barney, Wilson, and the three sailing masters—would have escaped.[61]

As soon as Wilson disappeared, Barney told his men to run off and save themselves. To a man, they refused. Barney was their leader who had inspired and dazzled by personal courage, and none of the sailing masters was about to abandon him. But when the commodore made it an order, two of them left reluctantly. The third disobeyed and remained steadfast by his side.

In the final moments of the battle for Barney's redoubt, British forces swept in with fixed bayonets, skewering gunners even as they stood with lit fuses in their hands.[62] One defender shot a British sailor in the face. Then, brandishing a sword in his other hand, the American slashed at

Midshipman Samuel Davies. The English country parson's son parried the blow with his own cutlass, but not before the other's blade sliced the middle finger of his left hand. Though wounded, the Englishman rammed his cutlass through the sailor's guts, killing him instantly.[63]

Barney, spotting a British officer, asked for him to be brought over. American sailing master John Webster, retreating "in double quick time" after having his horse shot through the head and another bullet passing through the crown of his hat, glanced back in time to see a British officer supporting the crippled commodore.[64] Unknown to Barney, the officer was Lieutenant Scott, the aide-de-camp to Admiral Cockburn. The lame Baltimorean introduced himself and asked Scott if he would stay. Scott assured him he had nothing to fear in his condition. The lieutenant, who was one of only a handful of British naval officers on the battlefield, left briefly to bring over Ross and Cockburn. Both British commanders were gracious, courteous, and in unabashed admiration of Barney's conspicuous bravery.

"Well, admiral, you have got hold of me at last," said the commodore.

"Do not let us speak on that subject, commodore," Cockburn replied. "I regret to see you in this state. I hope you are not seriously hurt."

"Quite enough to prevent my giving you any trouble for some time," said Barney.[65]

Ross was full of praise for the commodore's courage. The general summoned an English surgeon to dress the wound, then surprised the American by announcing he was paroled and at liberty to choose whether he wished to go to Bladensburg or Washington. He offered the middle-aged sea dog any help he needed and ordered a stretcher brought to carry him off the battlefield. By the time Ross and Cockburn said their farewells, Barney had already formed a favorable opinion of the two British commanders. He would remember for long afterwards how they had "behaved to me with the most marked attention, respect and politeness." Capt. John Wainwright, who was delegated to stay with the American, was so solicitous of his comfort and well-being that Barney thought he behaved "as if I was a brother."[66]

It was an isolated embrace of enemies. Elsewhere, off the battlefield, a thirsty grenadier of the Royal Scots Fusiliers stopped to fill his water canteen from a well some distance from his unit when he was pounced upon and captured by two Americans. They took his musket, tied him by the arms, and marched him away. But after a while they untied him briefly to let him eat a biscuit. The prisoner made his move after one of the captors went ahead to reconnoiter and the other sentry fell asleep. He cut the new cord around his hands, grabbed his musket, and bashed the sleeping American to death. Then he waited for the other captor to return, and shot him dead. When Admiral Codrington learned of this incident, he told his wife it might seem like legal butchery but it was really "well-performed duty. Were it not so estimated, England would not be what she is."[67]

The invaders suffered far more casualties than those they routed. A definitive account was never made because decomposing bodies continued to be found on farmland as long as two weeks after the conflict.[68] The best estimates of British losses, compiled by Dr. Catlett at the battlefield before the dead had been buried and the maimed tended to, amounted to 180 killed and 300 wounded. But the British reported only 64 dead and 185 wounded.[69] Catlett estimated American casualties at 10 or 12 killed and about 30 wounded.[70] General Winder believed his army suffered between 30 and 40 killed and 50 to 60 wounded.[71]

8. The Capital Abandoned

*A*t noon on Wednesday, with the British only minutes away from Bladensburg, Dolley Madison sat down to continue her chronicle. "Since sunrise," she wrote her sister, "I have been turning my spy glass in every direction and watching with unwearied anxiety, hoping to discern the approach of my dear husband and his friends; but, alas, I can descry only groups of military wandering in all directions, as if there was a lack of arms or of spirit to fight for their own fireside!"[1]

Even as she fretted for her absent spouse, she ordered a dinner table prepared for about forty guests, since she still expected the entire cabinet, military officers, and other guests for lunch at the usual hour of 3 P.M. Fifteen-year-old Paul Jennings, a slave in the Madisons' personal service, brought up large quantities of ale, cider, and wine and placed them in coolers.[2]

Later, as the boom of the cannons echoed from the fields of Bladensburg all the way to the President's House, a wagon was found and loaded with a fraction of the Madisons' belongings, including silver plate, some books, and a small clock. Also packed for the flight were crimson velvet curtains taken down from the elegant oval drawing room, where they had hung for the past five years.[3]

Now she waited, unaware of the course of the battle and too preoccupied with the desperate present to be concerned with the nebulous future. At this moment of limbo, Sukey, another of the servants, was leaning out of a window when the first of two horsemen galloped into view. James

Smith, a freed slave, waved his hat wildly as he shouted, "Clear out! Clear out! General Armstrong has ordered a retreat!"[4]

The First Lady refused to be rushed and ignored those who implored her to leave. One of her friends, wealthy landowner Charles Carroll of Bellevue, grew visibly angry when she insisted on remaining until her orders had been carried out to save Gilbert Stuart's full-length portrait of George Washington.[5] In 1800 the U.S. government had bought the framed portrait for the President's House, paying $800.[6] On this afternoon of 24 August 1814 it was attached to the west wall of the large dining room when two New Yorkers entered and offered to help Dolley in any way they were able.[7] One of the newcomers was Robert DePeyster, and the other, Jacob Barker, a shipowner, was an intimate friend of the Madisons and, like Dolley, a Quaker.

"Save that picture!" cried Dolley. "Save that picture if possible. If not possible, destroy it. Under no circumstances allow it to fall into the hands of the British!"[8]

When she saw Jennings and another servant taking too long to unscrew the giant frame from the wall, she instructed them to break the wood and take out the linen canvas. But French John entered the room as the first blow was struck and, seeing the potential for permanent damage to the painting, ordered Jennings to stop. With Dolley's approval, tradition holds, the Frenchman used a knife to cut the heavyweight English twill fabric from its frame. It now measured ninety-five inches by fifty-nine and three-quarter inches.[9] He handed it to Barker, who started to roll it up until French John quickly stopped him for fear this would crack the paint.[10] Barker and DePeyster left the portrait with a farmer they lodged with overnight. It remained there for a few weeks until Barker retrieved it and returned it to Mrs. Madison.[11]

While remnants of exhausted American troops paused outside the mansion to receive refreshments, Dolley completed the letter to her sibling. "And now, dear sister, I must leave this house, or the retreating army will make me a prisoner in it, by filling up the road I am directed to take. When I shall again write you, or where I shall be tomorrow, I cannot tell!!"[12] She then went to the dining room and stuffed some silverware into her old-fashioned reticule. Finally she grasped her copy of the Declaration of Independence before taking her seat in the carriage with Charles Carroll, Sukey, her female servant, and brother-in-law Richard Cutts, superintendent general of military supplies. Jo. Bolin drove them across Rock Creek to the heights above Georgetown, where they stopped first at the home of Navy Secretary Jones, then at Bellevue, Charles Carroll's stately brick mansion, with its sweeping view of the Potomac and the distant Capitol.[13]

Back at the President's House, a butler, John Freeman, drove away with his wife and child. The feather bed lashed to the back of the coachee was the only furniture anyone managed to save before the mansion was abandoned.

A mile away, on the corner of 1st Street and A Street SE, across the road from the majestic east front of the Capitol, Dr. James Ewell stood at a third-floor window of his comfortable brick home and looked out in the direction of Bladensburg with mounting trepidation. At forty-one, he was the capital's preeminent physician and well known beyond Washington since publication of his *Planter's and Mariner's Medical Companion* seven years earlier.[14]

Dr. Ewell's social and professional standing was of no use at this moment. His wife of twenty years, Margaret, trembled uncontrollably, and his two daughters were plainly terrified. Though they were a good half dozen miles from the battlefield and it was midday in the hottest month of the summer, they saw the Congreve rockets cutting fiery trails after launch. More fearful were the crump of cannons reverberating for miles around. And then suddenly all was quiet. Ewell did not know which side had been victorious, but his suspense was short-lived as dust clouds billowed above the forest of oaks. American horsemen fleeing the battlefield passed by his house. Among them were the secretary of war and his entourage. Other mounted militiamen galloped past, warning all and sundry, "Fly! Fly! The ruffians are at hand! If you cannot get away yourselves, for God's sake send off your wives and daughters, for the ruffians are at hand!"[15]

Ewell was horrified as he watched the long line of tattered infantry emerge from the dust clouds. He fretted for his family and others trapped in the capital. Had not the newspapers carried terrifying accounts of

British brutality along the shores of the Chesapeake Bay? As his daughters cried hysterically, his wild-eyed wife moaned and wailed, "What shall we do? What shall we do? Yonder they are coming!"[16] Trapped in the city because there were no wagons in which to flee, Ewell had decided they would be safer by moving in with a bedridden neighbor about a hundred yards away. The enemy would surely be more compassionate toward those at the side of a frail, sickly person. Besides, the woman had pleaded with Ewell to stay with her after her own husband left and the servants ran off.

Soon the remnants of the American military gathered in dribs and drabs at the Capitol. Initially, Winder had told them to regroup on the heights west of the turnpike gate, about a mile and a half from the Senate and House wings, where the general hoped to make another stand. But he changed his mind, and when only half a mile from the Capitol he crossed paths with Colonel Minor, commanding the 60th Regiment of the Virginia militia. The seven hundred men had finally been equipped with weapons and ammunition and were en route to fight at Bladensburg when Winder told them to stay and cover the retreating army, then march back to the Capitol.[17]

By the time he reached the twin wings of the federal legislature, the commanding general of a broken army had made a momentous decision not to stand and fight there, even with its advantageous height. He would sacrifice the city to save the lives of his battered forces. If pursued, he might perhaps turn and face the British, but only once he had reached the elevated slopes of Georgetown.

Stark reality left Winder no choice. His ranks were thinned and scared. Many had scattered after the rout at Bladensburg. The first line and some cavalry had taken routes north of Washington and away from the Capitol. Others had headed to their families or scavenged for food in the countryside. Many Baltimoreans had gone north to their homes. His bone-weary troops were in worse condition than they had been before the conflict. He had no reasonable hope of fighting off a determined assault by the enemy. To make a last-ditch stand inside the Capitol or any other enclosure in Washington would have bottled up his men, allowing the British to starve them into submission while giving the invaders a free hand to subdue the rest of the city. When he asked Armstrong and Monroe for their opinions, they both argued for rallying the troops on the heights of Georgetown, where the enemy would be at a geographic disadvantage and vulnerable to counterattack from the right flank or rear.[18]

As the first units trudged west from Capitol Hill, down along Pennsylvania Avenue and across the creek to Georgetown, other footsore contingents arrived from the battlefield. Uncoordinated and disjointed, the segmented lines relied on word of mouth and bystanders to find the route taken by earlier arrivals. A dejected George Hoffman surveyed the depressing sight of troops passing through the capital. It "made me regret that I survived the disgrace," the Baltimore militiaman told his father.[19] When sailing master John Webster arrived in command of about fifty of Barney's seamen, he spotted four mounted 18-pounders in front of the Capitol. Accompanied by a petty officer, Webster hurried across to the navy yard, where he stole eight harnessed horses readied to haul wagons. Once back at the Capitol, he spiked two of the guns with rat-tail files, hitched the horses to the other two fieldpieces, and hauled them down Pennsylvania Avenue on the way out of Washington. When they got to the front of the President's House they paused just long enough to add an abandoned, mounted 6-pounder to their collection.[20]

News of the collapse of the American army surprised Mordecai Booth at the navy yard. He had not even expected a battle, let alone this disastrous outcome. Hastily he ordered four newly arrived wagons to the magazine. But already there were signs of chaos among the few men remaining out of several hundred mechanics, laborers, seamen, and marines who were away in combat units. He saw men and wagons "flying in the utmost confusion."[21] Subordinates fled the scene, even as he tried to give orders. Booth hastened to lock the doors of his own house. When he found Commodore Tingey, the navy yard commandant let him into a closely guarded secret that left him reeling: in the event of an American retreat or defeat, he had orders to burn the navy yard. Compounding the shock, the sixty-three-year-old Tingey now ordered Booth to stay and help wreck the pride of the U.S. Navy.

The clerk hurried to the stables to saddle his horse and hand it over to the supervisor of laborers for safekeeping, but then he had second thoughts. Why not mount up and reconnoiter the area for military intelligence? Tingey agreed and Booth rode off, certain that he had heard cannonballs whistling over the marine barracks. When he got to the turnpike gate with its commanding view of the hills beyond, his heart ached with the depressing sight of hordes of his own countrymen in disarray and full retreat, some hobbling, others running, and even more breaking in apparent panic.

Some of the troops told him the army was rallying at the Capitol, and Booth rode back to tell Tingey, urging on all those he passed who looked fit enough to point a bayonet to make haste. But since he saw no sign of the British army, he decided the Americans could not have been vanquished. Some defenders must have blunted the attack. They *must* be holding the enemy at bay.

When he reported back to Tingey, he was ordered to turn around and find out what was going on near the Capitol. On his way, Booth saw that many of the soldiers had broken ranks and were visiting their families before pressing on for Georgetown. Some of the men had received permission. Others did not even bother to ask. Many of them acted out of scorn for their military leaders. General Smith, commanding the 1st Columbian Brigade, well understood the mood. "The idea of leaving their families, their houses, and their homes at the mercy of an enraged enemy, was insupportable," he would claim later. "To preserve that order which was maintained during the retreat was now no longer practicable."[22]

At the Capitol, Booth found 250 to 300 weary troops, many of them sailors and marines from Barney's contingent. When they told him units of the army had already reached Georgetown, Booth was incredulous. "It had in appearance, something too dastardly to be believed."[23]

Again he wheeled off to scan the fields from the turnpike gate a mile and a half away. Finding no sign of the telltale redcoats, he convinced himself that men who deserved to be called soldiers still held their ground between Washington and Bladensburg. It was about 4 P.M. when Booth sped back to the navy yard, but he was stopped short by a powerful explosion. The Eastern Branch bridge disintegrated before him, its wooden planks snapped into jagged fragments, hurtling high above the horizon. The bridge had been deliberately blown up by his own countrymen. Flat-bottomed scows and other boats laden with barrels of explosives under the bridge since dawn had been as devastating as Winder had planned. The long link spanning the banks of the Eastern Branch River was severed. Enemy troops would have to find another way into the capital.

When he reached the navy yard, Booth found Tingey being briefed by a young officer sent by Secretary Jones. Tingey had just learned that the U.S. military "could protect me no longer."[24] He was still recovering from this blow when he heard the explosion at the Eastern Branch bridge. Booth arrived as the officer was reporting that masses of British troops had penetrated the city limits and had even neared or reached the Capitol. Outraged by what he knew to be false, Booth let slip a stream of profanities. Later he apologized to Tingey, saying he had not meant to be disrespectful but had feared that the commandant might order destruction of the navy yard based upon incorrect information.

Again he offered to go out on reconnaissance. This time his burden was far greater, for Tingey said the fate of the navy yard, and even the life and reputation of the commandant himself, rested entirely on information Booth would bring back. The English-born Tingey, who had served in the British navy before immigrating to the New World while still in his twenties, was a highly respected naval officer. In 1799, while captain of a 24-gun warship in the Caribbean, he had defied the captain of a British frigate who wanted to board and search for English sailors. Newspapers had glorified Tingey's bold declaration that he considered every crewman to be an American. He had assured all on board that he would rather die than submit to the search. And he had vowed not to allow one sailor to be removed from his ship "by any force whatever." Such stout leadership had been rewarded with his appointment as commandant of the sprawling navy yard in 1804.[25]

As Booth rode off again, Tingey told other subordinates to get word out among nearby residents that the navy yard might soon be torched. The advance warning would give them a little time to take precautionary measures for their own safety and the protection of some of their belongings. Tingey's good intentions provoked furious opposition. Homeowners and neighboring residents clamored for him to hold off. Amid the hysteria, Tingey also had to listen to "a deputation of the most respectable women" pleading with him to defy his orders. After a while the commandant, whose own wife had died just four months earlier, could take it no longer.[26] With his patience exhausted, he abruptly pulled rank, threatening to light the fuses immediately unless they quit pressuring him. He would delay the fires as long as he could justify it—but only if left in peace.

Booth had ridden no more than a few minutes and could see the turnpike road when he saw a man whipping his horse on at full speed. When Booth caught up with him, the rider introduced himself as Thomas Miller, a Georgetown butcher who had also volunteered to collect intelligence. He had seen the British army and offered to pinpoint their whereabouts. They rode to the top of a hill, took a left turn, crossed a wide, open plain, and climbed a hill beyond a farmhouse. From there the butcher pointed to a column of men who looked to Booth as if they were dressed in blue or dark clothes. Many, however, had red coats, and he thought they were drummers and fifers, though Miller insisted they were officers. As the glaring sun was setting, Booth suggested they wait a little longer on the ridge for a clearer view. Soon, however, Booth changed his mind about the identity of the military unit below. He now thought the advancing column was a company of Georgetown riflemen and decided to close within three hundred yards for a better look. Together they reached a fence with some of its pickets scattered about, leaving a small gap. Miller dismounted and held it open for Booth, who asked him to wait while he rode up the hill. Before he reached the summit he heard Miller calling. He looked down and saw the butcher beckoning to him, but he continued on up. Miller mounted his horse and rode furiously to catch up, all the while yelling, "Hello! Hello!" When they were level the butcher said he had seen several men running off into the bushes, apparently to target Booth. A cornfield lay between the hill and the road, and Booth suddenly saw the men dart from the bushes toward him. He rode off evasively, thinking he was out of range, though one of the attackers opened fire. The butcher was quick to chide, asking Booth whether he needed any more proof that the troops were British.

Wary now of being intercepted on their way back, the two Americans kept to low ground, coming out near the Capitol and making for the sweeping view from the turnpike gate. The British had not yet passed the hill, so Booth rode on to report to his superior. He offered to make a written report, on the basis of which Tingey and Marine Corps Commandant Franklin Wharton could later justify having set fire to the yard. But Wharton was nowhere to be found. Faced with making the momentous decision alone, Tingey, who held the rank of captain in the navy, became excessively cautious. He knew he could be court-martialed if he let the public shipping and navy yard property fall into the hands of the enemy.[27] And he worried that the force of the wind blowing from the south-southwest would almost certainly fan flames from the navy yard across to neighboring private homes in the north and east. If only he could hold off setting the fires until nightfall, when the winds might calm down. Tingey was also awaiting the return of Captain Creighton, who had gone out in search of the American army. The captain had arrived at the navy yard at about 5 P.M. with the men he had commanded in blowing up the Eastern Branch bridge. Like Booth and Tingey, he was loath to see the navy yard in ruins. Still hopeful that the British may have been repulsed, he rode off to try and find them.[28]

As the butcher had told Booth that the Americans had already passed through Georgetown, the navy yard clerk now proposed riding as far as the President's House, where he hoped to get reliable information, failing which he might meet up with the reconnoitering officer. With Tingey's agreement, he set out. At Jersey Avenue he met an American cavalryman, Maj. Walter Cox, who reported he had left the broken army at Tenleytown, a hamlet two miles from Georgetown en route to Montgomery Court House in Maryland. Both men rode down to the President's House, where they found a uniformed horseman, apparently a field officer, by the steps. When Booth asked him his name, the colonel grew agitated and drew a pistol from his holster, but replaced it when Booth announced himself as an American scouting on behalf of the commandant of the navy yard. The officer said he did not think anyone was inside the mansion because he had summoned French John and no one had answered. Nevertheless, the colonel dismounted, walked up the steps, yanked the bell, knocked at the door, and called out for French John. "But," Booth well remembered, "all was as silent as a church." The colonel spoke cryptically of having had the power to detain General Ross and would have engaged Booth's companion in private conversation, but the navy yard clerk said they must not delay and the two of them rode off without the colonel. At this moment Booth realized the brutal truth. "Then, and not until then, was my mind fully impressed that the metropolis of our country was abandoned to its horrid fate."[29]

Almost all business was at a standstill. Shops and offices were shut and locked.[30] But Thomas Hughes kept his grocery store open as units of the demoralized military slogged past on the south side of Pennsylvania Avenue between Sixth and Seventh Streets, almost halfway between the Capitol and the President's House. At one point General Van Ness, one of the wealthiest men in the capital, stopped by and personally paid Hughes $25.31 for a barrel of whiskey, which he dispensed to grateful troops at the nearby water pump.[31]

The superintendent of patents, Dr. William Thornton, had returned home at midnight after dining with the president in a private home near Bladensburg and then going on mounted reconnaissance with a small party of prominent Washingtonians, including the attorney general. Though a Scottish-trained physician, the West Indian–born Thornton was better known as the man who had won the competition to design the Capitol. He had also designed the double town house on North Capitol Street for George Washington, and the Octagon House, the city's first privately owned mansion.

Both Thornton and his wife of twenty-four years, Anna Maria, like their next-door neighbors, Dolley Madison's sister and brother-in-law, remained in the city well after most of their friends had scattered. In midafternoon they sat down to dinner, but Mrs. Thornton had no appetite. Even though rumors reached them that the opposing forces were locked in battle, they remained restlessly housebound. But they prudently harnessed their horses to ride off at a moment's notice. They saw a rider gallop past as hard as he could for the President's House, yet it was not until American troops trudged in full view down the city's main thoroughfare that the Thorntons hastened to join the evacuation. They stopped at the President's House to look for Dolley Madison, and discovered that she had not been gone long because they caught up with the wagon transporting the portrait of George Washington.

Thornton separated from his wife in Georgetown, where an acquaintance told her to go no further as the road was jammed with soldiers and rumor had it that the British planned an attack in the area. Mrs. Thornton found refuge near the crest of Georgetown heights at Tudor Place, the neoclassical mansion designed by her husband for Martha Washington's granddaughter, Martha Custis Peter. Dr. Thornton joined her much later that day, having ridden as far as Tenleytown before his servant caught up with him and told him his wife was behind, not ahead of him.[32]

The chaos and turmoil were widespread, and some individuals exploited the breakdown of order and discipline for personal gain. In upper Georgetown, one tired officer stopped a horse-drawn cart driven by a black man and, unhitching the animal, announced that he could not walk any further and must have it. Without giving his name, address, or any payment for the horse, he mounted it and rode off.[33]

The president, meanwhile, accompanied by Attorney General Rush, General Mason, and businessman Tench Ringgold, arrived back at his official residence not long after his wife's escape. Madison had sent a message to Secretary Jones, who was then with his wife, Eleanor, and Dolley Madison, at Charles Carroll's home in Georgetown, telling him to rendezvous at Foxall's Foundry.[34] But the president changed his mind and sent Ringgold to Carroll's elegant mansion with another message, instructing Jones and Dolley to find refuge on the Virginia side of the Potomac and to meet the following day at Wiley's Tavern, the landmark inn close to Great Falls and sixteen miles northwest of Georgetown.[35]

The president and his entourage lingered at the executive mansion just long enough for refreshments before riding off toward Mason's Ferry to cross into Virginia. While at the residence, Madison took off his holsters holding the pair of dueling pistols given to him that morning by Treasury Secretary Campbell. He did not put them on again before leaving, and they were either stolen or consumed in the fire that later gutted the building.[36]

French minister Louis Serurier had either witnessed Madison's departure or had it described to him, for he reported to Paris that the president "proudly got on his horse and, accompanied by a few friends, slowly reached the bridge separating Washington from Virginia."[37] But by other accounts Madison crossed by ferry, squeezing his slight frame into a boat so small that it had to return several times to convey his entourage across.[38] Not long after, Dolley crossed over in the company of female members of the Jones and Carroll families. Their journey was painfully slow along a darkening road jammed with baggage wagons and throngs of desperate refugees in disordered flight.

William Simmons, who claimed to have saved James Madison from falling into enemy hands at Bladensburg, dismounted outside the President's House not long after the chief executive abandoned it. Simmons did not want the two 12-pounder cannons at the front gate to be captured by the enemy. Entering the mansion, he found that everybody was gone except for French John, who had apparently returned after Booth's stopover. Simmons told him to take brandy outside and pour drinks for the thirsty militiamen straggling by on their way to Georgetown. When this was done, Simmons successfully coaxed a number of reinvigorated troops to tow the cannons out of the city. It did not require much effort to pull them by hand, since both were already mounted on wheeled carriages. Simmons delayed his departure until he felt sure there were no U.S. military left in the capital. It was twilight as he rode out on Pennsylvania Avenue, past the brand new Press and Eagle tavern one hundred yards west of the President's House, and on into the security of the countryside.[39]

Almost five dozen mounted cavalrymen had escaped his notice. They were waiting on Capitol Hill for an expected regrouping of American forces. Their squadron leader, Colonel Lavall, could not remember whether he had been ordered to remain at Capitol Hill or if it had come to him as rumor, but for half an hour he waited in vain to be joined by other troops. Then, having heard that the army was re-forming outside the President's House, he signaled his men to follow him down Pennsylvania Avenue. They waited outside the lofty mansion for about three-quarters of an hour without seeing any defenders. Lavall was puzzled and then upset. "I could not, nor would not, believe that the city was to be given up without a fight." At length he received orders to join the army, which, he learned, had passed through Georgetown two hours earlier. With his back to the enemy, Lavall led his cavalrymen out of Washington, feeling "sorrow, grief and indignation."[40]

Dr. Hanson Catlett, staff surgeon attached to the 1st Infantry Regiment, was one of the last Americans to pass through the city from the field of battle. All the troops had dispersed by the time he reached Capitol Hill. The few citizens he saw further on by their houses appeared to him "as if resigned to meet an awful fate." A rumor that the British were somewhere near the race ground proved false from his personal observation, but whoever spread this tale had, in the surgeon's opinion, "only intended to produce panic."[41]

There were others in the city who had waited for the hour when the streets would be empty, the houses deserted, and troops out of sight. Now they were free to steal and run, with no one about to safeguard property or enforce law and order. Young Paul Jennings had stayed behind in Washington because Richard Cutts had told him to go to a stable on 14th Street and get his carriage. From his vantage point, the teenage slave was able to report later that "a rabble, taking advantage of the confusion, ran all over the [President's House], and stole lots of silver and whatever they could lay their hands on."[42]

Residents of Capitol Hill faced a more immediate terror. With the militiamen having long since skulked out of the city, the small band of defenseless, distraught civilians faced an unopposed foe, poised to invade. One old-timer, William Pumphries, tried his best to calm two hysterical women, Betsy Brown and her sister-in-law, Kathy Brown, telling them Commodore Barney was advancing, not the British. But the women would not be fooled. "They were ringing and twisting and screaming, calling the Lord, 'What is to become of us all,'" according to Michael Shiner, an eyewitness.

Shiner was riveted by the unfolding drama, and even though he wrote phonetically with the barest of grammatical accuracy, the untutored slave had a notable gift for sensitive expression. Years later he set down his recollections, remembering how he had heard the even tread of infantry and seen forward units of the victorious British army looming at the turnpike gate. "A colored man and myself with a old lady by the name of Mrs. Reid on Capitol hill and as soon as we got sight of the British army raising that hill they look like flames of fire, all red coats and the stocks of their guns painted with red vermillion, and the iron work shined like a spanish dollar."[43]

Adm. George Cockburn was the driving force behind the capture of
Washington.
Mezzotint by C. Turner 1879 after J. J. Halls. From Prints and Photographs
Division, Library of Congress.

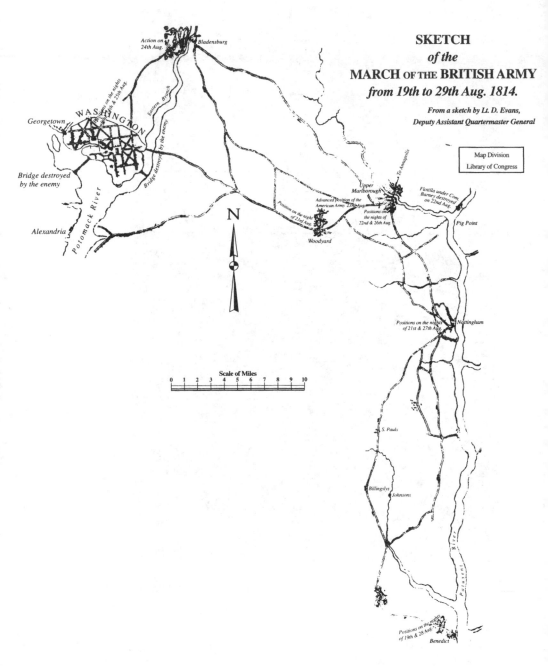

A sketch by Lt. George de Lacy Evans, British deputy quartermaster general, of the route taken by British troops on their march from Benedict on the Patuxent River to Bladensburg and Washington.

From Geography and Map Division, Library of Congress.

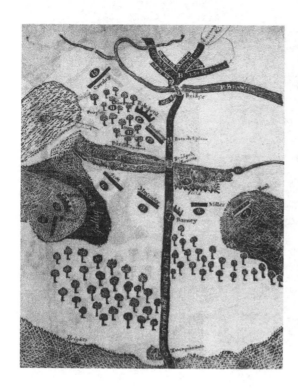

A contemporary drawing of a plan of the battle of Bladensburg, with the American forces arrayed on both sides of the main road to Washington (*center, forefront*) and the British troops beyond the river at the top of the drawing.
From Prints and Photographs Division, Library of Congress.

British commanders at Bladensburg admired the battlefield bravery of their wounded captive, Commodore Joshua Barney, seen in a 1785 painting by Charles Wilson Peale.
Photo from Prints and Photographs Division, Library of Congress.

President James Madison escaped capture by fleeing to Virginia just hours before British troops seized Washington.
Painting by James Vander-lyn. Courtesy of the White House. Copyright by White House Historical Association.

Dolley Madison, the most beloved of all First Ladies, in an 1804 painting by Gilbert Stuart.
Courtesy of the White House. Photo from Prints and Photographs Division, Library of Congress.

BRITISH BURN THE CAPITOL · 1814

British arsonists torch the Capitol in this 1974 fresco by Allyn Cox on the ceiling of a ground-floor corridor in the House wing of the U.S. Capitol. From the Office of the Architect of the Capitol.

A watercolor by George Munger, 1814, shows damage to the House and
Senate wings after the British burned the Capitol.
Courtesy of Kiplinger Washington Collection.

An 1814 watercolor by George Munger of the hollowed-out ruins of the
President's House after fires set by British troops. The twisted wire on the
roof is a lightning rod.
Courtesy of Kiplinger Washington Collection.

Saved from flames by Dolley Madison, this portrait of George Washington by Gilbert Stuart now hangs in the East Room of the White House.
Courtesy of the White House.

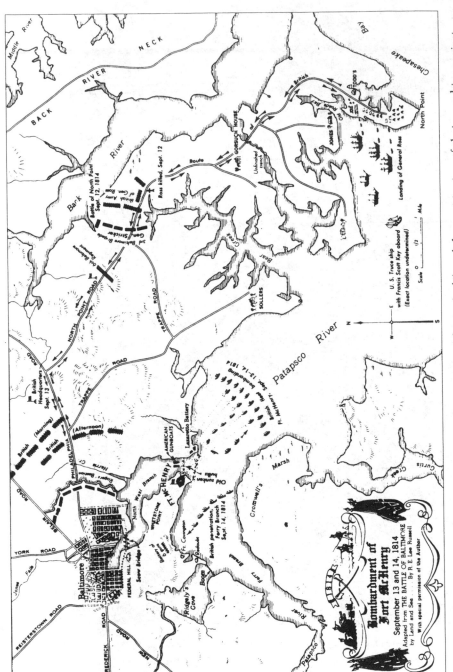

A map of the Baltimore area showing the route of British land forces (*right*) and the positioning of their warships against Fort McHenry (*left*).

From Geography and Map Division, Library of Congress.

Three weeks after capturing Washington, Maj. Gen. Robert Ross,
commander of British land forces, fell mortally wounded on the outskirts of Baltimore.
Engraved after a painting by Alonzo Chappel, published 1859 by Johnson,
Fry & Co. From Prints and Photographs Division, Library of Congress.

Maj. Gen. Andrew Jackson commanded American forces against the
British in the battle at New Orleans.
Engraving by T. Phillibrown after a painting by D. M. Carter, published 1858 by
Johnson, Fry & Co. From Prints and Photographs Division, Library of Congress.

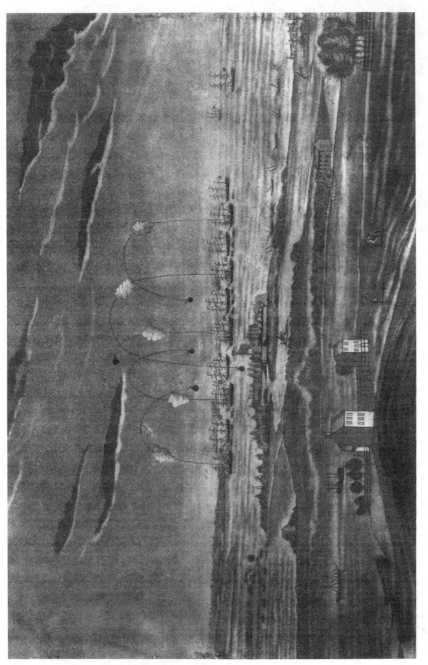

British warships bombard Fort McHenry in this aquatint engraved and published by John Bower, Philadelphia, 1814. Courtesy of the Peale Museum, Baltimore City Life Museums. From Prints and Photographs Division, Library of Congress.

9. Washington in Flames

*A*s the British rested at Bladensburg for several hours before marching on Washington, some of their troops lagged behind to steal from surrounding farms. But with the American military gone and most remaining Washingtonians cowering in their homes, no one came forward to respond to emissaries sent ahead by General Ross. They carried a flag of truce and were prepared to announce that the British would respect the private property of all who "remained quiet in their houses." But they would feel free to target every public building and store.[1]

Ross and Cockburn rode into the American capital at the head of a small group of officers flanked by guards. They were only several hundred yards from the open space in front of the soaring Capitol when shots rang out from a brick house on their right. Ross tumbled off his horse unscathed as the animal buckled and dropped dead from a bullet wound. It would lie where it fell for four days before anyone had time to remove the carcass. One invader was killed and at least one other wounded in the burst of fire.[2]

The veterans of multiple European campaigns did not flinch. They responded swiftly, Cockburn ordering Scott to lead an attack on the building from where the shots had come. Unknown to the British, the large fourteen-year-old town house had been the home of Albert Gallatin before his move to Belgium the year before as one of the U.S. commissioners trying to negotiate an end to the Anglo-American war. Though Scott's party quickly broke into the house, the assailant had already fled out the back. In keeping with their practice for over a year in the Chesapeake Bay, the British immediately set fire to the house because it had been used for hostile purposes.[3]

Martha Custis Peter, granddaughter of Martha Washington, was in her Georgetown mansion during the British invasion, and four days later she apparently knew the identity of the man who shot Ross's horse. In a letter to a friend, Mrs. Peter, who was outspokenly against the war and so enamored of British culture that she named a daughter Britannia and her private estate Tudor Place, identified the man as "a worthless hairdresser. . . . [T]he British soldiers were so enraged they would have torn him to pieces —but Ross remarked he was certainly too worthless to live—but he might live *here*."[4] However, another rumor that reached as far as the Chesapeake's northern shore had it that the sniper was an unidentified woman.[5]

The British presence was still unknown to the small band of Americans scouting the capital. Mordecai Booth and his companion, Major Cox, had been joined by Captain Creighton and two others. All five were reconnoitering together on their ride from the President's House via Capitol Hill back to the navy yard. In the fast-fading light Cox bent forward level with his horse's neck, straining to see what lay ahead. He thought he saw cows, but he may have been mistaken because the shapes rising up from the hollow in front of Long's Hotel looked more like men coming straight at them. His colleagues pressed forward with extreme caution until separated from the shadowy presence by a mere forty yards. All at once the shapes were defined. They were the enemy! The Americans dug in their heels, gave their horses free rein, and galloped off as musket shots blasted behind them.[6]

At the navy yard, Tingey was in a quandary. Creighton had been gone so long that the commandant feared he had been captured.[7] Rumors abounded. At one moment the enemy was reported near the marine barracks. Then the British were said to be on Capitol Hill, and even advancing on Georgetown. Tingey set a deadline for 8:30 P.M. If Creighton was not back by then he would put the terrible orders into motion.

Meanwhile, he instructed a handful of marines and other men to cast off in one of the small galleys. He was glad of this move, for the boat would be one of the few to survive. During this uncertain lull, Marine

Commandant Wharton and his paymaster fled north for Fredericktown, Maryland, in a light boat Tingey had set aside for them earlier in the day.

Booth and Creighton arrived within half an hour of Tingey's deadline. They were blunt, their evidence compelling: Bladensburg had been a disaster, the British were occupying the city, and the unguarded navy yard was in imminent danger of capture. These were the very preconditions set by Navy Secretary Jones about 2 P.M. that day when he had verbally instructed Tingey to lay the fuses and be prepared to burn the public shipping and stores.[8]

The moment had arrived, and the three men were appalled at what they were about to do. The navy yard had been envisioned even before the government moved down from Philadelphia in 1800. It was historic acreage. This was where the fledgling navy's warships were built. Twice as much money had been plowed into its development than for any other American navy yard.[9] Thomas Jefferson had personally selected Benjamin Henry Latrobe to design and oversee its growth, from the wharf, building slips, and multiple workmen's sheds to the commandant's house, guard quarters, and even the surrounding wall. Characteristically, Latrobe had brought art and elegance even to this noisy construction site, designing a handsome main gate with twin Doric columns for the carriage entrance. Tingey and his staff were keenly aware of the navy yard's place in the tiny capital. It was not only the workplace for hundreds of Washingtonians, but was also one of the most familiar landmarks in their hometown.

Tingey hesitated before giving the awesome command. He asked Booth and Creighton how they hoped to escape, whether on horseback or by rowboat. Creighton opted to go with Tingey by boat. Booth elected to gallop off because his horse "was too good a one to be lost." Untended horses were being snatched by complete strangers during the stampede to escape.[10]

Then it was time to burn. The arsonists set about their grim business, setting alight fuses leading to storehouses stuffed with ordnance, cordage, sail loft, and provisions. The largest ignited almost instantly. Next, they raced to the wharf where the new frigate *Columbia* and the sloop of war *Argus* lay motionless. The *Columbia's* hull was almost finished and her bottom ready for coppering. She would have been launched with traditional fanfare in ten days. There was enough timber on the wharf to complete her masts and spars. Her largest boats were themselves almost ready to be launched. The *Argus* lay at the wharf with all her armament and equipment on board. Her provisions were already lost in the burning storehouses. Like possessed pyromaniacs, the government employees set fire to the ships and watched pitifully as the flames devoured months of fine workmanship in the brilliant nocturnal pyre.

Shocked by the catastrophe of his own making, Tingey hesitated before moving against the new schooner *Lynx*. A faint hope stirred that perhaps he could save it. Illogical though it may have seemed with flames spreading so close, Tingey hollered to the others to back away and spare the *Lynx*. It was his only act of defiance against orders still fresh from the secretary of the navy.

The fires took a disastrous toll in his territorial fiefdom. Large quantities of timber and planks stacked in sheds and other locations were crumbling as fires roared unchecked. Two armed and rigged row galleys disappeared in the searing flames, together with three scows loaded with heavy guns. Fire spread to the mast and timber sheds, the joiners' and boat builders' shops, and the mold loft. Like a wheat field bending under fierce winds, most buildings caved in one after the other: administration offices, the medical store, the plumbers', smiths', and blockmakers' shops, the sawmill and block mill with all their specialized tools and machinery. So great was the fire that the only buildings untouched were the homes of the commandant and the lieutenant of the yard, the guardhouses and gateway, and one other edifice.[11] The heavy steam engines buckled and blistered, and combustible parts popped in the heat. The inferno spread to gun-carriage shops and into work areas where painters applied finishing touches. Flames licked the night air even higher after wrapping around the hulls of the old frigates *Boston* and *General Greene*. Solid sheets of bright orange flame enveloped the private apartments of the yard's master and boatswain, destroying in a whoosh their furniture and personal mementos.

Miraculously, some property survived. Large amounts of canvas, twine, lines, bunting, and colors did not burn in the navy storekeeper's detail-issuing store. Neither did the supply of mathematical instruments and nautical apparatus required for navigation, together with ship chandlery, tools, nails, and paint.[12] It seemed that at least two of the gunboats would be saved, but one of them, laden with provisions and gunpowder, ran aground before it cleared the Eastern Branch and was plundered by residents living near the navy yard. The other, weighted down with salted goods, sank in the Potomac.[13]

By the glow of monstrous fires, Tingey bade farewell to his faithful clerk. The British might well be closing in, and there was not a moment to lose. The commandant urged Booth to take good care of himself and his horse. Booth remembered clearly how at that moment the commandant of the navy yard took out his pocket watch and remarked that it was twenty minutes after eight.[14]

When he reached the long bridge over the Potomac, Booth had to order the south drawbridge cranked down. As he crossed over he glanced backwards and saw lights flickering in the Capitol. When he reached the Virginia shore he turned around and saw the navy yard burning. More than half a million dollars' worth of buildings, supplies, and shipping, not to mention books and papers detailing their value, were being reduced to ashes.[15] He rode on until he passed the causeway when a deafening explosion resounded across the Potomac River. It was so powerful that Booth imagined it could only have come from an ordnance store.

A quarter of an hour later he reached a hill and gasped at the devastation. The Capitol was burning. As the flames took hold, the magnitude of the calamity struck home. The landmark, notable as much for its artistic beauty as for its symbol of democratic freedoms, was doomed. Booth watched as the dancing flames spread unchecked. Soon the familiar wings were shrouded in flames and belching smoke. It was a conflagration of unprecedented scope. The majestic building atop its hill burned like an incandescent beacon. Booth felt pain and revulsion. It was a sight "so repugnant to my feelings, so dishonorable, so degrading to the American character, and at the same time so awful."[16] In the company of many women and children also immobilized by the horror, Booth watched from his hilltop vantage point for almost three hours as the flames soared.

Tingey scanned the wrenching scene as his rowboat cut through the Eastern Branch waters. He had intended anchoring in the river during the night, close by the yard over which he held administrative sway. However, the boat was cramped and overloaded with others, so he steered for the Alexandria shoreline.[17]

The British had earlier closed in on the undefended Capitol, its deserted twin wings linked by a one-hundred-foot, unpainted, covered wooden walkway. The enemy troops were dwarfed by identical sixty-seven-foot-high buildings, the Senate in the north and the newer House of Representatives in the south. Architectural details of the three-story Capitol were lost in the quickening darkness, but having broken in through the eastern entrance doors, which soared as high as a child standing upon the shoulders of a man, the foreigners were stunned by the dignified interior. They passed by finely fluted columns below vaulted brick ceilings, through arched entrances and up grand staircases into elegantly domed vestibules. The village below might be small and insignificant, but the legislative seat was noble and stirring even to haughty men of fine British pedigree. The effect was so unexpected that years later Lieutenant Scott would remember clearly how the building, far from being suited to "pure republican simplicity," seemed to exude "an unseemly bias of monarchical splendor."[18] A number of junior staff officers felt revulsion at what they were about to do. Captain Smith thought it barbarous. "I had no objection to burn[ing] arsenals, dockyards, frigates building, stores, barracks etc. . . . but we were horrified at the order to burn the elegant Houses of Parliament," he wrote.[19]

Work had all but ceased on the Capitol since the declaration of war two years before. Minor repairs had been done, finishing touches made to the Senate chamber, and some sculptural work done for the House.[20] Latrobe, the architect in charge for the past decade, had created a colossus of formidable beauty. It was to be expected from a man who boasted that the motto of his family, his art, and his duty was "Anything can be done."[21] Always opinionated and often blunt, he cared little for rivals whom he scorned openly as amateurs masquerading as professionals. Of Dr. William Thornton, who designed the Capitol, and James Hoban, the immigrant Irishman who once offered his services as a "house carpenter" before planning the President's House and becoming Latrobe's predecessor as surveyor of the public buildings, he scoffed: "General Washington knew how to give liberty to his country, but was wholly ignorant of art.

It is therefore not to be wondered that the design of a physician, who was very ignorant of architecture was adopted for the Capitol, and of a carpenter for the President's House."[22]

Latrobe was born in England in 1764 of an American mother and a Moravian clergyman. His father's religious travels in Europe enabled the young Latrobe to become fluent in English, German, French, Italian, Greek, and Latin. At thirty-two he was already a widower and a moderately successful architect when he immigrated to America, where, in 1803, President Jefferson appointed him surveyor of public buildings and architect in charge of construction of the U.S. Capitol.

In all the Capitol's vastness, nothing was more awesome than the chamber of the House of Representatives. Little did the Englishmen know how many years of creative energy had gone into it. As they entered, they faced the Speaker's canopied chair at the south end of a crimson-draped chamber. The room was shaped like an oblong octagon and measured eighty-five feet by sixty feet. Ten feet inside the outer walls were another set of semicircular walls, seven feet high on the eastern and western sides, each topped by ten fluted Corinthian columns, two feet, eight inches in diameter at the bases and twenty-six feet, eight inches high.[23] Latrobe had exerted himself with tireless zeal to bring this into being. He had searched abroad for superior sculptors, looking to the land of Michelangelo and Donatello, of da Vinci and Cellini. And after he hired two worthy Tuscans, he supervised with a perfectionist's rigor, even though moody from chronic headaches brought on, he imagined, by hard work, fatigue, and anxiety.[24]

He thought the richly ornamented columns, sculpture, and natural light displayed "great magnificence."[25] This was of no consequence to the single-minded British. They tried to burn it all by firing rockets through the sixteen-inch-thick domed pinewood roof, pierced with one hundred squares of imported English plate-glass sun lights. When the roof failed to ignite, a few soldiers clambered up, only to find it covered with sheet iron. Undeterred, they made a bonfire of wooden furniture in the center of the chamber, setting it alight with the rockets' combustible material. Flames quickly engulfed the mahogany desks, tables, and chairs, as well as two raised wooden platforms on which they stood.

At about this time, several miles away, the campus of Georgetown College was almost deserted. It was vacation time at the Catholic institution, and forty-five students had left for home. Father Giovanni Grassi, the college president, and John McElroy, in charge of the college accounts for the past eight years, looked eastward across Rock Creek to the hilly overlook. They had a good view because the campus lay on the heights of Georgetown, and they stood at the eastern window of the new building's upper dormitory.[26] The priest and the bookkeeper saw flames silhouetting the familiar outlines of the Capitol. McElroy had feared the worst. Earlier he had watched the sorry passage of routed American militiamen on their way through Georgetown to Montgomery Court House, Maryland. In the habit of keeping a daily record of events, McElroy looked at his watch. Later that night, in his familiar neat penmanship, he made a new entry under 24 August 1814: "This evening about dark the British arrived in W.C., fired the Capitol about 9:06."[27]

As the arsonists hurried to other parts of the Capitol, flames raced up the heavy green-lined crimson silk curtains draped between the columns to muffle echoes. Years before, sculptor Giovanni Andrei had exasperated Latrobe because he worked so slowly. But when the architect saw the first completed column he was overjoyed, telling all and sundry about this "artist of first rate excellence."[28] Now all was lost. The artwork baked and broke apart. The ancient Virginia freestone, hauled so cautiously from an island on Acquia Creek, cracked under the searing heat. The outer stone expanded and fell off, leaving the columns wobbly, their shafts burned into fragments of stone barely resting atop one another. Somehow they continued to hold up the six-foot-high stone entablature.

The fire raged indiscriminately. Above the Speaker's canopy it annihilated a cluster of sculpture below a crimson curtain, drawn aside between two columns to reveal the larger-than-life-size marble statue of *Liberty* sitting on a pedestal. In her left hand, supported by a carved eagle, she held a cap of liberty, and in her right a scroll representing the Constitution of the United States. Her foot trod upon an upside-down crown, the symbol of monarchy and oppression.

Sheets of flame mutilated the prized stone carving of an American bald eagle on the frieze above *Liberty*. Its outstretched wings spanned a full twelve feet, six inches. Latrobe had once halted Giuseppe Franzoni's work on the model because the eagle looked too foreign. Latrobe wanted nothing less than the American bald eagle, sculpted correctly to the minutest detail so that nobody, not even congressmen from western states who knew the eagle well, would be able to criticize him for mistakes. He pleaded with the eminent artist Charles Wilson Peale for "a drawing of the Head and Claws, of the Bald Eagle, of his general proportions with the Wings extended and especially of the arrangement of his feathers below the wings when extended."[29] Latrobe received much more than he asked for. When the stagecoach arrived one day with mail from Philadelphia, there was a small box addressed to him. It contained the preserved head and neck of a bald eagle. Peale's drawing followed a few days later, though it would be better, the artist suggested, to shoot a bird of prey for a close look at the arrangement of its feathers.[30]

Armed with this new information, the twenty-eight-year-old Franzoni had begun again. But he was weak and sickly and would die less than a year after the burning of Washington. One day he was unable to work as he coughed up blood. Yet Latrobe had needed no more than a glance at the unfinished work to claim "there is not in ancient or modern sculpture, an eagle's head, which is in dignity, spirit, and drawing superior to Franzoni's."[31] Now, however, with the Capitol in the hands of a reckless enemy, the great eagle was doomed. As the flames began to obscure it, Lieutenant Scott looked at the clock below the sculpture. It was exactly 10 P.M.[32]

The flames split and ravaged Franzoni's twenty-five-foot-long personifications of agriculture, art, science, and commerce chiseled in high relief in the frieze above the doorway through which the British had swarmed into the House chamber. The intense heat would result in the total loss of all the work in freestone in the House of Representatives and in part of the freestone dressings of the windows on the south and east sides.[33]

So fierce was the heat that glass oil-burning lamps and the plate glass on the ceiling melted into the sizzling debris.[34] When the roof crashed down, the glow from the burning landmark swelled as if fanned by a pair of bellows.

Once the flames reached the public galleries, seven feet up, they made short shrift of the timber and yellow pine flooring and seats. But the cool stone spiral entrance stairs and their wooden dressings at the south end of the building escaped. Six committee rooms on both sides of this wing, and even the handsome circular vestibule through which congressmen entered the chamber, owed their survival to Latrobe's masonry vaults spanning the ten feet between the columns in the House chamber and the outer walls of the building. All the other brick vaults in the building survived and, acting as firebreaks and fireproof supports, helped spare more rooms immediately overhead.[35]

The British had to work harder on their destructive swath downstairs, where there was less furniture and no wooden platform to kindle the flames. They pulled out window frames, shutters, and doors, chopped them up with an ax, emptied the contents of rockets into buckets, and spread the flammable mix onto the woodpile. It took time and was haphazard, with the result that some wood survived unscathed in every room.[36]

Cockburn, looking through other offices on the ground floor of the House wing, stepped into the high-ceilinged room set aside for meetings of the Committee of the District of Columbia. It doubled as a presidential office when Madison visited the Capitol.[37] Cockburn picked up a slim volume fifteen inches long and nine inches wide. It was bound in quarter sheep with marbled sides. Stamped in gilt over a green leather label on the front cover were the words "President of the U. States." The title of the book, written on the spine in gilt on a red background, read "RECTs & EXPENDs U S FOR 1810." This was Madison's personal copy of the government's receipts and expenditures for the year 1810, printed in Washington in 1812. The seventy-nine numbered pages noted payment of $25,000 to President Madison for compensation and expenses, and $1,000 "for trying the practical use of the torpedo or submarine explosion."

Cockburn decided to keep the book as a memento of his triumph. At that moment, or more likely at a later date, he wrote in a steady hand on the inside front cover, "Taken in President's room in the Capitol, at the destruction of that building by the British, on the Capture of Washington 24th. August 1814." Even later, he added an inscription below: "by Admiral Cockburn—& by him presented to his Eldest Brother Sir James Cockburn of Langton Bart Governor of Bermuda."[38]

The clerks' office suffered greatly because it had more furniture. One desk drawer that burned to ashes held the secret journal of the House of Representatives. It had been overlooked by clerks Burch and Frost in their frantic attempt to save paperwork before fleeing the city. The same panic accounted for the loss of records of contingent monies of the House for the eight previous months. They were locked in the private drawer of the chief clerk, Colonel Magruder, who had taken the key with him when called up to command the 1st Regiment of the 1st Brigade of the District of Columbia militia. Burch and Frost had intended forcing the lock just before fleeing but forgot to do so.[39]

Then, suddenly, the British plans went awry. The fires they had stoked sent out waves of unremitting heat. They were forced to back off. They could not even cross over to the western side of the building, so the ground floor rooms there were saved.[40]

The north wing sustained even greater losses, which must have been felt more keenly because Latrobe had spent several years ripping out masses of rotting timber in the ceilings and floors. The original builder may have been a scoundrel and at fault, but by the outbreak of war Latrobe had rebuilt the eastern half of the north wing, which held the Senate chamber and the Supreme Court.[41] Confidently, he had reported to President Madison, "All the east side of the wing is safe against fire or decay."[42]

Not surprisingly, catastrophic damage was done to the vulnerable western half overlooking the President's House and Georgetown. Here the heavily timbered Library of Congress burned to oblivion. Without vaulting, it had no protection against fire. The lofty, airy room had been favored for its two ranges of windows bringing in natural light even when the blinds were drawn against the afternoon sun.[43] It was a grand room by any standard, stretching eighty-six feet along its length and thirty-five feet across. The ceiling reached up thirty-six feet. Representatives had met in the library before their wing was ready, then it had become the Senate debating hall while their chamber was renovated in 1809. With no public library in Washington, congressmen used this perk for both reference and relaxation and were so jealous of their privilege that they passed another law shutting out everyone else, be they cabinet officers, Supreme Court judges, or even foreign ministers.[44]

The old shingle roof covering the library and most of the wing became mere tinder for the sparks. Falling bolts of timber smashed against walls and arches, leaving burn marks and smoldering surface scars. But the highest toll was in books. Almost three thousand perished in the fire.[45] Ironically, most were printed in London and many of the legal and history texts were by British authors. A number of volumes were even about the British parliamentarians and their laws.

Wind steered the huge flames into the Senate chamber, where they quickly incinerated blue mantua curtains lined with buff silk—colors chosen by Latrobe because of their association with Revolutionary War uniforms.[46] Elegant drapery, hangings, and carpets which five years earlier had moved a visiting Irish priest to swoon over their "superior style of splendour and brilliancy" were also snuffed into oblivion.[47] The overpowering heat cracked everything made of freestone. Marble polished columns crumbled into flaky lime and fell off the fourteen-foot-long shafts.

The foreigners were determined to destroy the Supreme Court, where the Senate had met before it moved into new quarters upstairs. But there did not seem to be enough firewood on hand. The only furniture in the courtroom had been hastily acquired by Latrobe after urgent pleas from justices who had been holding court sessions in a tavern while their new quarters were under construction.[48] The British hauled in more furniture from nearby rooms and made a fiery pile on the floor of the highest court of appeal. It was a death knell for the Doric columns and their rows of classical balance. The crackling fury burned them into rickety uselessness.[49]

But again, as if to vindicate Latrobe's faith, the graceful vaulting held firm. He had pioneered regular use of vaulting as a building technique in America, but he was not without critics who thought it too dangerous and costly. They got their chance to weigh in when vaulting collapsed in the Supreme Court in 1808, crushing the life out of Clerk of the Works John Lenthall. Even though the mishap occurred because wooden supports were removed prematurely during construction, Latrobe's reputation suffered severely. He was not in Washington when it happened, but he did not hesitate to accept responsibility.[50]

Outside the courtroom, the great staircase swept up with a flourish in a double dogleg pattern. Surrounding brick vaulting held the fire at bay until a flaming wooden lanthorn tumbled down from the crown of the brick cupola. It thudded onto the stone stairs but curiously left nothing more than scars easily capable of repair.[51]

Their work done, the British escaped into the brightly lit grounds through the lofty doorway leading out of a vestibule. Happily for posterity, the rare and serene vestibule survived, no doubt because of the vaulted ceiling. A quiet corner of the Capitol, it held half a dozen sandstone columns looking like stylized cornstalks, each topped with distinctly American "corn-cob capitals." Legislators had showered praise upon Latrobe for his original designs. Instead of conventional Greek and Roman acanthus leaves, Latrobe's capitals were carved with native American corn, their husks pulled back to show part of the kernels.[52] They were not only the first of their kind but arguably the most aesthetic.

Both the House and Senate wings were now burning with a brilliance all the more illuminating because of the darkness elsewhere. Horrified residents in the widely dispersed homes of Washington and Georgetown were only used to the pale flicker of candles and oil lamps after dark. Before the night was out, they would be able to read by the unnatural light of a city in flames.[53]

Dr. Thornton and his wife looked on helplessly from Tudor Place atop the heights of Georgetown. Later he would record only his "deep regret" on seeing the destruction of the handsome legislature he designed, but a brief mention in his wife's diary reflects their sad resignation: "We stayed all night at Mrs. Peter's (Mrs. Cutting with us) and there witnessed the conflagration of our poor undefended and devoted city."[54]

Latrobe was not in Washington when its grandest twin buildings burned. But months later, after walking through the awful wreckage within the roofless, outer walls, he could only lament the "melancholy spectacle."[55]

Still at the home of his bedridden neighbor, Dr. James Ewell looked on with disbelief as the Capitol burned. As one of the closest American eyewitnesses, not more than several hundred yards away, he saw flames bursting through the windows and rearing high above the roof. The lively mass of crunching, roaring flames sounded to him like thunder, and he was overcome with feelings of utter sadness and heavy gloom.

Suddenly Ewell was startled by banging on the front door. When it was opened, half a dozen British troops begged with effusive politeness for something to eat. They were given a cold ham with bread, butter, and wine. Ewell watched them set upon it with the "utmost good behavior."

But then he was distracted by lights in the rooms of his own house. It looked like the building was on fire. As he had not removed any of his property and wanted at the very least to save his medical books, he asked the Britons for help. The sergeant doubted the house was alight but agreed to go with him. At that moment, Ewell's servant entered and said the home had been plundered, though it was not on fire.

Simultaneously, Rev. McCormick arrived and said he had just been talking to Cockburn and Ross, a pair of "perfect gentlemen," whom he would introduce if Ewell wished. The doctor was quick to accept, hoping the British commanders would order protection for the remainder of his possessions.

McCormick thought he was introducing Ross, but Cockburn corrected him. "My name is Cockburn, Sir," he said in his clipped manner. Ewell told the admiral that he thought the British would respect private property, yet some of his furniture, clothing, and plate had been stolen.

"With whom did you confide your property, Sir?" asked Cockburn.

"With my servants," replied Ewell.

"Well, Sir," Cockburn chided, "let me tell you it was very ill confidence to repose your property in the care of servants."

Ross apologized for the apparent theft and asked Ewell to point out the house so he could place a guard outside.

"This is my house, Sir," said Ewell, pointing to the front door next to them.

Surprised and embarrassed, Ross said, "Why, Sir, this is the house we had pitched on for our headquarters."

Ewell could not contain his pleasure. He told them he only wished they had taken it earlier, as his possessions would then have been saved. Ross became even more apologetic, saying he could never think of moving into the home of a private family. He would give orders for the immediate removal of his gear. But in a scene almost comical for the swift reversal of roles, Ewell implored the invaders to remain.

"Well, Sir," Ross declared, "since you are so good as to insist on my staying at your house, I consent; but I will endeavor to give you as little trouble as possible. Any apartment under your roof will suffice me."

The physician conducted him to his own bedroom, the best-furnished in the house. Ross would not hear of it but accepted after Ewell insisted.

Then the general told him to go and tell his wife that she should return to her home, where she would be as safe as the night before when the American army had camped in Washington. "I am myself a married man, have several sweet children, and venerate the sanctities of the conjugal and domestic relations," said Ross.

Ewell was enchanted by their chivalry. He no longer feared for the safety of his family or for his property. Later he would have to explain his fraternization with the enemy to many of his angry countrymen, but for now he felt comfortable in having offered hospitality to those who were destroying the city's landmarks. He walked back to his wife and daughters feeling he had made a virtue out of necessity.[56]

About this time, a home north of the Senate wing went up in flames. It is not clear whether the house—once owned by George Washington—was burned willfully or by winds carrying the deadly flames across two hundred yards. However, some of the minor records of the House, stored there when clerks tried to empty the Capitol of paperwork prior to the invasion, were destroyed.[57]

With fires raging on Capitol Hill and at the navy yard, units of the British expeditionary forces marched southwest to attack the arsenal at Greenleaf's Point. Colonel Wadsworth, in charge of ordnance, had worked frantically that evening trying to spirit away some of the arsenal's stockpiled weaponry. Keeping one step ahead of the invaders, he had managed to load three fieldpieces and a quantity of ammunition onto a boat. They were taken upriver and deposited behind Mason's Island opposite the Georgetown ferry.[58] For Wadsworth, however, the night would bring nothing but frustration in a vain search for wagons to cart off supplies at the arsenal. He went as high up as the bridge over the Little Falls but again drew a blank. By then it was too late. The British had crossed into the city.

Cockburn and Ross meanwhile had targeted the President's House just over a mile west. An officer wearing the three-cornered *chapeau bras* on his head led a force of about a hundred soldiers and sailors tramping in two columns down the graveled breadth of Pennsylvania Avenue. Two men in the middle of the columns each carried a dark lanthorn. As they distanced themselves from Capitol Hill, there was something incongruous about the havoc behind them and the untouched orderliness of the double rows of

Lombardy poplar trees flanking the avenue. Resident slaves scurried ahead in the darkness, spreading word that the British were on their way to burn Mr. Madison's house and the homes of all government officials.[59] The columns moved briskly, but at one point the lead officer overheard some of the men talking. "Silence!" he barked. "If any man speaks in the ranks I'll put him to death!"[60]

William Gardner watched from the open window of his Pennsylvania Avenue house as the twin columns passed below. They were followed by four officers on horseback, all of whom doffed their *chapeaux bras* to bid him good evening. Gardner and his family returned the greetings. "Gentlemen," said Gardner, "I presume you are officers of the British army." When they replied affirmatively, Gardner addressed himself to Cockburn, who steered his horse under the window. "I hope, Sir, that individuals and private property will be respected."

"Yes, Sir," Cockburn assured him. "We pledge our sacred honor that the citizens and private property shall be respected. Be under no apprehension. Our advice to you is to remain at home. Do not quit your houses." Then Cockburn asked, "Where is your president, Mr. Madison?"

Gardner said he did not know but guessed he must be far away. When Cockburn asked what force he had, the American said it would be impossible for him to say because there were various estimates.

"We have got your Commodore Barney prisoner with us," said Cockburn.

"So I have heard, Sir, and that he is badly wounded," Gardner replied.

"Yes, Sir," Cockburn declared, "he is badly wounded, but I am happy to inform you, not mortally. He is a brave man, and depend upon it, he shall be treated with the greatest humanity and kindness."

At this point Ross interjected, "Yes, Sir, he shall be taken good care of."[61]

Saying that they were on their way to pay a visit to the President's House, the admiral and the general again told Gardner to stay indoors where he would be safe. Then, after bowing and bidding good-night, the officers continued down Pennsylvania Avenue. Some of the weary contingent led the way wielding long poles topped with flammable balls the size of large plates.[62]

The conquerors trod past the neighboring homes of two young married women, one cradling an infant, the other gulping camphor to still her frayed nerves. Alone since their husbands' mobilizations, and abandoned by their panic-stricken servants, the women had only each other's closeness for comfort. When it was obvious the British would descend down the avenue, a trembling, almost incoherent Mrs. Bender had gone next door clutching a camphor bottle in one hand and a handkerchief in the other. "There is but one power that can save us," she wailed to her neighbor, Mrs. Varnum.[63] "What shall we do?" And then, answering herself, she moaned, "We will stay together." They lit the lamps in both houses and returned to Mrs. Bender's to await their fate. The enemy passed by without incident, but then came Hinckley, the neighborhood drunk. An intelligent man when sober, he now entered their house cursing the British for what they had done. Terrified of the repercussions, the women hustled him to bed and to sleep, out of sight and out of harm's way.[64]

In another home, Mary Hunter waited fearfully. She had been separated from her family since morning, when her husband had scooped up their young children and taken them and the servants to safety a few miles off. She had elected to stay in the home with their housekeeper and a single black servant until he returned. But at midday she had heard cannon fire in the direction of Bladensburg, and some hours later saw militiamen "running in great numbers in a disorderly manner."[65] At sunset she watched aghast as the Union Jack flew atop Capitol Hill and British troops walked about brandishing rockets.

Suddenly "a grim-looking" officer rode up to her door and plied her with questions. Where was her husband? When did he leave? Why had he gone just at this moment? "I looked him fully in the face and very deliberately told him that my husband was gone to take a family of young children from witnessing such a horrid scene," she wrote to her sister, Susan Cuthbert, in Princeton, New Jersey. She said she had expected him back by evening, but that was hardly likely under the circumstances. Even though he left with assurances for her safety, she could not sleep. She looked out on a scene so "awful" that "no pen can describe the appalling sound that our ears heard and the sight that our eyes saw."[66]

Chester Bailey, an American mail contractor visiting the city, got a close-up look at the first detachment led by Ross when the invaders stopped opposite McKeowin's Hotel on Pennsylvania Avenue, almost halfway to the President's House. Though he did not know the exact nationality of the Frenchmen and Spaniards marching with the British, Bailey thought they were "the most hellish-looking fellows that ever trod God's earth."[67] Ross told the onlookers that private property and individuals would be respected, a pledge repeated by Cockburn when he brought up the rear. These were not glib promises. Ross had detailed a Scottish officer, Maj. Norman Pringle, to command a company of soldiers for the express purpose of protecting private property along Pennsylvania Avenue. They would perform so honorably that Americans, even combat veterans, would remember them respectfully for years afterwards.[68] Invading British troops caught violating the self-imposed restrictions were dealt with swiftly and harshly. Two soldiers caught stealing were punished with one hundred lashes each.[69] A third was shot.[70]

The phalanx of arsonists pressed on along the 160-foot width of Pennsylvania Avenue. Between 14th and 15th Streets they passed by the Washington Hotel on their right, better known as Macleod's Hotel after the owner, John Macleod, who six weeks earlier had opened new rooms where patrons could take a bath for fifty cents.[71]

Diagonally opposite, on the corner of Pennsylvania Avenue and 15th Street, was the long, low brick building which Mrs. Barbara Suter had rented for the past two months for her boardinghouse.[72] It occupied a prime location, being one of the closest lodgings to the President's House and major government departments. The widow Suter had passed a fitful week. Her permanent boarders, Postmaster General Return J. Meigs and two navy pursers, were out of town. People were fleeing the city and, understandably, no visitors had checked in. Her son, Alexander, was on active duty in a volunteer company. That afternoon he had passed through Washington with the defeated American units, and she had managed to see him briefly. "It was a whole week of great trouble, hardly sleeping at night, and all the day time spent in fright," she reminisced later.[73]

About an hour from midnight, Mrs. Suter was alone with a single female servant when the foreign troops took up positions around her house. A British officer who entered and introduced himself as General Ross said he had "come, madam, to sup with you."[74] More scared than ever, Mrs. Suter said she had nothing to eat and tried to steer him to Macleod's Hotel across the road. But Ross would have none of it and began teasing her. He told her he preferred her house because of the view it had of the public buildings. Playfully, the general said she was not a stranger to him. He even hinted to the flabbergasted woman how his spies had been at her boardinghouse. As soon as Ross asked after an elderly lodger who had objected to her feeding an apparent British army deserter a few days earlier, she recalled the incident vividly, realizing now that she had been duped. She remembered lunching with her family and boarders when a shabbily dressed Briton, claiming to be a deserter, had knocked at her door and begged for something to eat. Nobody was alarmed by the man's presence because desertion from the enemy's ranks had become common. Only Postmaster General Meigs had sounded a warning, arguing that she should not feed the man because there were too many vagrants about and surely some of them must be frauds or even spies. But Mrs. Suter had taken pity on the wretch and given him food, which he ate under the shade of a nearby tree.

Nervous and agitated, Mrs. Suter had no choice but to take orders from the British commander. He said he would be back for supper later that night with a number of fellow officers. When he left he had to walk only several hundred yards to reach the President's House. The minute Ross was gone, Mrs. Suter and her female servant killed some chickens in the backyard, then cooked them while they warmed up bread for the expected return of the unwanted guests.

When the advance units entered the chief executive's mansion, they found it deserted and quiet. All the staff had fled, leaving the dinner table handsomely laid for forty people and the rooms temptingly open to thieves and vandals. The Britons were famished, thirsty, and tired. Their long day had begun with the forced march to Bladensburg many hours before the midday battle, after which they had slogged another half dozen miles into Washington. But the sight of such abundant food and wine exhilarated them and they feasted inelegantly, gorging themselves at the banquet table as if it held the most prized spoils of war. "Never was nectar more grateful to the palates of the gods than the crystal goblet of Madeira and water I quaffed off at Mr. Madison's expense," Lieutenant Scott remembered.[75] The advance party, including Cockburn and Ross and companies from the 21st and 85th Foot Regiments, poured wine from cut-glass decanters to drink to the health of their Prince Regent and the success of His Majesty's land and naval forces.[76] Someone poured wine into a silver cup and toasted "peace with America and down with Madison."[77]

Cockburn was in a freewheeling mood as he jested and mocked the Madisons in the coarse lingo of a common sailor. The admiral had hauled in an innocent American bystander along the way and now tweaked his honor with mischievous relish, telling young Roger Chew Weightman, a bookseller married just three months, to sit down and drink to "Jemmy" Madison's health.[78] Then he looked around the palatial setting and told his unwilling guest to take a souvenir. Weightman, who had been Mrs. Suter's commercial neighbor in the building now occupied by the Bank of the Metropolis, wanted to save something of value.[79] "No! No!" Cockburn reprimanded. "*That* I must give to the flames. But here," he said, grabbing some ornaments off the mantelpiece, "these will answer as a memento." Cockburn scanned the room again, murmuring, "I must take something too."[80] He picked up a cushion and an old hat, a *chapeau bras* that must have been the president's. These, he bragged to Weightman, would be his personal trophies.

Cockburn's underlings scurried through the rooms, looting and snatching souvenirs. Scott looked in at the president's dressing room. There was evidence of frantic packing and sudden abandonment, but the mess could just as well have been the work of thieves seen earlier in the day by the young slave, Paul Jennings. Drawers were open and portmanteaux half filled. Scott tore off his filthy upper clothing and slipped into a stolen shirt. The clean clothing felt as good as the wine. Both were unaccustomed luxuries.[81] One of the raiders reportedly found a ceremonial hat belonging to the president. Raising it up by the tip of his bayonet, he boasted that if they could not capture "the little president," they would parade his hat in England.[82] Other vandals removed Mrs. Madison's portrait from her sitting room,[83] saying they would "keep Dolley safe and exhibit her in London."[84] Another looter seized a small wooden medicine chest with compartments for upright vials, slip-out drawers, and a latched door. The lightweight container, a bare eight and three-quarter inches high and only six and a quarter inches wide and five and a quarter inches long, could easily be cradled in an arm and carried away.[85] Lt. Beauchamp Colclough Urquhart, heir to one of the finest Elizabethan mansions on a vast Scottish estate through an aristocratic lineage traceable to the twelfth century, spied an enviable trophy of lasting value. The twenty-three-year-old officer with the 85th Foot Regiment promptly carried off President Madison's fine dress sword. It would make a handsome addition to treasures accumulated over the centuries by his noble forebears.[86]

French minister Serurier had watched quizzically as Capitol Hill burned. The flames were so brilliant that he could not tell if it was a general blaze or confined to one of the large public buildings. He had never seen a sight that was at once so terrible and yet so magnificent. But now that he could see the torchbearers headed in his direction, he grew more anxious. His temporary diplomatic quarters were in a darkened neighborhood. He occupied the Octagon, the capital's oldest private mansion, built by wealthy Virginian Capt. John Tayloe as a winter residence a few hundred yards west of Madison's official home. While Tayloe was in Virginia trying in vain to round up more militiamen to defend the capital, his wife, Ann, fled the city for Virginia after arranging with Serurier to move into the Octagon. Having the French occupy the home would give it greater protection from the invaders.[87] The French, in turn, had already offered a number of Washingtonians the chance to hand over personal possessions for safekeeping in the diplomatic "asylum."[88]

As the British closed in, Serurier had nothing to rely on except reports and rumors spread by fearful blacks. But he refused to remain a passive onlooker. He hastily dispatched a messenger to Ross with a written plea for armed protection against accidental firing of the French mission.

The courier found the British general still in the presidential residence. He was ordering furniture gathered in the resplendent oval drawing room to start a fire. Ross read the letter and offered assurances. He said he had ordered the diplomatic quarters to be respected as much as if the French monarch himself resided there. He also promised that if he was still in Washington the following day he would call on the French ambassador.[89]

There was no shortage of kindling wood in the President's House. Thomas Jefferson had turned over to the Madisons twenty-three rooms exquisitely furnished with crimson sofas, writing tables, window stools, card tables, commodes, and ornamented beds.[90] Dolley Madison and Latrobe had transformed the oval drawing room from a barren vestibule into a graceful venue for fashionably dressed Washingtonians, and sometimes even for those "in beards and boots,"[91] to make merry with chitchat and amorous intrigue, or merely to feel good in the confirmation of their social standing. But the oval room's three dozen gilded chairs with red velvet cushions, all hand-carved in Baltimore with the country's coat of arms, were about to become a British bonfire.[92]

Midshipman Samuel Davies, son of a country parson, raced through the mansion with four sailors, up the grand U-shaped staircase to a hall, then into the second story's more numerous but smaller rooms.[93] Randomly, they set fire to beds, curtains, and other fixtures and fittings.[94] "Our sailors were artists at the work," Captain Smith recalled.[95] The President's House was quick to catch fire. Flames licked indiscriminately at the choice contents, some of which may have been in George Washington's possession when Philadelphia was still the capital.

Many of the doomed artifacts had been selected and bought by the Madisons' agents, Latrobe and his wife, Mary, a friend of Dolley's since childhood. They had picked the dinner and dessert china, a silver service, lamps, kitchen furniture, a washing machine, copperware, and even a wig, hat, and turban.[96] All were consumed in the fires raging through the abandoned mansion. The heat made short shrift of glass mirrors set in a frame specially designed by Latrobe for the oval drawing room. Most vulnerable were the sunflower yellow damask curtains with valances of swags and draperies in Mrs. Madison's parlor, sandwiched between the dining room and the drawing room. Once a guest had delighted in setting eyes on the room's "elegant and delicate furniture."[97] Now the cheery yellow satin upholstery on the formal sofas and upright chairs instantly blackened and disintegrated. The smooth and polished wood became mere tinder to nourish the flames. So, too, did the guitar and pianoforte, personally chosen by Mary Latrobe, herself an accomplished guitarist.[98] The bulkiest furniture fell victim to the fire in the majestic east corner dining room, the third of the splendid trio of adjoining rooms. A sideboard, big enough to fit the length of a wall of a large contemporary parlor, disappeared in the flames.[99] Nothing would be left of the Madisons' unguarded personal possessions, nor of the furnishings, fixtures, and fittings paid for out of the public purse.[100]

An eyewitness reported how the President's House was quickly engulfed by fire and smoke. "The spectators stood in awful silence, the city was light and the heavens reddened with the blaze!"[101] It had been just twenty-two years since James Hoban, an immigrant from County Kilkenny in Ireland, had chosen a medal instead of $500 for submitting the winning design for the President's House. Three months later a procession of dignitaries led by the Freemasons in hierarchical masonic order had filed out of Georgetown's Fountain Inn, laid the foundation stone at the southwest corner, then returned to the inn for an elegant dinner and sixteen formal toasts.[102] The flames that now swept through the mansion consumed great quantities of woodwork that had arrived as heavy beams of yellow poplar and white oak from Light-Horse Harry Lee's ancestral lands in Westmoreland County, Virginia, by an agreement of sale signed with Hoban shortly before Christmas 1793.[103]

However, the great sandstone walls withstood the heat. The thick stone had been cut, set, and refined with elaborate carvings by fewer than a dozen skilled Scottish immigrants.[104] Jefferson had wanted the great walls built of brick, but both he and Hoban had deferred to the personal preference of George Washington for stone.[105] A great portion of the light gray stone blocks survived undamaged, particularly those in the basement where a great stone arch gave access from the north front to a long, rectangular room. But the blaze took its toll on the walls' weaker sections, and an expert would later recommend their removal.[106]

Not all the British rejoiced over the demolition. Charles Furlong, an officer who had just eaten so well at the president's table, felt sorrow at the fiery destruction of yet another magnificent building.[107] But he was powerless to halt the ruin. So, too, were others close by. From their hiding place in nearby woods north of the blaze, a small group of hushed American militiamen looked on. Fearful that they might be seen by the enemy in the brightening city, they lay face downwards, hugging the ground closely. Though armed, the raw recruits were no less scared, aware that capture would make them instant prisoners of war. One of them, twenty-year-old Edward Simms, a carpenter from Fredericktown, Maryland, had been enrolled so quickly that he still found it hard to adapt to his military status. Throughout the night the little band of witnesses lay motionless, and at times even breathless, as the enemy methodically sacked the grandest structures of the captured city.[108]

Countless other civilian refugees wandered within the thick woods around Washington and Georgetown. Tired and hungry, they preferred the safety of the wild to the insecurity of their homes. For more than a year the newspapers had reported on the suffering of American victims in the Chesapeake Bay. It was like a monotonous drumbeat that now built to a crescendo. The woods were alive with women and children, old men, remnants of the militia, and slaves, all drawn to the dark enclosures to hide and survive.

The raiders moved next to the brick Treasury building on the eastern flank of the President's House. George Washington had personally ordered this, as well as other government offices on the western flank, erected close to the chief executive's mansion and distant from Congress. He wanted to keep members of Congress at arm's length. Experience in Philadelphia had shown how legislators and their aides too often pestered heads of government departments. The cabinet, on the other hand, needed to be conveniently close to the president, whom they had to confer with daily.[109]

It did not take long for the Treasury to burn, or for Anna Maria Thornton to pass on graphic details of its demise. Though she had fled to Georgetown, the English-born woman later described to friends how British torchbearers, on command, had broken windows and hurled their burning poles inside.[110]

As flames spewed out, the British caught sight of a strong iron door which they thought gave access to valuables. When all efforts to pry it open failed, they broke a window and an officer climbed through and dropped down. He found himself in a chamber with a number of weighty boxes, but flames held back troops trying to reach him through a connecting passage. He managed to lift a suspected treasure chest through the broken window, but the dangerous mission was aborted when they discovered, according to Lieutenant Scott, "that the contents would by no means compensate us for our exertions and possible suffocation."[111] Most of the important documents had been removed from the Treasury in the nick of time before the occupation, but a large quantity of paperwork was burned, including the principal ledgers and journals from 1789 through 1798.[112]

Ross returned to Mrs. Suter's boardinghouse accompanied by ten other officers, including the spy who had posed as a deserter a few days earlier. The naval commander, in a show of boorish devilry, rode through the low front door on his mule and introduced himself as the much-maligned Admiral Cockburn. He blew out the candles, saying he preferred the light from the burning President's House and Treasury, which not only illuminated the room but outshone the pale moonlight. Eavesdropping on table talk during the quick meal, served without wine or liquor, Mrs. Suter got the impression that despite their playful merriment they were anxious and even worried about making good their escape. They had planned on synchronizing their presence with the arrival of the British squadron sailing up the Potomac, but the ships were nowhere in sight. They felt cheated that President Madison had escaped capture, as they had hoped to parade him in England. The president's whereabouts became the subject of many wild guesses and theories.

Another officer entered the room as they ate and asked whether they were going to burn the War Department.

"Certainly," said Cockburn.

But Ross squelched the idea. "It will be time enough in the morning as it is now growing late, and the men require rest."

The admiral, however, was not quite ready to call it a night. "There is a bank, too, near here," he said. "That ought to be burned."

Ross asked Mrs. Suter whether the Bank of the Metropolis was a public or a private bank. Though she may have known its real status, especially since it had bought and occupied the building where she used to run her boardinghouse, and notices had appeared recently in the *National Intelligencer* announcing dividends to shareholders, Mrs. Suter said she thought it was a private bank because it was in a private house. Few people may have known its status, as the bank had been open for business a mere four months.[113]

They had eaten their fill, and it was time to go. There is no record whether they paid for their meal or whether any kind of recompense was offered.

In all probability, some of the officers may then have walked across Pennsylvania Avenue and retraced their steps one block north, still intent on burning the Bank of the Metropolis. Their target, a three-story federal-style building bought four months back by the bank for $8,000, stood at the northeast corner of 15th and F Streets.[114] The bank had been closed since 2 P.M. that day when employees fled and the cashier, Alexander Kerr, scooped up the currency and other notes and deposited them in a bank at Hagerstown, Maryland.[115] Few details survive of the British presence at the bank, but a Mrs. Sarah Sweeny, described by the *National Intelligencer* as "a lady in reduced circumstances," somehow persuaded them not to torch the building.[116] The bank's board of directors met seven months later to vote Mrs. Sweeny a gift of $100 "for having been instrumental in preventing the bank being burned by the enemy."[117]

It was about midnight when Chester Bailey saw the British returning down Pennsylvania Avenue toward Capitol Hill.[118] Though done for the night, the invaders were awestruck by the conflagration and intermittent explosions from the navy yard. Colonel Brooke, commanding the 44th Regiment, thought it "one of the finest, and at the same time the most awful sights I ever witnessed."[119] Lieutenant Gleig had not witnessed anything "more striking or more sublime" since St. Sebastian's burned during the war in Spain.[120]

In the early hours of Thursday, 25 August, the sated vandals rested and fell asleep. But the citizens of Washington were wide awake. From the upper floor of her home, Mary Hunter looked across at the billowing fireballs in the navy yard and had the eerie sensation of standing within its perimeter. The blaze from the burning ships, houses, stores, and piles of dry timber was so huge that it seemed to her there was "an almost meridian brightness." She looked on stupefied. "You never saw a drawing room so brilliantly lighted as the whole city was that night," she wrote a week later. "Few thought of going to bed—they spent the night in gazing on the fires and lamenting the disgrace of the city."[121]

Ten miles into Virginia, above the Little Falls and close to the Potomac River, Dolley Madison stood by the window of a country mansion and looked out at the flaring night sky.[122] She and her party had found shelter at Rokeby, the home of her friends Richard and Matilda Lee Love. Twenty-three-year-old Matilda, daughter of longtime speaker of the Virginia Senate Ludwell Lee and niece of Light-Horse Harry Lee, was related through her stepmother to James Madison. She had been a frequent overnight guest at the President's House in Washington. Normally the blue-eyed, fair-complexioned hostess was bright and witty, but on this night she described herself as "in a peck of trouble" because her husband was away with the Virginia militia and she had to host the stream of dignitaries alone and without warning. Before Dolley's arrival a weary James Monroe had stopped by briefly, looking in vain for the president. He had eaten a quick dinner, during which Matilda had asked whether he thought she was safe in her home. "Madam," Monroe had replied, "as safe as if you were in the Allegheny Mountains."[123] But his words were hardly reassuring as Rokeby began to fill with tremulous women and their faithful servants.

The president and his entourage, who would spend most of that long night and the next full day on horseback, stopped often to look back at the burning city. Like others, they were numbed by the fires. Attorney General Rush remembered, "If at intervals the dismal sight was lost to our view, we got it again from some hill-top or eminence where we paused to look at it."[124]

According to teenager Paul Jennings, personal valet to Madison, the presidential party had gone about a mile into Virginia before the servants were abandoned. They met up again only after the chief executive and his colleagues "had been wandering about for some hours, consulting what to do."[125] No authoritative account is available on the president's precise movements that night, but Mordecai Booth arrived at Wren's Tavern in Falls Church around midnight and learned from a traveler that Madison was then less than a mile away. The anonymous traveler made threats against the president until quickly silenced by Booth.[126] Word also reached Wren's Tavern, a landmark inn recommended by Thomas Jefferson a decade earlier, that the presidential group had stayed a short time at Mrs. Minor's home, where many refugees from Washington and Alexandria were sheltering.[127] However, it may be that Madison's entourage stayed overnight at Salona, a 466-acre estate owned by Rev. William Maffitt.[128] The brick mansion, with a long T-shaped hallway linking wings at either end, lay just four miles from Washington on the road leading from the bridge over the Potomac River at Little Falls.[129]

In his spare comments on the president's movements that night, Paul Jennings recalled that after meeting up with Madison's mounted entourage, "I walked on to a Methodist minister's, and in the evening, while he was at prayer, I heard a tremendous explosion and, rushing out, saw that the public buildings, navy yard, rope walks etc. were on fire."[130] Though Jennings erred in Maffitt's Presbyterian denomination, it is plausible that the teenager would have gained admittance to the cleric's home only by accompanying the president, on whose estate he had been born into slavery, and whom he had served since early childhood.[131]

In remoter parts of Virginia and Maryland, glum and pensive citizens looked across the darkened countryside to the glow above the capital. It looked as if the Federal City was sending out a fiery distress signal. Daniel Sheldon Jr., an auditor in flight with the secretary of the treasury to Fredericktown, Maryland, stopped at 1 A.M. to look back at the capital twenty-eight miles south. Washington, he wrote to his father, was "most dismally and most distinctly visible."[132] Even further afield, in Leesburg, Virginia, people looked thirty-five miles to the east at the shimmering light over Washington.[133] It was a night of sorrow and dread. Within a few hours, rumor reached Sheldon that the British had burned down every building in Washington and Georgetown. "I do not believe it, but we cannot know with certainty for some hours," he wrote.[134]

The citizens of Baltimore also saw an ominous brightness at the end of a dark stretch forty-five miles to the southwest. At daylight, Baltimorean David Winchester wrote to his brother James in Tennessee that no one knew what had happened in Washington. "We only know from the light during the night that the city was on fire."[135]

Mordecai Booth went to bed at Wren's Tavern in the early hours of Thursday morning tired but filled with paternal relief. For hours he had worried about the safety of his own daughter and sons. He had even ridden six miles down the darkened road looking for them. When they finally turned up at the inn, he learned that Commandant Tingey had spirited them out of the capital while Booth was reconnoitering Washington. Booth felt such a debt of gratitude to his boss that he would thank him with unctuous excess, praising him as "an all wise being."[136]

At dawn, Booth rode off with the taverner's son in the direction of Mrs. Minor's, where rumor had it the president had stayed the night. But when they got there they were told the presidential entourage had stopped by only fleetingly the night before. As their present whereabouts were unknown, Booth returned to the tavern. There he met a guard of two dozen men and boys under a marine corps sergeant major who had come to take charge of the powder. Though Booth was hoping for presidential or cabinet-level instructions, he was not alarmed by the presence of 124 barrels and two quarter casks of gunpowder stored under his control at Daniel Dulany's farm. Others were more concerned. The large quantity of explosives held beyond military confines stirred a growing uneasiness among civilians and military men. To calm them down, Booth suggested that five notables, including Capt. George Graham, who had arrived with a troop of Fairfax dragoons, form themselves into a committee and authorize him to take the barrels of gunpowder further into the interior. Armed with this new authority, Booth directed the sergeant major to impress more wagons and haul the gunpowder four to six miles inland.

When he had overseen the move from Dulany's farm, Booth returned to Wren's Tavern, only to learn that he had just missed the president. Madison had stopped at the inn, then gone off in search of his wife at Salona, the home of Rev. Maffitt.

Booth rode hard to catch up with the president, but he had covered no more than a mile when he was forced to seek shelter from "the most tremendous storm I had ever witnessed."[137] While Booth ducked in at the home of Mr. McLain, the president found sanctuary at the Crossroads, five miles from the bridge at Little Falls. There he learned that his wife had already passed by on her way to Wiley's Tavern, their prearranged rendezvous on the road from Georgetown to Leesburg.

Dolley had reached the inn just before the storm broke, as gale-force winds tore apples off the trees in the surrounding orchard and flung them against the doors and windows. Her presence infuriated the female spouse of the family-owned tavern. "Miss Madison!" she shrieked on learning that Dolley was upstairs, "if that's you, come down and go out! Your husband has got mine out fighting. Damn you! You shan't stay in my house, so get out!"[138] But the First Lady's escort reportedly argued with the innkeeper and won a reprieve, as Dolley remained on through the storm and into the middle of the night.

The freak storm had barely passed when Booth met a man who told him the president was on his way to Wiley's Tavern. Shortly thereafter, the tireless navy clerk finally caught up with the elusive chief executive, accompanied by his faithful attorney general and a guard of two dragoons. They rode on together until just short of the tavern, when Booth lagged behind to give new instructions to passing wagoners. By the time the navy clerk dismounted at the tavern, Madison had been reunited with his devoted wife. Booth had come to the end of his odyssey. At last he was able to get instructions regarding the gunpowder. But he also got a welcome blessing from Navy Secretary Jones for having torched the navy yard. Booth had worried about setting it alight without written orders, but Jones set his mind at ease, saying the order to burn had been given in the presence of a third party, which was just as good as having it put in writing.

There was no respite that night for the grueling wanderings of the sixty-three-year-old president. When rumors swirled around midnight that the British were on their way to the tavern, the president's male entourage saddled up and rode further out of reach to Great Falls, where they planned to cross the Potomac River and link up with General Winder's reassembled forces at Montgomery Court House, Maryland. However, they were unable to cross and apparently passed the night in a hovel in the woods.[139] The following morning they crossed the rocky river at Conns' Ferry, just above the Great Falls and only a couple of miles opposite their destination.[140]

The president thought his wife would remain behind with the navy secretary, but her party backtracked a few miles to stay the next two nights at Mrs. Minor's, the refuge already crammed with families who had bolted Washington and Alexandria.[141] There Dolley cut such an elegant figure that her dresses bewitched seven-year-old Matilda Roberts, distracting the girl from the frightening noise of horse patrols and the chilling fear of being seized by British soldiers. Together with her brother, three sisters, and the neighbors, Matilda had been crammed into a wagon with trunks and bedding and hauled off by four horses all the way from Alexandria to Mrs. Minor's. When the First Lady came in and out of her room in the days to come, the little girl momentarily forgot about the loss of her favorite china toy tea set, spirited out of Alexandria but crushed in the comings and goings at Mrs. Minor's the night the capital burned. Yet even though the sight of Mrs. Madison was a welcome relief from the dreadful events, the child would never forget the night when she was plucked from her mattress and taken outside to see Washington burn. "At first I thought the world was on fire," she would reminisce decades later to her grandchild. "Such a flame I have never seen since."[142]

Dolley may have remained housebound because of the wild reports taking hold of a general uprising by slaves. Her friend Matilda Lee Love had left Rokeby by carriage early on Thursday morning hoping to get deeper into Virginia and further away from the British, but she and her sister had to turn around and race back home as the rumors gained strength. When the driver told them he did not think the horses would make it by nightfall, she guessed he might be in on the rebellion and made up her mind to shoot him if he reined in the horses. On their return to Rokeby they found everyone had acted on the rumors and fled to Falls Church, where there was safety in numbers. Matilda and her sister prepared for the worst at the sound of a persistent drumbeat, but it turned out to be nothing more than an old man making a noise to scare away rats at the nearby mill. He was made to keep a sharp lookout at Rokeby's gate all through the uncertain night.[143]

The following day Brig. Gen. Robert Young had to halt his brigade of militia near Carper's mills, opposite the Great Falls, when word reached him of the possible insurrection. Like Madison, he hoped to cross the Potomac River at Conns' Ferry, but the number and "respectability" of citizens flocking to him for protection compelled him to stay put while his infantry and cavalry scouts fanned out. Young's brigade lost valuable time, but he could not scotch the rumors until his men returned with negative reports of a rebellion.[144] The presidential party may well have lingered on the Virginia side of the river that day until confident the slaves were still quiescent, for they arrived at nearby Montgomery Court House as late as 6 P.M. that Friday.[145]

10. A Lightning Occupation

*A*round breakfast the morning after the Capitol burned, Ross shook the hand of Margaret Ewell, telling her how much he regretted her fear and explaining the necessity of burning the buildings in retaliation for the destruction of the British capital in Canada. She could only force a weak smile. Cockburn, sensing her fright, said, "Ay, madam, I can easily account for your terror. I see from the files in your house that you are fond of reading those papers which delight to make devils of us."[1] Despite his sneering manner, he was to make several visits during the day to try and console her.

With the earlier targets still burning and smoking, the refreshed enemy regrouped to attack what still stood of the city's public buildings. About nine hundred marched in three detachments to the offices of the State and War Departments, separated by a passageway in a building on the western plot next to the gutted blackness of the presidential mansion. Bringing up the rear were some thirty black men carrying powder and rockets to fuel the flames. Cockburn rode conspicuously upon a gray mare followed closely by her foal.[2]

Word of the British movement spread quickly to Georgetown, from where the mayor and a delegation of citizens had set out early under a flag of truce to speak to the English admiral. They said they would offer no resistance and hoped the British would spare the prosperous port city. Cockburn gave them the assurances they were hoping for, adding snidely that he would give them the protection which their own president had failed to provide. At 8 A.M. Father Grassi of Georgetown College passed the returning delegates and learned that Georgetowners would be safe as long as they remained in their homes.[3]

The superintendent of patents, Dr. Thornton, was breakfasting in Georgetown when he heard that the British were about to burn down his office building, together with models of original inventions and his own unfinished musical instrument.[4] He hurried off to try and talk them out of it. But even in his haste Thornton weighed the wartime risks of being seen huddling with the enemy. He decided to take along a witness to parry inevitable accusations of treachery. Fortunately for Thornton, one of the capital's most highly respected citizens, Charles Carroll, agreed to accompany him.

They arrived at the State and War Department offices just as troops were preparing to set it alight. The officer in charge, Colonel Jones, told him he was free to take away the musical instrument from the Patent Office since it was private property. Then Thornton and Carroll watched helplessly as the State and War offices blazed furiously. The building housed not only the offices of James Monroe and John Armstrong but also the president's own brother-in-law, Richard Cutts, superintendent general of military supplies. Ironically, Cutts had been so impressed with the quick turnout of five thousand militiamen during an invasion scare the year before that he had boasted the British would "pay dear for their audacity" if they dared enter Washington.[5]

Harried clerks had managed to remove nearly all the paperwork before fleeing, but furniture remained and now fueled the surging flames. Also lost in the inferno were recommendations for appointments in the army and incoming correspondence received before Madison's presidential inauguration. The most prized trophies—all the standards and colors snatched from the British during the Revolutionary War and the current conflict—had been spirited away.[6] Some of the old papers and army accounts from the War Department's accountant's office had been stashed in a fireproof room and survived the flames, only to be damaged and carried off by unknown scavengers soon after destruction of the building.[7] The adjutant and inspector general's office lost all files of muster rolls and recruiting returns up to and including the year 1813.[8] Also burned were valuable books in the ordnance office and many volumes in the State Department's library.[9]

As the arson took its toll, Carroll agreed to walk with Thornton to the Patent Office, but when they passed by the latter's house the dignitary begged off, saying he had to return. Alone, Thornton tried enlisting the mayor, but he was not at home. Eventually he recruited his model maker and messenger, Thomas Nicholson, and they raced to the Patent Office just as two columns of British troops marched on the same landmark.[10]

At the three-story building, ornamented with a pediment and six Ionic pilasters, they found Major Waters awaiting orders from Colonel Jones.[11] Four American bystanders moved closer to overhear the face-off with Thornton. A month later they would publicly come to Thornton's defense, denying insinuations that he had groveled and cringed before the major.[12] Thornton reasoned that everything of value in this museum of arts was privately owned and that it would be impossible to bring out the hundreds of models. Burning them, he argued, would be as barbarous as the Turks setting fire to the library at Alexandria in Egypt, for which they had been condemned by the civilized world. To save the building, which stood at the peak of a high swell of land amid wooded hills, Thornton pleaded with the major to remove anything considered public and burn it in the street.

The argument bought a reprieve. Waters wanted covering orders from his superior and told Thornton to follow him. They found Colonel Jones and others watching the invaders ransack the offices of the *National Intelligencer*, midway between the Capitol and the President's House. Cockburn was at last evening the score with the English-born publisher Joseph Gales, whose broadsheet had demonized him for so long before the American people. Of all the destructive acts perpetrated by the British in the American capital, this alone was based on a personal vendetta. The unforgiving Cockburn was determined to discipline Gales and hoped to silence the government mouthpiece by wrecking its plant and equipment.

Two women stepped forward and pleaded with Cockburn not to burn down the building for fear the flames would spread to their adjoining homes. Courteously, the admiral told them not to be alarmed. They would be just as safe with him as with President Madison.[13] Mary Hunter was one of the women who heard Cockburn say he admired American ladies because they made excellent wives and good mothers. But, he declared, they were prejudiced against him because Jo Gales had told so many lies about him. He asked Mary Hunter and the other women if they had been injured, or whether any soldiers had broken into their homes and stolen anything. He wanted them to report such violations immediately so that the offenders could be punished. The admiral's soothing words had an instantaneous effect. "I began to think ourselves happy," Mrs. Hunter later told her sister.[14]

Though Cockburn held back the torches, he now gave orders to tear down the building. At that point another bystander intervened, telling the admiral the building did not belong to Gales but to worthy Judge Cranch, who had been consistently opposed to war with Britain. Impressed, Cockburn once more scrapped his own orders and let the men continue to smash the windows, wreck the furniture, and strike at the paper's guts by stripping it of its presses and type.[15] He considered the type belonged as much to Madison as it did to "Josy" Gales. Contemptuously, he described Madison as the master workman and "Josy" as his printer. One bystander heard the admiral regret how he had not got hold of Gales instead of the type. He would then have cured the publisher of his two bad habits of "lying and dealing in vulgarity."[16] Cockburn told the bystanders he had paid back Gales by scattering the type.

The British threw out reams of paper, books, records, gazettes, files, and most especially the offending presses and type. One naval officer snatched an incomplete newssheet from the press as proof of the speed with which the printing staff had fled the day before.[17] The outdoor bonfire fed on the physical plant, early correspondence, and all the publisher's back issues of this, the country's first national newspaper.[18] A number of onlookers stepped in to try to save some of the material and probably accounted for the survival of the books of accounts and subscription lists.[19] An Englishwoman related to co-owner William Seaton picked up some of the type, though the publishers had to buy printing equipment to resume publication a week after the British departure.[20]

The spectacle of so much ruin provoked an American bystander to taunt the British admiral. "If General Washington had been alive you would not have gotten into this city so easily."

"No, Sir," Cockburn responded. "If General Washington had been president we should never have thought of coming here."[21]

Other British officers ridiculed the American secretary of war, telling spectators he must be a fool to have pitted raw militia against them, some of whom claimed to have fought in more than three dozen battles under the great Duke of Wellington. They had not expected the American militia to be any better than their own militiamen, whom they derided as "good for nothing."[22] The officers warned that if Americans did not remove Madison the war would be fought far more severely. They claimed to have more than 100,000 men on the coast who would burn all the towns. Only the name of Washington had preserved the capital from being totally destroyed. Other towns would suffer a worse fate.[23]

Colonel Jones, meanwhile, had mulled over Thornton's desperate plea and decided to spare the Patent Office and its priceless models. British troops were withdrawn, and Thornton returned to Georgetown. But unknown to him, one of his clerks, George Lyon, had locked the door to prevent theft by local residents. He had then given the key to a British officer so that if the soldiers changed their minds and returned, they would not have to break down the door, leaving it open to general plunder. Thornton approved of the arrangement when he learned of it later.[24]

Closer to the Capitol, thirteen-year-old Mary Ingle was sitting on the doorstep of her home on New Jersey Avenue, across from the old-fashioned neighborhood water pump, when a British officer rode up. He took out a silver goblet and spoke to his underling. "Here, orderly, bring me a drink of water in this goblet of old Jimmy Madison." Mary interjected, "No, Sir, that isn't President Madison's goblet because my father and a whole lot of gentlemen have got all his silver and papers and things and gone." Drowsy with drink, the officer ignored the remarks, but an arm extended out of the doorway and a hand clamped over the girl's mouth as she was yanked inside.[25]

Local residents were at that moment running gleefully wild in an orgy of theft at the unprotected navy yard. The mob burst into the grounds on the heels of a fleeting new raid by the British at 8 A.M. Within a quarter of an hour the enemy, led by the same Captain Wainwright who had treated the wounded Joshua Barney like a brother, had come and gone, setting fire to much that had escaped the flames the night before.[26] Their early-morning foray sent huge new flames leaping above the detail-issuing store. Nothing was left of its enormous inventory of canvas, twine, lines, bunting, and colors, nor of its stocks of mathematical instruments and navigational equipment. Ruin and fires were everywhere, among the ship chandlery, tools, nails, oils, and paint. Columns of dirty smoke rose above the coopers' shop, two small-frame timber sheds, and stores of tar, pitch, rosin, and other highly flammable supplies.

Commandant Tingey set sail in his gig from Alexandria at 7:30 A.M. As he crossed the Potomac he could clearly see the new fires, but the enemy had been gone half an hour by the time he landed at 8:45 A.M. He and his crew found the schooner *Lynx* unscathed but lying alongside the burning wharf. They hauled it out of harm's way next to the hulk of the *New York*, another intact vessel.

With relief, Tingey found his own home still standing, but only, he learned, because Cockburn had declared private property sacred. Local mobs, however, had already broken in and run off with some of the contents. A few people who lived outside the navy yard offered to hide his most valuable possessions in their own homes. Tingey took them up on their offers, rounding up some acquaintances to carry off the keepsakes. The commandant reckoned he needed only one more hour to save his furniture and everything else of note, but friends urged him to escape while he could. Cockburn had made no secret of wanting to capture him, and if the admiral did not already know of Tingey's return, it would not be long before he learned of it.

He fled in his gig while some of his men slipped off in a new launch lying close to a burning stage. Tingey's departure set off a new flurry of looting by people living close to the navy yard. He was the last figure of authority blocking their way. They set to with crazed abandon, swarming into homes, scurrying from cellars to attics, and snatching anything that could be carried away, even ripping fixtures off the walls and tearing locks out of the doors.

Tingey sailed up and down the Potomac until evening, resisting impulses to return to Washington yet keeping a watchful eye on enemy movements from a respectful range. At nightfall he steered for the relative calm of Alexandria.[27]

A lone British soldier armed with a musket was meanwhile robbing residents not far from the charred skeleton of the President's House. His first victim was John Macleod, proprietor of the Washington Hotel on Pennsylvania Avenue. After threatening to set fire to the building, the robber, assisted by a black man, moved on to the home of another victim as a neighbor sped to British headquarters on Capitol Hill to sound the alarm. William Gardner, who had spoken to Cockburn and Ross the night before, had raced to his Pennsylvania Avenue home from Georgetown, fearing that thieves might also be there. When he discovered that all was well, he took off his coat and waistcoat to cool off and was by his window overlooking the avenue when a British officer in his mid-twenties reined in his horse and asked directions to Macleod's Hotel. When Gardner pointed it out, the officer demurred.

"Sir," he said, "I have come on in haste from headquarters for the purpose of taking one of our soldiers who is robbing your citizens. But the distance is much farther than I was aware of. It must be upwards of a mile from our army and the probability is I shall be made prisoner by some of your troops."

Gardner said he had just come from that direction and knew for a fact that the soldier was not only robbing citizens but maltreating residents. "I pledge to you my honor there is not an American soldier or officer in that quarter of the city."

Another British officer racing down the avenue on horseback halted outside Gardner's house and exchanged words with his countryman. Then the first one on the scene said to Gardner, "I have every confidence in your honor. If you will immediately come with us we will proceed to the spot and take the villain. Do not stay to put on your coat or waistcoat. There is not a moment to be lost."

Gardner ran after them and they arrived at the home of a third victim as he was being robbed.

"You villain!" said the officer. "You have turned thief and are disgracing your country!"

The soldier denied taking anything, but Macleod said this was not true and offered to testify against him. The Russian consul, who was also at the scene, pointed to Macleod and told the British officer, "That gentleman is a man of respectability. Whatever he tells you is entitled to your confidence."

It was enough to infuriate the young officer. He clenched his fist and punched the thief so hard that the soldier staggered and his hat fell off. Gardner picked it up and found it stuffed with silk shawls and other valuable items. When the officer saw this he whacked the robber with the butt end of his pistol and threatened to shoot him on the spot unless he set off immediately for headquarters.

Before leaving, the officer offered Gardner his apology. "I am sorry our two nations are at war. I hope the time is not far distant when peace will be restored. We have not come here for the purpose of plunder, but to destroy all public property. If anything of the kind should take place again, such as you have just witnessed, I have to request that your citizens will assemble, seize the villains without delay, and conduct them to head-quarters. Depend upon it, Sir, they will be punished."

The soldier was set on his stolen horse and escorted up to Capitol Hill by the officers riding on each side of him. On the way he tried to escape several times, but his luck had run out. After being paraded at headquarters, he was summarily shot.[28]

Outside Dr. Ewell's home, a British officer pointed to the neighboring house of Elias Caldwell and bragged, "We shall be done with burning when the rope walks are burnt and that handsome building yonder."

"Why, certainly you are not going to burn that house, Captain?" Ewell asked.

"Yes, Sir, we shall."

"It is not public property," the physician insisted.

"No matter for that. There is public property at the house," said the captain, referring to cartridges and ammunition boxes found inside. "Besides, it belongs to a man who has been very active against us."

"It is true," Ewell replied. "Mr. Caldwell is captain of a volunteer company and a brave man. But brave men do not bear malice against each other for doing their duty. On the contrary, respect them the more for it, as General Ross yesterday did Commodore Barney. And, therefore, I hope that as this house is private property it will not be destroyed."

The captain paused for a moment before going off to consult with Ross. Ewell was not told of the outcome, but he guessed that the general spared the house, because it was not burned.[29]

Of all the fires set, the ones at the ropewalks owned by Tench Ringgold, John Chalmers, and Heath & Company caused the most stench and foul air from burning stockpiles of cordage, hemp, and tar. Once again Cockburn's aide-de-camp, Lieutenant Scott, oversaw the systematic wreckage. His detail broke open dozens of tar barrels, pouring their thick black ooze over cord and hemp spread down the center of the roofed walk. When they set it alight the flames licked at the long trail of fuel, moving rapidly down each of the long buildings.[30] Dense black smoke billowed above Washington. It was one of the few deliberate assaults on private assets during the twenty-four-hour occupation. The British justified it by charging the ropewalks were of use to the American navy.[31]

Meanwhile, an enemy detachment of about seventy-five men was laying waste the enormous quantities of munitions and defenses at the arsenal on Greenleaf's Point. This broad, flat finger of land jutted out at the confluence of the Potomac River and its Eastern Branch, less than two miles southwest of the Capitol. They put cannons out of action by aiming one of them at the muzzles of all the others and blowing out the breeches. Unmounted cannons were spiked and thrown into the water, together with quantities of shot, shells, and hand grenades.[32]

All went as planned until they came upon about 130 barrels of gunpowder, which they tossed one by one into a well. From whatever cause, most likely a spark from one barrel scraping against another, a thunderous explosion boomed across the city, jolting the land like an earth tremor. The blast left a crater some forty feet in diameter and almost twenty feet deep.[33] About thirty troops died instantly, some blown apart and others entombed below mounds of earth. One of those buried under the rubble, a captain in the Royal Engineers, was found a month later with pencil sketches in his belt pouch of each day's march from Benedict.[34] Another forty-seven suffered multiple wounds and mutilation. Mangled survivors screamed and groaned in the chaotic aftermath. A stunned officer heard the wail of the dying and saw others almost buried alive, their broken arms and legs askew and severed limbs lying haphazardly in and around the crater. The gruesome carnage was "a thousand times more distressing than the loss we met with in the field [at Bladensburg] the day before," the British officer wrote home.[35] Burning buildings were flattened and roofs torn off others. Huge clods of soil were flung high into the air, hurtling together with stones, bricks, shot, shells, and other debris which the soldiers had to dodge when they plummeted to earth. Days later, one of the corpses still lay exposed atop the rubble. "He was the most horrible sight I ever beheld," wrote the visiting editor of the *Winchester* (Va.) *Gazette*. He reported that the likely cause of the explosion was a lighted match thrown by a Briton into a dry well near the magazine, which had been filled earlier with powder by the departing Americans.[36]

The explosion heightened fear and terror in the occupied city. Young Mary Ingle froze momentarily, wondering whether the two armies were shooting at each other again.[37] In Georgetown, the few remaining residents expected an imminent British advance. Prudent householders and storeowners had already removed most of their furniture and stock to the countryside. John McElroy and clerics on the staff of Georgetown College hid the sacred vessels and other treasured articles of plate.[38] Many families took their own plate and other valuables to the college for safekeeping.[39]

Following the blast, Dr. Ewell set fractured limbs and dressed wounds in brick buildings adjoining his home. Later he would have to fend off charges of treason by some locals, but he had assured Ross he would treat all the injured, no matter which side they were on.[40] The general looked close to tears as he stood near the dismembered and disabled. In the days to come Ewell was helped by one of his friends, Georgetown physician William Baker.[41]

A storm packing the force of a tornado or hurricane struck the city early in the afternoon. The rains were seasonal and, as usual, battered the city without much warning. But the ferocity of the winds humbled the British and scared seasoned locals. It came upon Washington with an advance of thunder and lightning, swirling winds, and a darkening sky. The gusts hummed and whirred as they picked up velocity until they set off a frightening roar. Electrical storms were common to the area, but it was rare for the sun to be eclipsed so early. Bolts of lightning illuminated scenes of chaos. Tumultuous winds ripped off roofs and carried away feather beds. The violent weather toppled three chimneys off the common roof of the Patent Office and General Post Office.[42] A whirling, unseen force, it buckled the chains of the drawbridge across the Potomac so that the draw could not be raised on this river link between Washington and Alexandria.[43] Trees were uprooted and fences downed. A few houses collapsed upon the unsuspecting enemy. Some of the older homes were lifted off their foundations and dashed to pieces. Soaked British combat troops caught in the open lay flat on the ground, fearful of making a run for it. Others broke ranks and scattered for cover. One officer on horseback rounded a corner and caught the blast head-on. In an instant both he and his horse were blown to the ground. The winds scooped up several light cannons and bore them off like paperweights, dumping them at random in the turmoil.[44] Only the burning buildings benefited from the two-hour-long deluge. Soggy wood and wet brickwork checked the flames. The rains contained many of the fires and doused the weaker ones. An eyewitness, Michael Shiner, rated it "one of the awfullest storms which raged for a long time."[45]

The storm churned the deep waters of the Potomac. A few boatloads of refugees who had fled several miles upriver were forced to pull onto a bank, where they lashed their craft together and tethered them to trees. Lightning crackled repeatedly as trees bent low over the flimsy boats with their huddled human cargo. "The government papers and other valuables were covered with tarpaulins," the young Miss Brown later reported back to her family in New England. "Into the corners under these we crept, but failed to find entire protection from the deluges of rain."[46]

British sailors manning their idle fleet on the Patuxent River off Benedict soon felt the brunt of the savage winds. The normally placid river now roiled in the tempest, whipping up waves that drenched the rigging and decks. Two ships were tossed free of their moorings and driven ashore. The darkened sky rumbled and cracked as rain fell in loud torrents.[47]

Cockburn and Ross were sitting out the storm with Ewell in the doctor's dining room when a delegation of four Alexandrians arrived carrying a white flag. From close quarters across the Potomac they had seen the capital burn. Even more terrifying for them was the certain knowledge that British warships were sailing upriver toward their city. They feared both for the security of the citizens and for their warehouses swollen with valuable produce. Alexandrians had chosen a pair of physicians and two other respected notables to surrender the sixty-five-year-old city and find out what tribute they would have to pay in return for their lives.

The British admiral was brief and to the point. "Gentlemen," he declared, "I have nothing to say until you first tell me whether Captain Gordon is in sight of Alexandria or not."[48]

They replied that there were no ships of war at or in sight of Alexandria, and from information they had received that morning there were none within fifteen miles of Mount Vernon. The Alexandrians said many residents had fled, and most of those who remained were women and children and the elderly. They had made no preparations for defense, nor did they have the means for "hostile defenses."[49]

Cockburn was quick to set their minds at rest. If the inhabitants did not resist, and if they let his forces take quick possession of the city, then no one would be harmed. Private property would be respected, with the exception of provisions for the troops, for which a fair price would be paid. But, warned the admiral, all his assurances would be nullified if they made "secret or wicked" attempts on the lives of Britons. Alexandrians would then have to beg for clemency.[50]

As soon as the group departed, a British naval officer entered the room. He told Cockburn that if he carried out his orders to burn the Bank of Washington, the flames would engulf private property.

"Well, then, pull it down," Cockburn commanded.

Even though Ewell was in self-confessed awe of "this son of Neptune," he interjected. "Adm. Cockburn, you do not wish to injure private property?"

"No, I do not. But this is public property."

"No Sir," Ewell countered. "The United States have no bank here now. This is altogether private property."

"Are you certain of that?" Cockburn asked.

"Yes, Sir. I pledge my honor it is private property."

"Well then," said Cockburn, addressing the officer, "let it alone."[51]

A few miles southwest of Ewell's home, British troops holding the Washington side of the long bridge spanning the Potomac River opened fire on Americans guarding the Virginia end. Storm damage had crippled the chains connected to the drawbridge, and Americans no longer had the option of raising the draw to block any British attempt to cross over.[52] While the American end of the bridge was burning, the British torched their side to prevent a surprise attack from the south. At that moment a blind woman, apparently convinced that the entire city was about to be burned, ran onto the bridge with her children in a frantic attempt to flee. She ignored shouted warnings of American troops to halt, instead running even faster toward them. Three American soldiers risked their own lives in springing forward to scoop up the family to safety. It was a display of courage watched with admiration by Britons at the other end of the bridge.[53]

After the storm had spent itself, Mrs. Bender was in Mrs. Varnum's parlor when they heard horsemen approach. Someone outside shouted, "Let's have a pop at him." A gunshot followed, then the sounds of a man darting through their house and rattling down the kitchen stairs. Mrs. Bender swallowed more camphor, then offered the bottle to her companion. They looked out the open back window and saw the cellar door inching upwards. A head popped out, and they recognized the sandy-colored head of Moriarty, an old Irishman who ran a liquor store in the neighboring building.

"Lord, is it you, Moriarty!" said an exasperated Mrs. Varnum. "You have frightened us terribly!"

"Indeed," he replied, "and it's myself that was frightened, for I thought the British were at my heels, ma'am." He said he had been pumping water at the corner when he, too, heard someone shout out, "Let's have a pop at him." Thinking he was the target, he dropped his pitcher and ran into their house.

The British were actually aiming at a rider named John Lewis, a great nephew of George Washington. Recently escaped from impressment aboard a British ship, Lewis had vowed vengeance against his captors and had apparently cursed some of the sentries and exchanged shots with them. Mortally wounded, he galloped past the President's House but slipped off his horse and fell dead in F Street. No one picked up his body until the following morning.[54]

Enemy units began regrouping on Capitol Hill after the storm and before nightfall. They rode and marched from distant points of the smoking city. Their heavy tramp attracted the attention of one woman as they paused by a water pump to drink. As she stepped out of her house, Cockburn exclaimed, "Great God, Madam! Is this the kind of storm to which you are accustomed in this infernal country?"

"No, Sir," she answered, "this is a special interposition of Providence to drive our enemies from our city."

"Not so, Madam," he countered. "It is rather to aid your enemies in the destruction of your city."[55]

The admiral rode up to Capitol Hill and was not seen in Washington again.

Ross was formal and polite to the end. As he was about to mount his horse, he apologized once more to Ewell for the theft of some of his personal possessions. He promised recompense for this loss and for the treatment Ewell had promised to give to the severely wounded who would have to be left behind.[56]

It was already dark when Ross told the deputy adjutant general, Captain Smith, that he had given orders for the army to march.

"Tonight?" Smith asked incredulously. "I hope not, Sir." Quickly, he suggested why it would be better to sleep over in Washington and withdraw the following morning. "The road, you well know, for four miles to Bladensburg is excellent, and wide enough to march with a front of subdivisions. After that we have to move through woods by a track, not a road. Let us move so as to reach Bladensburg by daylight. Our men will have a night's rest and be refreshed after the battle. I have also to load all the wounded and to issue flour."

But Ross would not budge. His object accomplished, he wanted to move out before the Americans could regroup.[57] "I have made the arrangement with [deputy quartermaster-general George de Lacy] Evans and we must march." Remembering wiser leadership in Spain, Smith muttered quietly to himself, "Oh, for dear John Colborne! [a distinguished contemporary British field commander]."[58]

The occupying army left with residents confined indoors under an 8 P.M. curfew. But the retreating forces were not taking any chances. Alert to the possibility of surprise attack by night, they moved out with extreme caution and deception. They kept the campfires burning, with enough stockpiles of wood for the last man to throw on heaps before leaving. A few soldiers paced up and down near the fires, giving an impression that the army was encamped for the night. No one rode out for fear the horses might neigh or canter off and betray their whereabouts. Instead, about forty out-of-condition horses were corralled to pull the cannons and about a dozen carts and wagons, an oxcart, a coachee, and several gigs, all of which would carry the lightly wounded from Bladensburg to the ships. About sixty head of stolen cattle led the general exodus. The troops were under orders to keep strict silence and not walk haphazardly. They left the capital as they had fought at Bladensburg, with textbook precision and enviable discipline. Their departure was so quiet and ghostly that Michael

Shiner guessed they had muffled their horses' hooves and the wheels of stolen wagons. The last detachments to leave Capitol Hill shortly came upon camp bonfires deserted earlier by other units, who had retreated in the same stealthy manner. While they disappeared into the darkness they left behind a line of fires, stoked to keep the deception alive for hours afterwards.[59]

The ruse worked so well that in the early-morning hours their whereabouts were at first a mystery to many. Some thought they might have boarded ships in the Potomac until they realized none had been close enough to take them aboard. Even after skeptics made inquiries at Bladensburg, they were told that only about six hundred British troops had passed through that night. Three days after they departed the capital, a Baltimorean reported to his brother, a brigadier general living in Tennessee, that the military chief in Baltimore "does not now know what course they [the British] have taken."[60]

Meanwhile, the public buildings in Washington continued to burn and glow in the dark. Far to the east, aboard Cockburn's flagship HMS *Albion* on the Patuxent, a duty officer recorded his impression in the log book at 9 P.M.: "Observed a great fire in the direction of Washington."[61]

Along the way some units broke ranks to steal from the farms and cottages, just as some had done after the battle of Bladensburg en route to Washington. This time they destroyed furniture and rustled cattle.[62] But the vast columns pressed ahead with a steady tread until they came upon the sepulchral field lit by a pale moon. The dead, stripped of their clothing, lay bloated and bleached by the afternoon rain and the heat of the day. About one hundred bodies had already been buried by slaves belonging to neighboring plantation owner George Calvert, a pillar of Maryland society and close friend of the last British minister to Washington.[63] But dozens more British and American corpses lay stiff with rigor mortis where they had fallen. An odor of decomposition hung over the stilled tableau, mixing with the sharp smell of burned powder and scorched grass. Saddened by the melancholy scene, the survivors felt a mix of grief and a fleeting sense of their own good fortune. As they went downhill to cross the bridge into Bladensburg, the troops randomly picked up knapsacks filled with clothing, thrown away in the heat of battle to lighten their load.

While they regrouped at Bladensburg they were approached by a number of Americans holding a flag of truce, who impressed Captain Smith with their "gentlemanlike deportment."[64] Smith, in charge of secret intelligence, suspected they had come to size up the British army, though they said they were there to ask how private property had been respected. The British officer deliberately asked them numerous questions about Annapolis and Baltimore to let them think they were headed that way. If the bait was taken, Americans would divert forces to those cities, leaving the retreating British unchecked passage back to their fleet. The ploy worked, for that night word reached Smith that American troops were converging on Annapolis.

Meanwhile, surgeons selected all those with broken arms or other wounds which would not prevent them from walking, if need be. For now, they were hoisted onto one of the forty horses or seated in carts and wagons for the ride east to the Patuxent River. Dr. Catlett, the American staff surgeon allowed into Bladensburg to tend to his wounded countrymen, estimated the British had between three hundred and four hundred wounded.

Lieutenant Gleig, still suffering inflammation from his own thigh wound, went to Ross's Tavern, converted into a makeshift hospital, to comfort the seriously maimed.[65] They numbered about ninety, and deep concern was felt over their fate.[66] Because of the gravity of their injuries and limited transport, they would be left behind. They would have to depend on the mercy of their enemy. Gleig's company sergeant, bedridden with wounds in both thighs, broke down in tears, saying he would rather be dead. He was unmoved when Gleig told him senior officers, including Colonel Thornton, were also remaining behind. Gleig barely had time to shake the hands of officers in their separate ward when, at about midnight, a bugler sounded the call to prepare to move out.

They had been in Bladensburg only an hour, but few had rested. The dead were mourned, the wounded helped into wagons, and barrels of flour opened for hungry soldiers to line up and fill their haversacks. Again they departed with characteristic order. The third brigade led the horse-drawn artillery, followed by the second brigade, light infantry, and mounted drivers flanked by more foot soldiers. Bringing up the rear were the marine artillery, ready to launch Congreve rockets at the slightest alarm. Everyone moved in silence, expecting Americans to launch hit-and-run attacks all the way back to the ships.

They had not gone three miles through darkened woods with barely visible paths when Smith felt totally vindicated in trying to get Ross to delay the withdrawal until daylight. Exhausted men stumbled and wandered out of line in the blackness. Had it not been for the heavy white flour they threw away to ease their burden, they would not have been able to follow the track. The lines stretched longer as more stragglers lagged behind and fell by the wayside. Some of those unable to endure any more motion had slipped from sight at Bladensburg and resumed the long flight late the following morning. Cool night air helped keep the bulk of the army on the march, but by 7 A.M. Ross was forced to call a halt. They had marched all night, with only a brief respite in Bladensburg. Within minutes the slumbering British resembled hordes of battlefield dead. Guarded only by a few sentries too tired to be on maximum alert, the victorious army slept until noon.

Then they slogged all afternoon and into the evening, arriving at the same site just outside Upper Marlborough where they had slept the night before the battle of Bladensburg. Gleig tried sleeping in an isolated house, but the cries and groans of wounded officers sleeping in the same room kept him awake until 2 A.M., when he left for the quiet of a nearby shed.

At first light the army was on the move again, retracing its steps to Nottingham. The further they distanced themselves from Washington the more relaxed they became. The expected pursuit never materialized, and the troops were no longer cautious in raising their voices. Confident that there were no Americans nearby in any number to threaten the troops, Ross rested his men overnight at Nottingham and for the whole of the next day. The onerous task of lifting the wounded and artillery into a gun brig, barges, and other small craft rowed upstream was left to the boat crews, who also loaded some of the vessels with tobacco and flour seized in Nottingham.

But a handful of stragglers, looking suspiciously like potential thieves, had been seized in Upper Marlborough by a few locals led by Dr. William Beanes, the same wealthy Scottish immigrant who had hosted Gleig more than a week earlier.[67] One of the prisoners escaped late at night and alerted British horsemen sent back to Upper Marlborough to see if American forces were following. The horsemen rode into the village, broke into the doctor's house about midnight, and took him back to Nottingham, barely giving the sixty-five-year-old enough time to change from his nightclothes.[68] Two other Americans apparently involved, Dr. William Hill and Philip Weems, were also roused and taken away.[69]

An angry General Ross ordered the physician held for hostile conduct.[70] Within days Hill and Weems were released after a personal appeal by Gov. Levin Winder of Maryland. But Beanes, a warden of Trinity Church, continued to be held in harsh conditions. Officers refused to talk to him, and he was kept in a forward part of the ship among the lower ranks of soldiers and sailors, who treated him with contempt. Beanes would not even be given a change of clothing for the next two weeks. Ross showed no leniency, not even when Winder pleaded that "a respectable and aged old man . . . would not have been guilty of any act intentionally and knowingly contrary to the usages of war."[71] Ross had apparently decided the doctor was guilty of a breach of good faith because he had so recently hosted the British in his own home. He would therefore treat Beanes as a culprit rather than a prisoner of war.[72]

The long rest prepared the army for the final stretch all the way to Benedict, a distance they had covered in two days at the start of their invasion. After nightfall they reached the ridge of the same hill at Benedict where they had set up camp immediately after disembarking from the ships. In the short span of ten days they had walked about a hundred miles and fulfilled Admiral Cochrane's desire "to give them [the Americans] a complete drubbing."[73]

Boat crews rowing them to the fleet the next day hailed the returning conquerors with boisterous cheers for a job well done. Ross's deputy, Colonel Brooke, thought the achievements of the past ten days "as fine a thing as any done during this war, and a rub to the Americans that can never be forgotten."[74] Cochrane himself was well satisfied, reporting estimated losses of no more than three hundred, "astonishingly few considering what the troops had to perform."[75]

Ross could scarcely believe the magnitude of the lightning campaign, telling one senior naval officer, Rear Adm. Pulteney Malcolm, that he would have been forced to retreat if the Americans had confronted him with three thousand troops "well posted."[76] Malcolm, aboard his flagship

Royal Oak, was bursting with admiration for Cockburn. A few days later he wrote home saying, "He is a dashing fellow and I attribute our excursion to Washington to his sanguine advice."[77]

The rank and file were also well pleased with themselves. In boastful letters home they exaggerated the scope of their gains and the strength of their opponents. "We completely defeated them and burned down the City of Washington, destroyed twenty thousand stand of small arms, two hundred pieces of cannon. In short, we totally destroyed that part of the United States of America," wrote Pvt. William Kirke, of the King's Own Regiment, to his father.[78] Midshipman Samuel Davies bragged to his mother and brother, "We were surrounded by twenty thousand soldiers but they would not engage us the dam [*sic*] rascals."[79]

As they were about to board the ships, Ross took Smith aside, telling him he would have the honor of conveying the general's formal dispatches to London. Smith was overjoyed. Seven years had passed since he had last set foot in Britain. He would be homeward bound within days, accompanied by Captain Wainwright, who would deliver Admiral Cochrane's own summaries of the campaign to the Admiralty.

But at that same moment, Ross told the young captain that both Cochrane and Cockburn were urging him to swing north and attack Baltimore. He was against it and asked for the young officer's opinion. Smith, too, was firmly opposed, believing it must by now be well defended and that British failure at Baltimore would only restore American self-confidence.

"I agree with you," said Ross.

"Then, Sir, may I tell Lord Bathurst you will not go to Baltimore?"

"Yes," said the general.

But Smith was not convinced. A few days later, as he prepared to set sail, he brought up the subject again. "Dear friend," said Smith, "may I assure Lord Bathurst you will not attempt Baltimore?"

"You may," said Ross.

Smith would remember the words well. They were the last he ever heard from the general he admired so much.[80]

It would take a month for the British people to learn of the surprise swoop on the American capital. At 5 A.M. on 27 September, printers stopped the press at the venerable *Times* of London to insert a rare bulletin.

It was from the Admiralty Office: "Captain Wainwright of his Majesty's ship *Tonnant* arrived early this morning, at this office, with dispatches from Vice Admiral Sir A. Cochrane, Commander in Chief on the American station, with an account of the capture and destruction, by his Majesty's forces, of the City of Washington."[81]

Later, in London, Harry Smith was conducted from the Colonial Office in Downing Street to a private audience with the Prince Regent. He was nervous and giddy at the prospect of coming face-to-face with the acting monarch. No one had even hinted that he might have to brief such an exalted person.

"I know nothing of the etiquette of a court," he whispered to Lord Bathurst.

"Oh, just behave as you would to any gentleman," the aristocrat coaxed. "His Highness's manner will soon put you at ease. Call him 'Sir' and do not turn your back on him."

The guns outside Parliament and at the Tower of London boomed a salute to the astonishing British achievement as Smith was ushered into the royal dressing room with its perfumes, snuff boxes, wigs and silken finery. The prince, fifty-two, ruling as regent during the illness of his father, King George III, looked intently at Smith's map of the American capital. He asked the name of each of the public buildings marked in red to denote its destruction. "In his heart I fancied I saw he thought it a barbarian act," Smith reminisced later.

When the brief audience was over, Smith began to back out of the room but checked himself when the Prince Regent spoke again. "Bathurst," he ordered, "don't forget this officer's promotion."[82]

While British troops rejoiced, many relatives of those supposedly trapped in Washington lapsed into anxiety bordering on hysteria. In Winchester, Virginia, more than seventy miles west of the capital, Sarah Young fretted for the well-being of her sister, Maria Nourse. Having learned only sketchy details of the capital's fate from a frightened refugee, she feared for her sibling's safety. "Why do not you write?" she asked in a letter full of foreboding four days after the conflagration. "No regular dispatches have been sent. No mail. No private letters. Where are you? . . . This suspense is horrible. I sometimes think I would rather be in the battle than sit waiting here for the news of it."[83] In Philadelphia, Jane Clarke suffered the same jitters as she wrote to her friends Navy Secretary Jones and his wife, Eleanor. "Where are you? Not a line to say you are in safety."[84]

They would have been surprised at how faithful the British had been in their promise not to harm Washingtonians. But they would have been mortified by the misconduct of their own countrymen. The morning after the British left the capital, hordes of citizens swarmed over the remains of the President's House, the Capitol, and the navy yard. The streets were empty and most houses abandoned. Without any means of law enforcement, the city was open to looters and thieves. Like vultures, they descended on the open ruins to pick and pluck at random. Unchecked, they violated the sanctity of private homes, snatching and hoarding items of value and even of worthless sentiment.

Access was easy. The handsome interior of the President's House, put together almost entirely of flammable material, had been burned away. Great damage had been done to the superstructure of the outer walls, but the better part of the walls and of the basement level stood unscathed. Government offices flanking the President's House fared better because the upper parts of their outer walls were made of brick. In time they would be more easily repaired because of the relative ease with which bricks could be removed and replaced. The Capitol had fared less well. Its massive walls had withstood much of the fire, but the glorious chamber of the House of Representatives had been mutilated to such an extent that when architect George Hadfield got his first close-up look he bemoaned "the loss of that sublime specimen of architectural excellence."[85] The looters had no difficulty raiding the ground-floor level because the vaulted ceilings had stood firm against the blaze.

That same morning, the superintendent of patents rode into Washington from his country retreat eight miles out. Dr. Thornton wanted to make sure the Patent Office had been spared, as promised by senior British officers. He worried that a junior officer, unaware of the pledge to protect the building, might set it alight. To his relief, he discovered that the enemy had gone, but to his horror he learned of the wholesale theft in progress. With Mayor Blake still absent across the Potomac in Virginia, Thornton, a justice of the peace, took charge to stem the lawlessness. He stationed guards at the President's House and at the Capitol and ordered the gates slammed shut at the navy yard just as Commodore Tingey arrived to regain authority over the vandalized shipyard.[86]

Thornton's visit to the British casualties on Friday, 26 August, sparked such an ugly public feud with the mayor in the weeks ahead, with Blake even questioning his patriotism, that the *National Intelligencer's* exasperated editor called for an end to "this sort of badinage . . . unsuited to the times."[87] Thornton had been so moved by the misery of the captives that he decided they "were no longer enemies."[88] In the name of the city, he even thanked Dr. Ewell for treating their wounds. The senior British non-commissioned officer, Sergeant Sinclair of the 21st Regiment, who had been left behind in charge of the few sick and wounded and their attendants, first heaped praise on Ewell, then asked Thornton to guarantee protection for the British. Thornton, who had seen four British stragglers near the navy yard, promised more than the sergeant could have expected when he suggested that a British soldier join each of the six-man American night patrols in every ward as a hedge against dispersed Britons being shot on sight.

But the mixed-nationality patrols were not to be. At about 3 P.M. on Friday, Mayor Blake crossed over from Virginia by Mason's Ferry to set foot once more in the rubble of his gutted city. By his estimate, nine-tenths of the inhabitants had fled and were still absent, yet he rushed to protect those whites who had stayed put. Chilling rumor had it that quantities of arms and ammunition had fallen into the hands of slaves. Sensing "great agitation and alarm," the mayor called an emergency meeting of citizens for 5 P.M. at McKeowin's Hotel. As he walked to the landmark venue he crossed paths with Thornton, who claimed later that Blake told him he approved of everything Thornton had done in the mayor's absence. Blake, however, would flatly deny this. "I never gave my assent to the British soldiery or any part of them patroling our streets. On the contrary, it is well-known that I contended they were our prisoners and reprobated the idea of placing ourselves under British protection."[89]

The citizens' forum moved quickly to guard against the possibility of a slave rebellion by calling on all white males to patrol the streets throughout the night. Within hours Blake was among those armed with muskets walking up and down the darkened roads. But Thornton was conspicuously absent. He had not even stayed for the meeting, claiming he had to ride back in the dark to rejoin his family in the country. He left no doubt that his attendance would have been a waste of time. An earlier town meeting, he sneeringly reminded his critics, had attracted only three people while "resolves and addresses proceeded from them in great style."[90] Though the minutes of the meeting were soon lost, Blake said participants vetoed Thornton's plan for joint Anglo-American night patrols. Those present also voted to send a burial party to Bladensburg the following day to clear the battlefield of rotting corpses. And mindful of the possibility that legislators might want to move the capital out of the wreckage of Washington, they directed the mayor to let the president know that many buildings still remained to accommodate Congress.[91]

About sunset, while Blake was still at the hotel, a Captain Caldwell arrived at the hostelry with his unit. As Caldwell was then the highest-ranking military figure in Washington, the mayor told him about Thornton's plans for joint patrols. "He agreed with me as to its impropriety, observing that we would disarm the British guard in the morning," Blake recounted.[92]

The night passed without incident, and no stragglers were spotted. On Saturday morning Blake did as Thornton had done, visiting the sick and wounded of both sides in the capital and at Bladensburg and authorizing supplies for the hard-pressed surgeons.

At about 5 P.M. everyone's attention focused on the rumblings coming from the direction of Fort Warburton on the east bank of the Potomac River, about a dozen miles south of the capital.

11. A Flag Furled in Darkness

*M*ultiple rumors had reached Capt. Samuel Dyson of the invading force marching on Fort Warburton, the understaffed garrison of eighty men which he had assumed command of less than two weeks before. The gloomy masonry fortress stood sentinel 185 feet away from the high-water mark on the Maryland shore, over a site selected by George Washington in 1794. The parapet of this squat and sprawling fort was a solid ten feet, four inches thick and soared forty-one feet above the river.[1] It had a commanding view up and down the Potomac, with Washington's own estate at Mount Vernon partially visible three miles downriver. On a clear day the spires and rooftops of Alexandria were easily recognizable six miles upriver on the west bank, as was the capital itself on the opposite side. Only a thousand yards of water separated the five-year-old fort from the closest part of the forested Virginia shoreline.

At about the time the two armies squared off at Bladensburg, Dyson had been tipped off by the military in Alexandria that the squadron of British warships had passed through the treacherous Kettle Bottoms on their way up the Potomac.[2] They would have to pass between the fort and the Virginia shore en route to Alexandria and the capital. If rumors of a land march toward the fort were correct, Dyson might find himself wedged between a British land army in his rear and enemy naval forces in front.

Any dilemma he may have felt should have been dispelled shortly after midnight on Wednesday, 24 August. At that time Maj. Robert Hite, assistant adjutant general for the 10th Military District, rode into the fort, led Dyson into a private room, and passed on a secret verbal message and order from General Winder. The enemy was within ten miles of the capital, Hite said, and Fort Warburton could be one of the targets. If Dyson was "pressed to extremity in his *rear* by the enemy," he should spike his guns, blow up the magazine, and cross the river with his garrison.[3] The order emphasized he was to evacuate only if pressured by land forces in his rear. There was no mention of what to do about the naval squadron that would bombard from the front.

But based on a glowing report on the fort's location and defenses, written a year earlier when the British were first expected to strike at Washington, Dyson should not have worried about a threat from the river. "Its situation is so elevated, the result of a cannonade by ships from the river should not be dreaded," Colonel Wadsworth, chief of ordnance, had written to the secretary of war. Wadsworth was so confident of the fort's muscle that he had dismissed as "trifling" any threat by land. But the colonel had based his cocksureness on American land forces remaining "decidedly superior to that which the enemy can oppose to it." He was not out of line with popular opinion. Even in 1813 it would have been fanciful, even lunacy, to imagine the British marching unopposed on a fifty-mile incursion, then routing American troops within sixty minutes at Bladensburg. Wadsworth had given such high marks to the river bastion that he told the secretary of war, "I am therefore of opinion an additional number of heavy guns at Fort Warburton and an additional fort in that neighborhood are both to be considered unnecessary."[4]

But Dyson had a poor opinion of the fort's equipment. He thought even less of the manpower, one-quarter of whom were raw recruits, even though they were drilled three times a day in manning the guns. According to his predecessor, there was a shortfall of about 190 men who would be required to man all the guns if bombarded from the river.[5]

Dyson shared the confidential order with one of his four junior officers. He called in Lt. James Edwards, who had commanded the fort from 11 May through 5 August, prior to Dyson's arrival, and told him to plan the trail of gunpowder in case they had to demolish the fort themselves.[6]

While keeping a watchful eye out for enemy sails, Dyson tried to keep track of British infantry through daily intelligence reports from his picket guards and neighborhood residents visiting the fort. But much of this was rumor and speculation. No one had seen the enemy marching down. They had only passed on scuttlebutt, hearsay, and guesswork.

Lt. Thomas Harrison, on picket guard about three miles up on the road to Washington from about noon on Friday, 26 August, to 9 A.M. the following morning, was convinced the British were approaching Fort Warburton. This was what he had been told by travelers coming down the road and what was also expected by several neighborhood residents he talked with. But again, no one had actually seen the enemy.

Out of curiosity, Dr. William Marshall of Piscataway, a port settlement a few miles southeast on the Potomac, rode to the fort. When Dyson asked if he had heard of any British movements on land, Marshall said they were either at or near Upper Marlborough. The doctor had also heard rumors that some of the British had divided their forces after withdrawing from Washington and that some of the troops were marching on Fort Warburton. This only strengthened Dyson's belief that he would soon have to face a rearguard action. He warned the doctor to return home to avoid being captured.

At 2 P.M. that Saturday, Dr. William Fitzgerald made another of his almost daily social calls at the fort and told Dyson he had met two Methodist preachers who had recently been in the vicinity of Benedict. They had not seen the landings, only heard of them, yet they firmly believed the British would fan out as far as the fort.[7] But when Lt. Walter Berryman returned to the fort from his guard duty two miles up along the same road later that afternoon, he reported that a vidette said the British had left the capital and returned to Benedict. Dyson had heard only of the landing at Benedict, but he still expected the enemy to assault the fort that night.[8] He had made up his mind that the information had to be correct because so much of it added up to the same conclusion even though it came from different sources.[9]

When he looked toward Washington, Dyson could see the smoke still rising from its ruins, even though the flames had been lit two or three days before. He believed the British were still in the capital or marching out of it, and if they were not on their way to the fort they were at least not far from it. "Was I not justified," he asked later, "in concluding that the overwhelming force of the enemy had driven back all opposition and that my miserable post and little band was all that survived the general wreck? I had neither time nor chance of destroying the fort and withdrawing my garrison if I remained longer in such a position."[10]

Late that Saturday afternoon the British squadron appeared downriver less than three miles south of the fort. Dyson immediately ordered the men to their stations. There were only enough healthy, able forces to man five of the guns.[11] The commander also sent a sergeant to recall Lieutenant Berryman from picket duty two miles north on the road to Washington and to let him know the enemy had been sighted. Berryman had expected to see the colors flying from Fort Warburton when he returned, even though it was customary to hoist them only on Sundays. But when he looked up the flagstaff was bare.[12] No flag of challenge flew above the lone bulwark standing in the way of Gordon's squadron.

Only two small British ships were at anchor within the three-mile range of the fort's 32-pounders. The rest of the enemy vessels were further behind and not yet in line of battle. About twenty barges were also visible. Instead of going on the attack and launching a barrage of heavy ammunition at the exposed ships, Dyson called his officers together to vote on whether to abandon the fort. It would provoke bitter condemnation from his critics. "Why not now begin the combat?" Judge Advocate General R. H. Winder later fumed at a court-martial. "The fort had now but a small part of the fleet to contend with. A heavy fire might have produced difficulty and confusion in forming the line of battle. The *Seahorse* frigate is said to have grounded near the fort. Other accidents would probably have happened—independently of the great execution which the length and caliber of the guns, and the ardor and discipline of the men would have insured at all events. The enemy would have been repulsed—at least crippled and cut to pieces as to be unfit for any ulterior project."[13]

When the four junior officers were assembled, Dyson told them of the secret order from General Winder to evacuate and destroy the fort if pressed severely in the rear.[14] He told them there was an enemy force behind them and that they could not defend against the naval squadron. Dyson seemed neither scared nor nervous. But he did look very perplexed.[15] The captain then asked his lieutenants whether they should blow up the fortress. Berryman claimed he did not vote, but others said the vote was unanimous in favor of quitting the post and blowing it up.[16]

A flurry of activity followed. The fleet was abreast of George Washington's stately white mansion at Mount Vernon at about 5 P.M. when the garrison was told to spike the guns and abandon fort.[17] Lieutenant Edwards went with a sergeant to lay the trail of gunpowder to explosives in the magazine.[18] A cannonball might not penetrate the fireproof magazine from outside, but if all the explosives were blown up from within they might blow open the three- to four-foot-thick arch below the shingle roof and also demolish the double brick wall around it. Meanwhile a messenger was sent a quarter of a mile away to the Thomas Digges family home, where George Washington had visited often and on whose land the fort's horses were pastured, to tell them to look out for their windows because the garrison would soon be blown up.[19]

The order to evacuate without a fight was met with deep misgivings and open grumbling. "We ought at least to give them one shot," lamented a man named Riley.[20] Even Lieutenant Harrison, who did not think the fortress was defensible, was heard to say, "We should give it to them directly."[21]

When the enemy had come into sight, Dr. John O'Connor, hospital surgeon at the fort, had gone to his room to make a last-minute check on operating equipment he might have to use on battle casualties. The first he learned about an evacuation was when he came out and heard talk about spiking the guns. Incredulous, O'Connor went to see for himself before he could be convinced of the truth.[22]

As they left the fort, Dyson looked melancholy.[23] They had left behind all the artillery, some twenty-seven guns, and taken with them only about four dozen muskets. He had not fired a single shot from the redoubtable garrison, and the enemy had not yet opened fire as he led his men out of harm's way. But they had gone no more than fifty paces when the first British shell landed in a creek beyond the fort. The second shell crashed only thirty paces from the front guard. Aboard the *Seahorse*, Captain Gordon looked through his telescope and saw the Americans retreating, but he kept up the bombardment because he suspected "some concealed design."[24] The line of escapees, many deeply resentful at having to make such a shameful withdrawal, had walked about an hour and were almost three miles beyond Fort Warburton when the powder magazine blew up, destroying the inner buildings.[25]

Despite lobbing mortars and rockets, the British intended to launch their full-scale assault only at daylight the following morning. The explosions took them completely by surprise. They did not even know whether their shells had hit an ammunition store or whether the Americans had lit their own fuses. The general opinion was that the defenders had self-destructed and that they need no longer fear a trick.[26]

Thomas Digges, sheltering inside his house about four hundred yards away, saw dozens of shells and rockets pass so close that they very nearly sailed over his roof. He witnessed or heard others falling on his front fields and not far from his well. But this was insignificant damage compared to a recent thunderbolt which, he told his friend James Madison three days later, "did me more mischief than all their firing."[27]

The blasts reverberated for miles upriver. In Washington, Commandant Tingey had just finished writing a report on the navy yard's destruction when he heard "a smart cannonading."[28] He knew the enemy's frigates had targeted the fort, and he took note of two or three distinctly powerful explosions, but he could only guess at the outcome when the guns fell silent after 7 P.M.

Aboard the *Euryalus*, Lt. Charles Napier could not understand why the garrison had taken "such an extraordinary step."[29] The fort was well positioned, and he calculated that its capture would have cost the lives of at least fifty Britons—even more had it been properly defended. The attackers were handicapped by an unfavorable wind, and Napier guessed that other advantages and chances also lay with the Americans. He was convinced that the fort could have been destroyed only by a successful naval assault.

On land, the retreating column walked with mixed emotions over another four miles along the road to Washington before turning off to take the ferry across to Alexandria. They did not halt that night until reaching Sebastian Springs, almost four miles beyond Alexandria.[30]

Dyson was deeply troubled by his actions. Even though he knew he had not acted out of "base or unmanly motives," he felt he had "reluctantly yielded to a sense of duty in violation of every wish and feeling of my heart."[31] He seemed to want to convince himself that he was not a coward. Some hours later, Dr. O'Connor heard him say he could fight as well as anyone.[32] Later the captain would conclude that he had done the right thing in walking away from what would have been a futile defense. The country's honor could not be preserved "by an idle attempt" to do what was evidently impracticable. Nine weeks after shying away from the scrap, Dyson came out fighting to defend his conduct. "A mere nominal resistance firing a gun or two for the name of the thing is folly and more frequently the refuge of cowardice than the effort of courage. Surely an officer should never be condemned to undergo the mortification of hoisting the standard of his country when he knows that he cannot defend it."[33]

This did not sit well with the prosecution. Judge Advocate General Winder branded Dyson in language of utter contempt and loathing for his lack of backbone. "The star-spangled banner, under the auspices of this commander, instead of being planted on the rampart, proudly to wave defiance to the foe and light Americans to victory, lies furled in darkness, a council called and the fort abandoned. Whilst the enemy is arraying himself for battle, instead of animating his men for the conflict, with the looks and language of a hero, he marches the unwilling fugitives away without firing or receiving a single shot."[34] The panel of judges would agree, finding Dyson guilty of running away and shamefully abandoning the fort. It would banish him immediately and forever from service in the United States military.

The British closed in for the kill at dawn on Sunday. They moored under the fort's battery and pounded the sullen and empty river guardian until much of it lay in ruins. When they landed they swept past the battery on the beach, into the heart of the fort, and up into the martello tower, all along mutilating the spiked artillery and destroying the gun carriages so that none would be reusable after they left. When they finally rested, the interior of the fort was wrecked. Every fieldpiece had been rendered useless, with the exception of the two large 52-pounder columbiads. But surprisingly, the walls were unscathed by the pounding, save for the ribband edge of the topmost brickwork, which had been knocked off.

British officers, impressed by the fort's strategic location, told Digges that only one hundred British artillerists would have been needed to quickly destroy a squadron even larger than their own attacking force.

Digges was told not to worry about the safety of his own home and property, but he remained on guard, wondering what they would do on their return downriver. Cryptically, he would warn President Madison, "I nevertheless fear they have an eye to the negroes hereabouts."[35]

The naval force had overcome its last obstacle, and the path was now open to Alexandria and the capital.

12. Refuge among Pacifists

*G*eneral Mason's wife, Anna Maria, had fled Washington with her three eldest daughters and two servant maids, finding refuge with "a poor but respectable family" at a farmhouse four miles from the Quaker village of Brookville.¹ She lay ill with a fever and a pounding headache that no amount of forced bleeding could relieve. Though too ill to talk, she welcomed the presence of her good friend Margaret Bayard Smith, who had come from Brookville to nurse her all through Friday and into Saturday morning, 27 August.

But the tranquillity of the humble refuge vanished with the arrival of Dr. Charles Worthington, the patient's wealthy Georgetown physician who was so old-fashioned that he wore his hair in a ponytail and dressed with knee breeches, long stockings, and buckled shoes long after they went out of style. He was outspokenly against the war with Britain and would soon take into his Georgetown home some of the British soldiers wounded at the battle of Bladensburg, an act that later prompted one of the officers to give him a gift of a gold snuffbox engraved in gratitude for the doctor's "extreme kindness and attention."²

Worthington did not care for diplomatic niceties. Instead of showing concern for his patient, he spoke gleefully of the rout of the American army and the fall of the capital. Tearfully, Mrs. Smith begged him, especially at this moment, not to rejoice over losses that should be mourned. Worthington let the matter drop, but Smith was shaken to the core. She could not believe that anyone, even a Federalist, could say such things. In the weeks to come, Worthington's patient was so miserable among teetotaling Quakers that she pleaded with her brother, Attorney General Rush, to send her some bottles of Madeira.[3]

Meanwhile, the president and his horsemen created a stir in the crowded village of Brookville when they arrived on Friday night during Margaret Smith's absence. They had continued on from Montgomery Court House after finding the army had quit the town six hours earlier for Baltimore.[4] The presidential party put up at the sturdy two-story brick home of the village postmaster, Caleb Bentley, and his wife, Henrietta, a friend of fellow Quaker Dolley Madison. The Quaker hosts and household staff fluttered in and out of the rooms preparing supper and making beds in the wood-beamed parlor. Ever since the village had filled with refugees in their carriages and baggage wagons, the hospitable Quakers had worked tirelessly to house and feed them. Mrs. Smith had "never seen more benevolent people." The tiny community was evidently driven by a common good nature. "It is against our principles to have anything to do with war," Mrs. Bentley explained, "but we receive and relieve all who come to us."[5]

As sentinels circled the house, bands of cavalry and infantry pitched their tents by the stream and beside the wall of a mill, piercing the darkness with myriad campfires and flickering candles. Curious knots of villagers of all ages bunched close to the Bentley home to try and get a glimpse of the president of the United States. With the nation's capital held by the enemy, the nondescript village of gentle pacifists was quickly transformed by Madison's presence into a makeshift center of supreme executive authority.

Madison retained much of his usual composure, and though distressed, he appeared to be far from dispirited.[6] At 10 P.M. he wrote a brief letter to James Monroe, asking whether he should remain in Brookville or journey to him. "If you decide on coming hither, the sooner the better."[7]

The following morning, Saturday, Monroe got word to the president that the British had evacuated the capital and were en route to Upper Marlborough. Madison acted quickly to summon his cabinet back to Washington. Couriers galloped off to Fredericktown to find Armstrong and Campbell. At 10 A.M. the president scribbled a note to Jones at Wiley's Tavern. Unaware that Dolley had moved to Mrs. Minor's, the president wrote, "I hope you will, with the party attached to your care, have remained at Wiley's and be so much the more quick in your return to the city."[8]

Then he wrote to Dolley. Since the chief executive's mansion had been gutted by fire, Madison told his wife, "I know not where we are in the first instance to hide our heads; but shall look for a place on my arrival. Mr. Rush offers his house in the six buildings and the offer claims attention. Perhaps I may fall in with Mr. Cutts."[9]

At noon the president, now joined by the secretary of state, set out for Washington. Five hours later they rode into the charred city.[10] It was a wrenching sight. The glorious landmarks, designed and crafted with obsessive passion and meticulous detail by Hoban, Thornton, Latrobe, Andrei, and Franzoni, lay open to the skies, their roofs burned off, their singular works of art reduced to rubble or cracked and blistered beyond repair. Scorched walls enclosed piles of ash. At the President's House, charcoal-black stains defaced the surface of chunky stone building blocks. Polished public buildings that once rivaled their weathered counterparts on the old continent of Europe stood hollow and wizened. The ruins were a telling commentary on the scale of the city's degradation.

The ache ran deep. There was a sense of profound personal loss. Richard Rush, a man renowned for his conspicuous good manners and even temperament, grieved when he surveyed "the disgraceful demolition."[11] It looked to him like "the most magnificent and melancholy ruin you ever beheld."[12] To former president John Adams he lamented, "How it will agonize your son [John Quincy Adams] in Europe when he hears of it. How it will make all our [peace] commissioners blush when the British commissioners hand them General Ross's dispatch."[13]

Misery would turn to anger. Successive observers decried the "wanton destruction."[14] Others scrawled graffiti on the walls of the Capitol, venting their rage and scorn at both British and American leaders: "James Madison is a rascal, a coward and a fool"; "Armstrong sold the city for 5000 dollars"; "The capital of the Union lost by cowardice." A pencil sketch showed Winder hanging from a tree. Another depicted the president fleeing without his hat or wig. Cockburn was made to look like a common thief robbing henroosts.[15]

The president took up temporary lodgings at the F Street home of his brother-in-law, Richard Cutts, only a brief stroll from the gutted executive mansion.[16] He was heavily guarded, at first by eleven horsemen and then by fifty militiamen. The next-door neighbor, Anna Maria Thornton, felt such pity when she saw the guards lying outside on beds of straw, in drizzle, during the night that she noted in her daily diary, "Even dogs have kennels."[17]

Madison left no record of his personal feelings when he surveyed the grim desolation, but he had little time to brood. The boom of British cannons rumbled all the way from the ships' line of battle near Mount Vernon until they were heard clearly by frenzied Washingtonians and Georgetowners.[18] When the magazine blew up at abandoned Fort Warburton, vibrations rippled for miles at breakneck speed. Georgetown produce merchant Thomas Beall interrupted the entry of routine daily expenditures in his ledger to record how the blast "jarred the windows and ground here."[19]

Fear of invasion again took hold after sunset. Terror stalked the isolated households. This time the British raiders might be as brutal as they were reported to have been in settlements along the banks of the Chesapeake. By sunrise many leading citizens were prepared to surrender Georgetown and the capital to spare their lives and prevent the destruction of their homes. Monroe took stock of the situation, realized Baltimore was also tottering, and came to the unhappy conclusion that "the infection ran along the coast."[20]

Washingtonians particularly feared the British sailors. When Dr. Thornton and Mayor Blake again crossed paths on the street, Thornton prodded him to get the president's consent for a delegation to call on the commander of the British fleet. Thornton did not consider it capitulation, even though he did not expect the delegates to oppose another occupation. He only wanted them to beg the British for a single favor: that they "would not permit their sailors to land."[21] Blake would have none of it, even as others pressured him to change his mind. He preferred stubborn resistance, and was even then gathering men to make a stand beside the smashed defenses at Greenleaf's Point.

The fainthearted citizens also came up against a robust, newly defiant executive. Madison was adamant: under no circumstances would he nod approval for a meeting with the British. Monroe, appointed acting secretary of war during Armstrong's absence, threatened a bayonet charge against anyone trying to contact the enemy. In sharp contrast with Armstrong's neglect, he rushed to mount batteries at Greenleaf's Point, at the windmill point, and near the long bridge over the Potomac. In a dramatic showdown, Monroe left no doubt that he was second only to the president in the chain of command. When a colonel refused to obey orders to move cannons from the Virginia shore to the southern tip of Mason's Island in the Potomac, Monroe rode up the riverbank and repeated the order in person. Still the colonel refused, saying he did not recognize Monroe as secretary of war or even as commanding general. It was his first and last act of insubordination. Monroe told him to obey the order or leave the field. When the colonel skulked off, Monroe had a free hand with the armaments and indisputable command over the troops.[22]

Dolley Madison returned to the dejected capital on Sunday even as a letter from her husband was on its way to her in Virginia. The president did not yet know the fate of Fort Warburton. If it had been captured, he feared British barges would row up the Potomac and once again "throw the city into alarm." If this happened, he warned, she might have to flee again. But if the British onslaught had failed, the president told his wife, "you cannot return too soon."[23]

Though beloved by so many for her good nature and stylish demeanor, Dolley Madison was disguised and uncharacteristically downhearted on her return. She had hidden her identity by wearing someone else's clothes and had exchanged her carriage for another's, on the instructions of her husband. By the time she arrived at the edge of the Potomac she was accompanied by a single bodyguard, the other weary eight having abandoned her after bouts of heavy drinking in the wayside taverns. When she tried to cross over, a one-eyed colonel had barred her passage, forcing her to reveal her true identity before he would allow the vehicle onto the ferryboat heading for Washington.[24] "I cannot tell you what I felt on reentering it," she later wrote to her longtime friend Mary Latrobe. "Such destruction—such confusion."[25] The high wind and heat may have helped deflate her spirits. After moving into her sister's home, she was so downcast that Margaret Smith, who had returned from Brookville that afternoon, observed "Mrs. M. seemed much depressed, she could scarcely speak without tears."[26] Another friend and eyewitness, Anna Maria Thornton, recorded in her diary: "She was very violent against the English and wished we had 10,000 such men as were passing (a few troopers) to sink our enemy to the bottomless pit."[27] The First Lady was not alone in her scorn. James Monroe, also visiting the house on F Street, cursed the enemy as "all damn'd rascals from highest to lowest."[28]

Navy Secretary Jones did not go home when he returned to the city on Sunday morning. His wife had fled to Baltimore, en route passing by the battlefield at Bladensburg, where she had the misfortune to spot a foot sticking out of a freshly dug grave.[29] The Joneses' absence from their Georgetown home had been costly. Mildew had damaged the dimity and chintz curtains, and personal possessions had apparently been looted.[30] Ten days would pass before the financially pressed secretary moved impatiently out of expensive public boarding rooms, with their "constant crowd and bustle."[31]

Domestic inconveniences were far from the mind of Attorney General Rush as he worried about the political fallout from the capital's destruction. By Sunday evening he knew what had to be done and scribbled it down for the most senior cabinet colleague. Rush urged Monroe to take quick action to show the government was back in control "after an event so very marked in our public affairs and destined to be always prominent in our national history." The executive "should be prompt to tell of the act ourselves and in our own way, without holding back as if from shame." A swift move would counter "malicious comments" sure to be put out by the British. If the proclamation came so soon out of Washington it would prove how promptly the city had been repossessed, undercutting talk about moving the capital elsewhere. "Holding a high and manly tone, it could not fail to help on the patriotism of the nation and certainly to rally the spirits of our friends."[32]

Rush did not have to wait long. Four days later the president signed a proclamation formulated by the attorney general and published throughout the land. It sought to discredit the British by highlighting their wanton destruction of costly buildings of artistic taste and public archives of worldwide interest. The enemy was excoriated for barbarism and uncivilized warfare. As nothing was now safe from the enemy's predatory and incendiary reach, the proclamation called for "a manly and universal determination to chastise and expel the invader." Appealing to the patriotism and pride of all Americans, Madison called on them not to forget "the glory acquired by their fathers in establishing independence, which is now to be maintained by their sons."[33]

Shortly after noon on Monday, 29 August, a brigade of about 450 District of Columbia militiamen tramped into Washington at the end of a twenty-mile forced march. They set up camp near the shell of the President's House, in full view of the British squadron anchored off Alexandria. Summoned by Monroe after midnight when he learned what had happened at Fort Warburton, the militiamen had marched down from Conns' Ferry, just above the Great Falls on the Potomac.[34] The executive was determined not to cut and run this time. If the British wanted to storm the nation's capital again, they would have to fight a revitalized military taking orders from a government eager to redeem itself. But many civilians who had returned to the capital remained scared and once more fled to the countryside.[35]

Secretary of War Armstrong arrived in the capital from Fredericktown at about the same time as the militiamen. He was now the most reviled man in the country and an abscess on the body politic. His stubborn refusal to defend and protect the capital in the face of overwhelming evidence of British intentions had led to the sorry outcome. No single individual was held more accountable than the secretary of war, yet he compounded his culpability by an arrogant refusal to admit blame. Within hours of Armstrong's return, the commanding general of the militia warned the president that every officer would tear off his epaulettes if the secretary of war continued to have supervision over them.[36] Returning residents trying to catch up on the dramatic events learned that Armstrong "would have been torn to pieces" had he passed through the city the day after the fiasco at Bladensburg.[37]

On his evening ride, Madison dismounted outside Armstrong's lodgings at the Seven Buildings, a few hundred yards west of the President's House. Fears were mounting of an imminent invasion from the British ships on the Alexandria side of the Potomac. Madison may have wished merely to sound out Armstrong's opinions, but the discussion led to a dramatic showdown. The mild-mannered president got straight to the point. Conquest of the city had ignited "violent prejudices" against the government, and particularly against Madison and Armstrong. He told Armstrong of the officers' ultimatum and disclosed that both of them had been threatened with personal violence. The mood of the troops was so antagonistic that, if possible, the secretary "should have nothing to do with them."[38] Monroe had acted in his stead during Armstrong's absence, but that was no longer possible now that the secretary of war was back. Madison, aware of the dangers of "any convulsion at so critical a moment," wondered how best to resolve the dilemma.

Armstrong offered little help, neither admitting his failures nor gracefully accepting responsibility. Instead, he argued as if standing above the fray, oblivious to multiple errors of judgment and idle stewardship of a powerful portfolio. He accused his critics of falsehoods and intrigue, declining to offer specifics because "this was not the proper time." Even now he remained anything but humble, telling the president he could not remain in Washington while his powers were divided or exercised by anyone else. His offer to resign was coupled with an alternative suggestion that he leave the capital immediately to join his family in New York.

Madison seemed taken aback, saying he had not even considered such a far-reaching action as resignation. Temporary absence was "less objectionable" because it would solve the immediate problem and leave all options open. But when Armstrong again insisted that he had done nothing wrong, the president took issue, saying that the conversation had now become "a frank one." Armstrong, he charged, had never appreciated the danger to Washington, nor the consequences of its being captured. He had failed to implement some cabinet decisions. Arms and equipment had not been brought in from distant depots, resulting in some of the local militia having to go all the way to Harper's Ferry for weapons.

Ever the gentleman, Madison confessed how difficult it was for him to make these observations. He had appointed Armstrong with confidence and out of respect for his talents. He reminded his secretary of war that he had always treated him as a friend. Then, delicately, the president said he had only a short time left until the end of his public career. His greatest wish, apart from leaving the country in peace and prosperity, was to preserve harmony. Armstrong acknowledged the president's friendliness and respected him for it. But Madison closed the dialogue by referring again to Armstrong's suggestion that he visit his family in New York. Madison would not object. In the morning, Armstrong, now a political pariah, sent word to Madison that he was off to rejoin his family.

The following Saturday, Armstrong completed a nineteen-paragraph letter to the *Baltimore Patriot*, going public with his reasons for quitting the cabinet. He swung out at critics on all sides, refusing to adjust his principles and conduct "to the humors of a village mob, stimulated by faction and led by folly." He declined comment on reports he found hard to believe, that shortly before his return to Washington a delegation of Georgetowners, led by Alexander Contee Hanson, had secured a promise from the president that Armstrong would not remain in charge of the District's military defenses. But he vigorously contested a string of outlandish accusations which he said had cost him the support of the president. His critics had stoked up such animosity toward him that he even had to deny ordering a retreat from Bladensburg, blocking defense of the capital, allowing Fort Warburton's destruction, and sanctioning fires at the navy yard. He rejected the common belief that he had stood idly by before the battle of Bladensburg. Had he not authorized Winder to round up supplies and a force of more than sixteen thousand defenders? Uncowed and even indignant, Armstrong saved his most scathing counterattack for the men who had run from the field of battle. "It is obvious," he concluded, "that if all the troops assembled at Bladensburg had been faithful to themselves and to their country, the enemy would have been beaten and the capital saved."[39]

13. Alexandria Surrenders

lexandria was doomed. It lay like cornered prey only six miles upriver from the desolate fort. The wretched moment had come for Mayor Charles Simms and the committee of vigilance to surrender the flourishing city. It was without credible defenses, and the squadron of seven warships had sailed past the fort, preceded at some distance by armed veterans on barges.

At about 10 A.M. on Sunday, 28 August, the mayor's group rowed downriver holding a flag of truce. Behind them, on the opposite bank, the Washington navy yard continued to burn, as if to remind them of the penalty they might incur if they did not succumb.[1] They boarded the *Seahorse* to ask Captain Gordon what fate he intended for their city.

One of the Alexandrians, hoping for leniency, said Ross and Cockburn had "immortalized their names" by respecting private property in Washington. Now would be "a fine opportunity" for Gordon to follow their example. The remarks stung the proud, one-legged sea captain as he faced the city notables. "I do not want any prompting to do what is right," he countered.

To make sure they all understood the definition of private property, he asked one of the Americans, Jonathan Swift, for his opinion. "All the vessels now laying off Alexandria and every sort of merchandise in the town," Swift answered. Gordon was quick to correct, saying he would seize every vessel off and near Alexandria. However, private homes and their furnishings would not be touched. Nor would the British raid any of the retail shops.

Swift complained that the intended confiscation seemed to be a special hardship for Alexandrians, "who were all Federalists." They would have to suffer more than their neighbors in Washington. His comment brought another sharp rebuke from Gordon, who said he would not take Swift's word for what Ross and Cockburn had done in Washington. But even if the British had not taken goods out of the capital, he said, it must have been because they lacked the means to do so. Gordon, on the other hand, had ample means and even considered it "my duty to distress the enemy of my country as much as possible."[2] To avoid any misunderstandings, he told them he would lay down his demands after his squadron anchored off Alexandria. Once the ships were in position, he knew the Alexandrians would have no option but to accept his dictates. Meanwhile, they could take comfort from his pledge that neither the residents nor their property would be harmed so long as the British under his command were not attacked.

When the mayor arrived back in his quaking city, he learned that a detachment of cavalry scouts from Gen. John Hungerford's Virginia militia brigade had visited briefly. Hungerford's infantry and cavalry, supported by two or three small pieces of artillery, had been stalking the British squadron along the western shore for a great part of the way up the Potomac. Hungerford, however, was still about sixteen miles south of Alexandria, too distant to be of any immediate help.

The seven ships which would hold the town hostage took their time in coming up. They did not arrive until the evening. The following morning Alexandrians awoke to find the formidable squadron arrayed a few hundred yards offshore in a threatening extended line, their guns able to destroy any part of the settlement.

About 10 A.M. on Monday, 29 August, an officer from the *Seahorse* handed the mayor Gordon's seven written conditions for sparing the city and its inhabitants. He gave the mayor exactly one hour to reply. Simms looked over the short list, which began with a demand for the immediate surrender of all naval and ordnance stores. The British would also take possession of all ships. Vessels sunk a week earlier had to be raised. Tobacco, flour, cotton, and other goods for export were to be forfeited. All merchandise taken out of the city in the past ten days had to be returned and surrendered. Refreshments had to be supplied to the ships, though they would be paid for at market prices. British officers would monitor compliance with every demand.

When the mayor and committee of vigilance said they had no power to recall merchandise sent out in the past ten days, the British officer scratched it from the list of conditions. And when they said they could not compel the residents to raise sunken ships, he told them English sailors would handle the salvage work.

The dreaded moment of servility had arrived. In a formal resolution, the Common Council of Alexandria bowed to Gordon's demands. But it absolved itself of any stigma, saying it had acted "from the impulse of irresistible necessity and solely from a regard to the welfare of the town." Its assent was merely a formality because "the enemy had it already in their power to enforce a compliance with their demand by a seizure of the property required."[3]

Virginia militiamen camping at Greenleaf's Point in Washington, about five miles north, had been keeping the enemy ships under observation with telescopes. At about midnight they saw Gordon's squadron fire half a dozen rockets high up into the night sky. Shortly afterwards the rocket signals were answered by booming guns from the direction of British warships on the Patuxent River. Militia captain Heiskell, called into action from his civilian job as editor of the *Winchester* (Va.) *Gazette*, marveled at modern warfare. In a dispatch to his paper he wrote, "It is truly astonishing to what a degree of perfection the art of war has been brought by the bold, enterprising enemy."[4]

That same Monday, Mordecai Booth rode from Falls Church into Alexandria. The navy yard's senior clerk could barely sit on his horse because of the festering boils on his thigh, hip, and wrist and the excruciating pain from a swollen leg and foot, the result of a boot cutting into the upper surface of his foot. He had expected to find the navy yard commandant keeping a watchful eye on the enemy's movements. Tingey, however, was nowhere in sight. On hearing of Gordon's "degrading" ultimatum, Booth rode down to the water's edge to size up the number and deployment of enemy ships. What he saw sickened him. He felt helpless and outraged. Later he reported to Tingey, "Again my feelings [were] most sensibly excited on seeing the British flag waving triumphant in the District."[5] Enemy craft were snaring hapless American vessels. One launch was towing a captured ship that had drifted well upriver. A sloop appeared to have run aground. Booth had seen enough. In acute physical pain he set off for Georgetown, where he rested briefly before continuing on to report to the commandant at the navy yard. There he was flabbergasted to learn that powder had been destroyed at the naval magazine during the occupation.

For the next six days, until their departure on Saturday, 3 September, the British plundered warehouses along the riverbank of their agricultural produce. Only because they lacked horse and carriage transportation did they not take anything from further inland. And they worked alone, watched by the passively indignant residents.[6] Editor Heiskell visited for a few hours on the third day of looting and wrote of "a melancholy scene. Figure to yourself the prevalence of the yellow fever in its most hideous form, and you will have an idea of the depopulated state of the place. The wharves exhibit a mere busy scene; but alas! It is the enemy who create the bustle! The merchants stand by, viewing with melancholy countenance the British sailors gutting their warehouses of their contents. Dejection was depicted in the countenances of all I met."[7]

The fragile calm was shattered only once, on the morning of the second day of occupation. Hungerford's troops had arrived the night before and stationed themselves atop Shuter's Hill, from where they saw flames still flickering across the river in Washington. They could also look down on the wharves of Alexandria, where the British overlords were loading tobacco and flour into the ships. Hungerford and the secretary of state made last-minute plans to deploy forces on both banks downriver to harass and possibly cut off the British squadron on its descent.

At this moment, two of Hungerford's officers decided to don the civilian clothes of country gentlemen and ride downtown to gather intelligence. The spies went unnoticed until they neared a wharfside warehouse on busy King Street. A young British midshipman, John Went Fraser, had apparently strayed from a squad of soldiers rolling out tobacco when the impulses of one of the American officers got the better of him. He rode up to the midshipman, clutched him by the clothing around his neck, and yanked him forward in an attempted abduction. The startled young officer, gasping for breath, might have been throttled if the material had not torn. He fell free and the British sounded an alarm, thinking they might be under an all-out attack because Hungerford's army had been visible even though immobile on Shuter's Hill. Some soldiers dived into the water. Others jumped into barges and readied the short-barreled carronades to open fire. At least one account says the British fired bombs and rockets into the town, setting several houses on fire. The mayor and committee of vigilance hastened to Gordon's flagship to tell him they had nothing to do with the isolated assault on the lieutenant. They did not think Hungerford would violate the terms of capitulation, especially since his forces had made no movement from the hill. To their relief, Gordon dismissed the scare as a single officer's high-spirited lark, but he cautioned that a repetition might lead to destruction of the town.[8]

The British stuffed twenty-one ships with looted cargo. All told they stashed away 16,000 barrels of flour, 1,000 hogsheads of tobacco, 150 bales of cotton, and some $5,000 worth of wine, sugar, and other items.[9] They had to leave behind another 200,000 barrels of produce for want of transport. Only one of the ships raised could not be made seaworthy, and this was promptly burned. When they finally set sail they were short four or five men who stayed behind as deserters.[10]

Gordon decided to cut and run when he got wind of rumors that "strong measures had been taken to oppose our return."[11] Their flight down the Potomac would not be as easy as the ascent. Hungerford's brigade, constrained from swooping down on the British by Alexandria's pledge to capitulate peacefully, braced for action along the high bank in thick woods above the Potomac. The general's troops had sped down the Virginia shoreline with Captain Porter's sailors and marines, hauling the weapons with which they hoped to savage Gordon's squadron: ten small horse-drawn fieldpieces, two 12-pounders, and three long 18-pounders. In their wild scramble over crooked roads and rugged hills, they risked overturning the artillery and injuring the horses. When they came to level ground they took greater chances by quickening the pace to a gallop. The desperate gamble paid off when they reached the White House, a large navigational landmark building by the water's edge, four miles below Mount Vernon. Behind it, on a steep forty-foot-high riverbank where trees had been hurriedly cleared, they positioned the guns. Vessels passing by in the Potomac had to come within three hundred yards of the Virginia shore as they clung to the narrow but navigationally safe channel.[12] The

British squadron would have to run a gauntlet of firepower launched at deadly close range.

As they waited for the enemy ships to come down from Alexandria, Booth pushed himself to the limit of his endurance to supply the White House battery with ammunition. He had been physically active since breakfast on 3 September, when he had ridden hard from Washington for the Dulany farm in Virginia. He galloped the whole distance and by 1 P.M. could look with satisfaction at the hasty departure for the White House battery of two wagons loaded with fifty barrels and two quarter casks of powder. Though the wagoners returned two days later reporting safe delivery of the powder, Booth's exertions had taken their toll on his feeble physical condition. "I paid severely for this ride," he recalled, "but by bathing and poultices got some relief."[13]

The man in charge of the White House battery, Capt. David Porter, was a naval commander fresh from recent glory in the Pacific. Three months earlier he had fought so valiantly against British ships attacking his frigate, *Essex,* near the port of Valparaíso, Chile, that although the ship was mauled and on fire, and many of the crew had drowned trying to swim to safety, Porter won high praise from the British for his courage.[14] His triumphant return to America brought cheering throngs into the streets of Philadelphia, where jubilant sailors unharnessed the horses so they could have the honor of personally pulling his carriage by rope.[15]

Porter now commanded the remnants of his crew at the improvised fortification on the west bank of the Potomac River. They had barely set up two small 4-pounders on the edge of the bank when the British brig *Fairy,* bristling with eighteen guns, came into view half a mile downriver.[16] It was apparently washday, for her rigging and yards were hung with the crew's flapping shirts and trousers. The deck was crammed with men as the vessel rolled in the swell. Ahead was a boat taking soundings and signaling back the depth of the water. Hoping to catch the British by surprise, Porter had his men lie down so they could not be seen from the brig. Then he gave the order to open fire with artillery. The first shot bounced off the water just ahead of the sounding boat. The next sliced the cord fastening the signal flag to the staff. It toppled into the river and the boat dropped back to the brig. Uncannily, the brig crew remained unperturbed on deck, apparently under the impression they were being fired upon by a small party of skirmishers. But as the brig sailed in front of Porter's battery a third shot pierced the hull. The brig opened up with a broadside, but the balls fell harmlessly on the bank below the battery. Simultaneously, the American infantrymen stood up and unleashed a withering volley of musket shot. One of the balls went wild and struck Porter's epaulette. Though unharmed, he would later complain of the men's careless aim.[17] But many others found their mark, and the shrieks of those struck on deck could be heard distinctly on land. More shots ripped through the hoisted laundry while a cannonball punched through the woodwork, smashing into glassware.[18] Holed, scarred, and splashed with the blood of her casualties, the *Fairy* squeezed through the trap with the help of a fine breeze and sailed up to Alexandria to warn of the guns downriver.

The following morning Gordon dispatched a bomb vessel, a gunboat, a mortar boat, and the *Fairy* to pound away at the White House battery in hopes of destroying it. But foul winds dogged the British. Their plans went further awry when the bomb ship *Devastation* grounded a few miles below Alexandria, causing the two frigates to anchor close by to shield her.

The stranded warship was targeted by forty-three-year-old Commodore Rodgers, a man so fearsome-looking that his wife-to-be thought "he must be a man of violent temper."[19] He had once looked over a rundown ship and pronounced it "as little like a man-of-war as I am like a saint."[20] And when war came he threatened to banish crewmen unwilling to die by his side.[21] Assigned by the navy secretary to harass the retreating British, Rodgers plowed down the Potomac in his gig on the morning of 3 September, followed by three small fire ships protected by four barges manned with about sixty seamen armed with muskets. He was confident the fiery hulls would ram at least two ships, but the wind dropped as the lead warship came within musket range. At the same time, British sailors rowed their barges toward the Americans, towed the flaming craft out of harm's way, and chased the assailants back up the Potomac with blasts from heavy guns.

At 7 A.M. the next day, Rodgers had to burn one fire vessel to prevent its capture. He ordered all other craft to turn tail in the face of overwhelming numbers of enemy barges. The pilots of Rodgers's burning vessels had to jump overboard to avoid being burned alive.[22]

When the winds picked up, the foreign fleet passed the ruins of Fort

Warburton and sailed down to within range of Porter's White House battery and Hungerford's camp guarding the rear against a possible landing. They rained down a day-long shower of rockets and 14-inch bombs. Shells fell near or burst over the battery, but others dropped harmlessly off target or out of range. In time the Americans lost their fear of the rockets. Some of them took to throwing sand and earth over the flames and black smoke. Then they playfully carried the balls of reddish brimstone in their hands, until one rocket exploded, tearing the sheet-iron cylinder into shreds.

Thomas Brown, one of Hungerford's aides, was delivering a message on foot when caught in the afternoon barrage. He was only twenty paces away from one shell which hit the ground with such force that it threw up clods of earth as large as barrels of flour. As he turned he saw another ball slam into a young boy's hip. Only his backbone prevented his being cut in half. The boy, who had befriended the troops in Alexandria, was the youngest fatality.

Hungerford was dictating a letter as he sat on a pile of mattresses in his marquee when an orderly shouted, "Ball coming!" The general threw himself to the ground and turned pale when he saw it cut through the tent at the exact spot where he had been sitting. Later that day he was riding with subordinates toward the White House battery when a bomb exploded high overhead. They charged for the cover of an oak, but a large shell fragment fell through the tree, slicing branches before landing between the trunk and the general's horse. "Well, I really believe they intend to kill me," said Hungerford.[23]

Some of the Americans were so worn out by lack of sleep that they became oblivious to the dangers. Thomas Brown had fallen asleep in a stockyard next to the White House battery when a rocket streaked in and set fire to a stack of straw. He was so tired that he fell asleep in the pandemonium of more incoming rockets and soldiers trying desperately to squelch the flames. When he awoke in the morning Brown was horrified to discover bales of smoldering straw where he had collapsed for "the best night's sleep."[24]

The broadsides continued against the White House battery for four days as Porter's unit fired beneath a white flag emblazoned with the words "Free Trade and Sailors' Rights." Noise from the cannons carried all the way up to Georgetown.[25] Smoke from the booming guns was so thick that at times it obscured the combatants until the wind cleared the air. Streams of incoming cannon shot, grape, and canister seemed like hail to Richard Norton, a volunteer in the Independent Blues attached to General Young's militia brigade. He was surprised at how soon he got accustomed to the terrifying screech and whine. "I never knew what it was to hear the whistling of cannon balls and shells," he remembered. "At first it was not very agreeable music to a raw soldier like myself but custom soon makes everything familiar to us."[26] While cannonballs severed pine trees, Norton's group rushed down the slopes to block incoming barges, but the British had second thoughts and turned around.

On Tuesday, 6 September, the squadron prepared to slip downriver with a fair wind about noon. A pair of British frigates opened up with deafening volleys for more than an hour. So many shot, shells, and rockets fell among Hungerford's troops that he could not redeploy them as British ships slipped away behind the anchored frigates. But sharpshooters aiming from the water's edge and behind trees continued to pick off targets on the decks and rigging and behind the portholes. One company of volunteer riflemen had come down from the small settlements of rural Jefferson County, Virginia, where they were as skilled in firing as in handcrafting their long-barreled weapons.[27] They paid dearly for their bravery, accounting for many of the fourteen dead and some thirty-two wounded.

The squadron was surprised about six miles further downriver when it came under spirited attack from Capt. Oliver Hazard Perry's artillerists on a high ridge of Maryland hills at Indian Head. They were no match for the warships, but a single 18-pounder, hauled in a half hour before the wild terrain echoed with gunshot, gave the makeshift battery a formidable boost. The *Fairy* and cargo ships anchored, but the rocket ship *Erebus* drew sharp fire when she grounded and was badly damaged before boats towed her free.

After more than an hour, the guns on land fell strangely silent. By then it was night and the British remained at anchor. Unknown to them, the Americans had used up their heaviest ammunition and almost run out of supplies for their light 6-pounders. Unable to retaliate during the continuing heavy British bombardment, Perry withdrew his forces out of range.[28]

With limited resources, he had displayed the same guts that won him victor's laurels on Lake Erie a year before.

When Gordon led the ships past in the morning he was surprised that no shots were fired. Only later did Napier, bringing up the rear, find out the real reason.[29] The shortfall in arms and ammunition scandalized the American government's sharpest critics. "The people of America will not believe it. Europe will not believe it," fumed the *Federal Republican.* "There were men enough, ten, twenty times over, but there was a deficiency in the munitions of war."[30]

The dramatic twenty-three-day expedition up the Potomac was over. However, back in Alexandria officials were so paralyzed that they would not raise the American flag even though the British were twenty miles away. "Rodgers had actually to swear he would fire into the town if they did not consent to his hoisting the American flag, which they had objected to even after the British had left the place," wrote Capt. Charles Nourse, aide-de-camp to James Monroe. Disgusted with the Alexandrians, Nourse wrote to his mother, "I wish the town had been burnt to the ground or blown out of existence."[31] Others of much higher standing shared his feelings. Even Dolley Madison told her friends the Alexandrians should have let their town be burned rather than submit to such humiliating terms.[32]

14. Baltimore Defiant

*M*ost Baltimoreans feared they were next in line to be crushed. The prosperous port city at the head of the Patapsco River high up the Chesapeake Bay was the third-largest settlement in the United States. It was particularly disliked by the enemy because so many of the fast clipper ships, known as privateers, had set sail from there to earn prize money from the capture of British ships. Even before British troops crossed the Atlantic, a London newspaper had reported they would "in all probability" target Washington, Philadelphia, or Baltimore, "but more particularly Baltimore."[1]

Though the city was still firmly controlled by Republicans, it no longer held sway over state government. Marylanders had been so horrified by the excesses of the Baltimore mobs in the riots of 1812 that they had voted in a majority of Federalist Party members to run the state legislature. Montgomery County had even elected to Congress the principal target of the mob's wrath, Alexander Contee Hanson, the outspoken editor of the *Federal Republican and Commercial Gazette*. But with the war now into its third year, fratricide had given way to a grudging alliance against the nation's common enemy.

Those Baltimoreans who could afford it fled to safer havens in the countryside and even beyond the Maryland borders. It now seemed as if the year before had been nothing less than a dress rehearsal for the looming disaster. Then, the British had sailed upriver and blockaded Baltimore, idling her ships, strangling her international trade, and scattering wealthier residents too fearful to stay put.[2]

When it was learned that the nation's capital had fallen, many were so disheartened that it seemed they would not even defend themselves.[3] Baltimore was a sad and frightened city, resigned to a dismal fate. Joseph Nicholson, chief judge of the Maryland Court of Appeals and a brother-in-law of Francis Scott Key, was so appalled by defeatist talk that he demanded better leadership. "For God's sake let us have a commander who has nerve and judgment," he wrote to Navy Secretary Jones, whom he knew from a decade earlier when they were both members of the Seventh Congress. The forty-four-year-old Nicholson had returned to Baltimore from New York the day after the capture of Washington. Despite a high fever, he spent the next three days alternating between his home and Fort McHenry, about two miles south of the city, clamped to the tip of a peninsula, where he commanded a volunteer company of artillerymen. Those seventy-two hours had convinced him that "there has been a deliberate plan to surrender it [Baltimore] without a struggle, and if General Ross had marched to this place instead of to Patuxent he would have been master of our city with even less trouble than he had at Washington."[4]

Others shared Nicholson's feelings. Pvt. David Winchester pictured only the worst scenario. The day after the battle of Bladensburg, he expected to get word that the British were marching on Baltimore. "If they do," he wrote to his brother, Gen. James Winchester in Tennessee, "we are gone. We have not a single company of regulars, either here or in our vicinity."[5] One marine arriving soon after the battle of Bladensburg expected to see a white flag flying over the city. "When we got to Baltimore the citizens had not determined to defend the town," Lt. John Harris wrote to a friend. "I believe had not Commodore Rodgers and his crew arrived there as soon as they did they would have capitulated."[6]

Rodgers, like others, had received a flurry of fast-changing orders directing him to hurry from Philadelphia to the defense of Baltimore the day the British landed at Benedict. Then Jones had sent him down to Bladensburg "to preserve the national capital from the ruthless hands of our vengeful foe."[7] But overlapping orders had left him stranded at Elkton, Maryland, during the battle of Bladensburg, to the dismay of the navy secretary. "Undoubtedly you would have turned the scale," Jones wrote to him four days after the battle. "You would have had the glory of saving the capital."[8]

The day after the battle, Rodgers returned to Baltimore and immediately took command of twelve hundred sailors and marines. The presence of such a redoubtable man was like a whiff of ammonia to the dispirited citizenry, and within forty-eight hours a dramatic change of mood overtook the city. "The citizens have recovered from their panic," Captain Porter informed the navy secretary.[9] Rodgers generated confidence because he thought the city now had muscle to flex. "Even in our present state I do not think the enemy dare attack us," he confided to his wife in his untidy scrawl.[10] Yet the commodore had no illusions about the stakes. If Baltimore fell, then Philadelphia was next, something he felt was "dreadful to ruminate on."

Less than four days after his arrival, Rodgers thinned his own ranks by sending Porter scurrying down to Washington with one hundred seamen and marines to protect government leaders and guard against "petty warfare which frequently takes place in the environs after sacking a town."[11] The very next day Rodgers himself was gone, pulled out with seven hundred of his men to jab at and even hopefully burn British ships departing Alexandria.[12]

Though vast numbers of troops streamed into Baltimore, nearly all were far below the caliber of Rodgers's departing force. George Hoffman, who had survived the battle of Bladensburg and watched the flames leap from Washington as he headed north toward Montgomery Court House, arrived footsore in Baltimore on the evening of Saturday, 27 August. The pathetic American performance at Bladensburg gnawed at him. He felt cheated at not having been given the chance of taking on the British at Washington. Though the movements of the British were uncertain, Hoffman watched American troop strength swell to his bloated estimate of twenty-five thousand. He was obsessed, however, with his own dire need for money. Hoffman had to pay cash for everything he bought, and as he did not anticipate being paid by the military at the end of sixty days, he pleaded with his father, "Be so good as to send me about $20. If I live, gratitude will reward you. If not, you will consider it trifling as a parting gift."[13]

Brig. Gen. Thomas Forman, commanding the 1st Infantry Brigade of Maryland militia, arrived the same day as Hoffman in a town which looked "gloomy and distressing."[14] Although he rode in with just one hundred cavalry and a body of troops, two days later he was confident of shortly being in command of as many as twelve hundred imminent arrivals from Cecil, Harford, Delaware, and Anne Arundel Counties and from the town of Annapolis. Little did he know how badly clothed some of them would be. Three weeks later their plight was so extreme that Maj. Gen. Samuel Smith suggested furloughing the men from Cecil and Harford Counties for ten days so they could go home and get shoes and clothing.[15] Forman was unaware of this serious drawback when he wrote to his twenty-six-year-old bride of only three months, on the eve of their arrival.[16] "The force at this place will soon be very great. Troops are flocking in from all points," Forman wrote, so overblown with confidence that he did not think the British would dare attack Baltimore. "I am certain that they will never willingly meet anything like an equal force." So high was his morale that he did not even mind the drenching rain that cooled and muddied the beleaguered city.[17]

Baltimore's Committee of Vigilance and Safety, hastily formed the day the British entered Washington, convened daily. Made up of representatives of the city's wards and precincts under the chairmanship of Mayor Edward Johnson, it acted boldly to quash the panic and impose discipline. One of its first moves was to endorse a call from four distinguished military officers for the appointment of General Smith as overall commander of the city's defense forces.[18] A popular choice, the sixty-two-year-old Smith had served with distinction in the Revolutionary War, receiving a vote of thanks and a sword from Congress for keeping the enemy at bay for over a month while commanding Fort Mifflin near Philadelphia. The son of a wealthy merchant, Smith had made his own fortune in land speculation. His popularity and prominence in Baltimore had won him five terms in the House of Representatives, then a seat in the U.S. Senate for the past decade.[19]

The committee of vigilance solicited tips on suspicious people and places, even hiring an individual to search for suspected strangers. If found, they were to be brought before, or discreetly reported to, the mayor.[20] Britons who had deserted were to be held in the jail. Residents were to surrender wheelbarrows, pickaxes, spades, and shovels at designated points so that work brigades rushing to build defenses would have the necessary tools. Hospital officials were alerted to stand by to admit as many as a thousand sick and wounded.

The committee was deeply troubled that free speech during the war might damage morale. Loose tongues could so easily threaten security.

Marylanders were urged to be especially guarded in what they said or wrote about enemy movements and local defenses. The governor was asked to remove Joseph Presbury as a justice of the peace for "expressing sentiments unworthy of an American citizen."[21] Witnesses said he had rejoiced at the government's difficulties and welcomed the enemy's reinforcements. Detention orders went out for other offenders.[22] No chances were taken. Three enemy deserters were given five dollars each and hustled out of Maryland.[23]

Basic services were so strained in a city now swollen with manpower that the military ran out of money to pay for supplies. Local bankers averted catastrophe by granting $100,000 in loans to the military purchasing officers until new funds arrived from Washington.[24] But not even a fresh infusion of money could outfit the hordes of reinforcements marching in from out-of-state. From far and wide a surge of patriotism took hold. Pennsylvania volunteers and militiamen entered the city daily. Among the first was twenty-three-year-old James Buchanan, who would be elected fifteenth president of the United States forty-two years later. As he recalled, the burning of Washington had "lighted up a flame of patriotism" and the young Lancaster lawyer found himself addressing his first public meeting, where he rallied men to volunteer for the defense of Baltimore. Among the first to sign up, he spearheaded the massive Pennsylvanian influx as a private in a company of dragoons.[25] By 3 September Smith estimated the Pennsylvanians would shortly top a thousand and would perhaps reach twelve hundred. But they were supplied only with muskets, as stocks of cartridges, bore ammunition, and even camp kettles and tents were exhausted. Other new arrivals, including two brigades totaling more than twenty-six hundred Virginians, were similarly weakened by lack of supplies.[26]

Meanwhile, the city was bustling with servicemen building a string of strongpoints. More than two hundred men reporting for duty at the crack of dawn were sent to fortify the western sector of the city, on Camp Lookout Hill near the magazine.[27] Also known as the circular battery, it lay northwest of Fort McHenry, below Federal Hill and just half a mile north of the Ferry Branch. When General Smith complained that he had seen no more than twenty men erecting breastworks at Hampstead Hill (now known as Patterson Park) on the eastern front,[28] the committee of vigi-

lance immediately hired another hundred men to complete the assign-
ment on the vital road leading toward North Point.[29]

The committee snubbed the War Department when it was told to surrender federally owned 18-pounder guns on traveling carriages. Smith was
authorized to do everything he could to prevent their removal. The powerful weapons were vital for Baltimore's defenses, and since the carriages
were owned by the city, the committee ordered them withheld as long
as necessary.[30]

With so many family breadwinners in military uniform and away from
their regular jobs, the committee looked to the needs of the poor. It
appointed a committee of relief to solicit donations in cash and kind to
help families hard hit by the emergency, especially those now lacking
their chief income-earner.[31]

Smith clamped down heavily to stem unruliness. When he heard militiamen firing their muskets in the city and near the headquarters camp, he
growled that "prompt punishment will cure the evil."[32] But a restlessness
spread among the outsiders, and they continued to waste ammunition by
firing festively when stood down.

Into the second week of September, Smith tallied up a rough estimate
of 15,500 men directly under his command for the defense of the port city
named after an English aristocrat.[33] Anxious that none of his officers relax
their guard, he forbade their leaving the camp for any reason. Inspectors
were posted every few miles on the roads leading out of Baltimore to block
servicemen from trying to skip town.[34]

But numbers alone did not give Smith the edge he sought. The advancing foe had shown a backbone and muscle that had made American
novices quake at Bladensburg. Samuel Smith needed regulars who would
not freeze with fear in the face of bayonet charges and the awful whine
of airborne shells. He wanted tough men who had already grappled with
the well-trained British killers. He desperately needed fighting men who
could give as good as they got. The American general knew that the men
who fit that bill were the seven hundred gritty seamen and marines under
Commodore Rodgers. Exasperated by their departure on 30 August,
Smith had since grown gruffly impatient for their return, together with
their artillery and ammunition.[35]

On 3 September, Jones ordered Rodgers back to Baltimore without delay. The British seemed bent on a rapid move toward the port city, and Jones knew what the commodore's presence would do for morale. Rodgers had no need of the secretary's flattering appeal to his efficiency, skill, energy, and influence.[36] He was spoiling for a fight, and everything pointed to an opportunity at Baltimore.

Once there, he deployed his men in a semicircle on the eastern defenses, facing the likely invasion path. The defensive pockets were studded with handpicked officers and veteran seamen from the lower ranks. They would be in the forefront of the battle, whether it came from the northernmost points above the Philadelphia road or from its southern extremity near the mouth of Harris Creek. Their batteries varied from a single gun with thirteen men to seven guns and a hundred seamen. Rodgers appointed three battle-tested officers to command batteries close to the shore, all of which looked out on the southern watery approaches. Lt. Solomon Frazier and forty-five of his flotillamen awaited the enemy by their three-gun battery near the Lazaretto, at the mouth of the North West Branch opposite Fort McHenry. Braced for action at Fort Covington, one and a half miles west of Fort McHenry, were Lt. Henry Newcomb and his group of eighty navy seamen.[37] Sailing master John Webster, who had led one of the flotilla's barges, watched and waited with seventy-five of his subordinates by the six-gun Fort Babcock battery, five hundred yards east of Fort Covington. Webster had walked to Baltimore from Montgomery Court House, where militiamen had stolen the eight horses he himself had illegally snatched from Washington's navy yard to pull artillery pieces.[38]

On 5 September a lieutenant and two men from the 3rd Brigade of Maryland militia rode down to North Point with several days' rations and a spyglass to scan the horizon for signs of the British fleet.[39] Even though there was not a sail in sight, their compatriots more than a dozen miles back prepared for action. The city's bulbous heights were slashed with soggy trenches. The heavy hills squelched with the comings and goings of a soaked and expectant army poking weapons toward the roads leading in from the east. Rifle pits were gouged out of the wet earth and a chain of redoubts appeared, connected by mile-long lines of breastworks behind sodden ditches. The semicircular batteries, at short distances from one another, were prickly with silent artillery pieces.[40]

Smith's experience fed his anxiety. Only a greenhorn would have been impressed by the more than fifteen thousand men under his command. He knew their limitations, and worse still, he was aware of the fragility of his defenses. The redoubts and lines had been thrown up hastily. They were shoddily built and consequently weak.[41] The west side of the city was most vulnerable: gun emplacements and bulwarks against invasion would not be ready by the time the British warships appeared on the horizon.[42]

The only stoutly reliable post was Fort McHenry at the western entrance to the North West Branch.[43] The star-shaped masonry fortress had been named after James McHenry, a secretary of war and Baltimore resident who saw all too clearly, at the turn of the century, the need for robust coastal defenses. It stood in the path of hostile ships, daring them to brave the guns they would have to pass if they hoped to capture Baltimore. Towering ramparts, packed tight with earth to blunt and muffle incoming explosives, soared above the dry moat. Firepower faced every direction from bastions atop each of Fort McHenry's five pointed stars. French military engineers had designed it so brilliantly that defenders positioned on any one bastion could clearly see and target enemy forces trying to scale bastions on either side of them.

The flagstaff near the entrance rose so high that its timber supports drove nine feet underground. Maj. George Armistead had ordered a flag so large "that the British will have no difficulty in seeing it from a distance." Baltimore seamstress Mary Pickersgill, already experienced in making ensigns and pennants for merchant ships, had obliged by using linen thread to sew a flag thirty feet from top to bottom and forty-two feet across.

There was more daunting firepower beyond the walls, with batteries lining the water's edge and even more higher up. If hostile forces managed to land they would have to overpower about six hundred regular U.S. infantrymen ringing the fort in the dry moat. With all his great guns at the ready, Armistead had under his command about a thousand regulars and volunteers.[44]

No one doubted that the fort would be broadsided from bomb ships on the Patapsco River. If the fort was subdued, the way would be open for the British to sail a mile up the North West Branch to Fell's Point, home of the naval shipyard, arsenal, and military recruiting offices. Nothing but feeble obstacles remained beyond this point to stop the foreigners from setting foot in the heart of Baltimore.

On the morning of Saturday, 10 September, Major Armistead woke up inside the lonely private quarters set aside for Fort McHenry's commanding officer. He had sent his pregnant wife, Louisa, out of harm's way to Gettysburg. But her flight had left a void and he had dreamed of her and the child she carried. Only hours away from the horrors of warfare, Armistead sat down to compose a few lines of tender feelings to his absent spouse: "I wish to God you had not been compelled to leave Baltimore. I dreamed last night that you had presented me with a fine son. God grant it may be so and all well."[45]

That night the anxious city learned that the advancing fleet of thirty vessels had reached the mouth of the Patapsco.[46] There was every reason to fear the ships of the line, heavy frigates, and bomb vessels whose decks were laden with Congreve rockets, long-range mortars, and thousands of shells weighing more than two hundred pounds each.

At 9 A.M. the next day, Baltimore's committee of vigilance met to endorse Smith's last-minute plan to sabotage the path through the main waterway. The committee named eight of its thirty-one members to seize at least thirty ships and deliver them as fast as possible to Commodore Rodgers. He would have the final say in where to sink them near Fort McHenry.[47] The wreckage would, they hoped, block enemy vessels from penetrating the watery arteries leading right up to the city's soft underbelly. Rodgers would know the instant the foreign fleet looked like it might be headed for this channel. Armistead and Lt. Solomon Rutter at the Lazaretto had already agreed to fire a single-gun signal if either bastion sighted the enemy ships or saw them approaching. In case either of their defenses opened fire by mistake, they would discharge a blue light repeatedly until answered.[48]

Having done what he could to defend against the powerful armada, Rodgers set up a last-minute ambush on the eastern hills. He had his men heap barrels of tar and combustibles within point-blank range of the main bastion. Gunners were briefed to target, explode, and ignite the pile if the British approached too closely. They would then be able to pick off the British troops in a brightly illuminated terrain.[49] With luck, the glare might even temporarily blind the enemy.

15. The Battle of North Point

*S*moke wafted from the charred ruins of Washington as the British ships idled in the Patuxent for a few days. Cockburn had pressed for an immediate thrust against Baltimore, arguing that its defenders would still be panic-stricken and reeling from the conquest of Washington, but he was overruled. A full week would pass before Admiral Cochrane reversed himself and impulsively recalled Cockburn, who had just set sail for Bermuda. They would, after all, target Baltimore.[1]

The delay had given exhausted British troops time to recover their strength from the hundred-mile tramp. Some stayed on board, others, flushed with new glory, strolled along the riverbank. A week of inactivity passed before the ships sailed down into the Chesapeake Bay. Twenty-nine, including frigates, transports, brigs, and tenders, continued up the Potomac in a ruse aimed at keeping the Americans guessing about the next target. They were spotted by an American spy keeping track of the British ships, but he reported the simultaneous movement up the Chesapeake of twenty-seven other enemy vessels, which also included frigates, transports, brigs, tenders, and seven double-deckers.[2] The feint worked, for when the fleet sailed up the bay toward Baltimore it passed the former national capital of Annapolis, where people were fleeing in wagons stuffed with furniture. Watchful horsemen galloped along the shore as alarm guns boomed from signal stations and warning beacons lit up on lighthouses.[3] The city was convulsed with the same frenzy that had seized Washington in the days before its destruction, only this time the brazen British could witness the havoc from the decks of their passing warships.

But some of the British warriors were themselves unsettled. A few days earlier they had massed on Tangier Island, their Chesapeake Bay headquarters about 150 miles south of Baltimore, hoping for spiritual comfort on the eve of battle. They had stood on the parade ground on the southern tip of the minuscule island, where they had built Fort Albion, a compound of barracks, a hospital, a storehouse, redoubts, and a guardhouse.[4] Each man held his hat in his right hand under his left arm and faced a raised platform. They had expected encouragement from the squat, stammering Methodist evangelist they had all come to know as "The Parson of the Islands." But Rev. Joshua Thomas had stunned and surprised them all, just as he had the year before when they swept ashore only to have him block their plans to cut down the pine, cedar, and wild cherry trees on the site of his revival-style meetings. Now he shouted at them, "Thou shalt not kill!" Before long the parson had unnerved some of the men, telling them "it was given me from the Almighty" that they would not overrun Baltimore. "You cannot take it!" he thundered with the same absolute conviction that drove him to preach. They had better prepare for death, he warned. The minister had a very real fear that they might "cut me in pieces for speaking the truth,"[5] but still he predicted that many would die soon. At the end of the Sunday service, some of the men stepped forward to say they hoped it would not go as badly as he had foretold. But Joshua Thomas shook his head and told them again that he was certain many had just received their last call.

The British, however, had good reason to be highly confident. Sir Peter Parker, captain of the frigate *Menelaus*, had gained valuable intelligence on the weak and desperate American defenses while attacking settlements and reconnoitering the Baltimore area in a diversionary move as Ross and Cockburn veered inland. Captured Americans confirmed that "the shores below Baltimore are left in a defenseless state."[6] Parker had even sailed rashly up the Patapsco River, where he eyed the few ships tied up in the harbor, took crucial depth soundings for Cochrane's navigators, and even captured a boat full of fruit near Fort McHenry. Annapolis was even more vulnerable. Two of Parker's officers had walked undetected in the city at night, around Fort Madison, allowing him to report that "Annapolis would face a very easy conquest."[7]

As Cochrane's fleet cruised past Annapolis, two prominent Americans stood on board one of the British frigates. John Skinner, United States agent for the exchange of prisoners, and Francis Scott Key, a Georgetown lawyer, had come to plead with the British commanders for the release of Dr. Beanes, the physician abducted from his home at Upper Marlborough. Key, a close friend of Beanes's, had a reputation for tact and persuasiveness, and one of the doctor's patients, Richard West, had ridden from Upper Marlborough to Georgetown to enlist his help. With President Madison's permission, Key had saddled up and gone to Baltimore on 4 September to rendezvous with Skinner, already well known to the British. They boarded a sloop flying a white flag of truce and sailed down the bay, expecting to find the fleet in the Patuxent but locating it instead at the mouth of the Potomac on Wednesday, 7 September.[8]

Cochrane and the army and navy officers received them courteously aboard the admiral's flagship, HMS *Tonnant*. However, there are conflicting accounts of what happened next. According to Key's brother-in-law, Roger Taney, the British reception turned frigid when the purpose of the visit was disclosed. Taney said Key told him less than two weeks after the incident that Ross, and particularly Cockburn, spoke of Dr. Beanes "in very harsh terms." Taney recalled that at this point Skinner handed over letters from gravely wounded British prisoners captured at Bladensburg, all of whom wrote of "the humanity and kindness" with which they had been treated.[9] And, according to Taney, Key spoke forcefully of the doctor's good character and high standing in his community. Ross at first insisted that Beanes deserved even greater punishment, but then he softened, saying he felt obligated to release him solely because of the goodness Americans had shown toward the British prisoners.

Skinner's recollection, thirty-five years later, says he alone pleaded for the doctor's release, which was discussed in private with Ross. According to his account, he and Key were invited to dine with the military leaders that first night aboard the *Tonnant*. Skinner was honored with the seat to the right of the commander in chief, Admiral Cochrane, while Key took his place next to the captain of the fleet, Admiral Codrington. Dr. Beanes was not discussed until much later, after an awkward moment when Codrington, in a talkative mood from a free flow of wine, disparaged Captain Porter for having flogged a British sailor. Skinner did not realize until that moment that the "plainly dressed officer" seated next to him was General Ross. As he turned toward the general, he was momentarily unable to take his eyes off the conspicuous, unhealed neck wound Ross had received in battling the French at Toulouse.

Ross, apparently aware of Codrington's insensitivity to the American guests, politely invited Skinner to join him in the admiral's cabin. Only now did Ross speak of Dr. Beanes. "Mr. Skinner," he said, "it gives me great pleasure to acknowledge the kindness with which our officers left at Bladensburg have been treated. I wish you therefore to say to him and to the friends of Dr. Beanes that, on that account, and not from any opinion of his own merit, he shall be released to return with you."[10]

But there was a surprise awaiting Key and Skinner. Neither of them, nor Beanes, would be allowed to leave the fleet until the end of the attack on Baltimore. They now had firsthand information on the fleet, the troops, munitions, morale, and even the target of the next assault. Clearly, they could not be freed and allowed to tip off their own people before the battle.

Cochrane, apologizing for not being able to accommodate them on the *Tonnant* because it was "crowded" with army officers, said they would be well taken care of in the frigate *Surprize*, commanded by his son, Sir Thomas Cochrane.[11] Early the following morning a mate and four marines boarded the truce ship, which was taken in tow by the *Surprize*.[12] But even though the two men were transferred with Beanes to the smaller frigate, both Key and Skinner continued to dine nightly with Cochrane and senior officers. As he got to know them better, Key grew to dislike most of the officers. Three weeks later he poured out his disgust in a letter to his close friend John Randolph, the unabashed anglophile who had led the congressional campaign against the war: "Never was a man more disappointed in his expectations than I have been as to the character of British officers. With some exceptions they appeared to be illiberal, ignorant and vulgar, seem filled with a spirit of malignity against everything American." But charitably, the pious Key qualified his remarks: "Perhaps, however, I saw them in unfavorable circumstances."[13]

As the fleet moved up the bay, Key had mixed feelings about the fate awaiting Baltimore. Though he loathed "this abominable war," he remembered how Baltimoreans had rejoiced at the declaration of hostilities two years earlier and "could not feel a hope that they would escape." But even if they deserved what was coming, Key thought they would probably be spared because of the prayers of the city's devout, "whose piety leavens that lump of wickedness."[14] He grew even more concerned after Cochrane gave him the impression the town would be burned. If Baltimore fell, Key was convinced it would be plundered. He believed such a promise had been made to the British troops. The prospect tore at him, for he knew there were still so many women and children in the city.

On Saturday, 10 September, Skinner once more asked to be freed. Cochrane smiled. "Ah, Mr. Skinner," he teased, "after discussing so freely, as we have done in your presence, our purposes and plans, you could hardly expect us to let you go on shore now in advance of us. Your despatches are all ready. You will have to remain with us until all is over, when I promise you there shall be no further delay."[15]

Convinced that Cochrane would not change his mind, Skinner insisted that he and Key at least be allowed to return to their own ship. This time Cochrane did not object, and they were ferried across to their sloop. But a guard of British sailors and marines went on board with them to enforce the detention and prevent them from signaling or helping the defenders in any way.

It was already dusk on Sunday, 11 September, when they anchored at the mouth of the Patapsco, fourteen miles southeast of Baltimore. They were two miles off the tip of a peninsula, to their right, separating the Patapsco and Back Rivers by widths as narrow as half a mile and no broader than a couple of miles. A signal had already gone out to the fleet: "Troops to be ready to land tonight if ordered."[16] They would not attempt a landing further upriver for fear the ships might get grounded in the shallows, as some had done for a full day on the way up. If that happened again, within range of American gunners, it could be fatal to the army stranded on board.[17]

On the eve of battle the men aboard Lieutenant Gleig's ship slept in their clothes, prepared for action at the blast of a bugle. Gleig sensed a stir, almost a nervous restlessness in the open darkness. Crude jokes helped relieve the tension. Later, as a full moon shone brightly in the clear sky, a stillness fell over the drowsy troops. The softest of sounds amplified in the broad silence. Even the rhythmic splashing of oars on a solitary boat going to and from the admiral's flagship carried across the tranquil water. The low voices of sentries changing guard on the decks of creaking ships drifted across the cool night air. Gleig savored the calm with pure delight.

At 2 A.M. gun brigs moved closer to shore to cover the mass movement of men from ship to shore.[18] Below the masts of the silhouetted ships an army sprang into action, shouldering knapsacks, clutching weapons, and lowering landing boats. By 7 A.M. all the fighting men, about five thousand, had landed on the mainland at North Point, together with horses pulling eight fieldpieces, including two howitzers. Their target was just a few hours' march northwest.[19] A boat carried Admiral Cochrane away from the *Tonnant*, and at 9:30 A.M. his flag flew aboard the *Surprize*, the lighter ship being able to sail further upriver.[20]

The British arrival had been something of a surprise because at one point on Saturday, eyewitnesses reported sighting the fleet of forty-seven ships moving down the bay. Momentarily lulled into a belief that they could relax, Baltimoreans dropped their guard. At Fort McHenry, Major Armistead allowed Judge Nicholson and his eighty volunteers to take a break in the city. They were warned, however, to remain on standby. The artillerymen had not been long gone when word arrived that the British fleet had turned around and was once more sailing toward Baltimore. By 9:30 P.M. that Saturday, noncommissioned officers had raced to the homes of the volunteers, summoning them to the corner of Howard and Market Streets for a combined dash back to the fort. Twenty-year-old Philip Cohen scurried to the meeting point and made it back to the fort by midnight, despite a drenching downpour.[21] But the long day had exhausted his younger brother, Mendes, who slept through the alarm. The following morning, as the teenager hurried to rejoin his company, he paused atop Federal Hill, several hundred feet above the harbor, and got a clear view of the British fleet anchored about a dozen miles downriver off North Point.[22]

Baltimore's vigilance committee tightened security, ordering night patrols for the city and suburbs.[23] Men and women gathered on the heights of Federal Hill to catch a glimpse of the frightening fleet.[24] Wealthier residents could no longer escape north by stagecoach, since regular service had been suspended between Philadelphia and Baltimore.[25] Alarm guns boomed across the city on Sunday at noon. It was the signal for men who had paraded earlier that morning to rendezvous without delay at predetermined rallying points.[26]

Two weeks earlier David Winchester had prepared for catastrophe, gloomily forecasting the imminent arrival of Britons who would sack the city. Now, as he watched the ships bunch in great numbers, he welcomed the contest of forces. "Great confidence prevails in our ability to repel them," he wrote to his brother in Tennessee, "and if our troops will but stand there can be no doubt of the issue being what every American could wish."[27]

At the end of the day, a Methodist minister, Rev. John Baxley, wrote in his private journal, "This has been a day of great alarm, and to some of terror and dismay."[28] Though fearful of the British presence, he went to bed confident that his God would spare the city and save its inhabitants.

At noon on Monday another Baltimorean, John Hewes, wrote an eyewitness account to his father in Wilmington, Delaware. "The British fleet, say about 40 sail of all sizes, are in full view of this city. They are actually landing men at and about North Point, the mouth of this river, 14 miles from town. 3 frigates are now at Sparrow's Point, that is five miles up this river, 9 from Baltimore." An hour later he added fresh details, underlining the words *"Invading Force"*: "47 sail bringing from 6000 to — [blank] men, unknown. I may stay till they are nearer, but not at night. I have some doubts of being in town tomorrow."[29]

At 2 P.M., Lieutenant Newcomb looked down the Patapsco and estimated that the squadron of warships which had detached itself from the fleet at North Point had come to within about six miles of Fort McHenry.[30] A short while later Cochrane dictated a communiqué to Ross from the *Surprize*, lying about four miles away, off Fort McHenry, as it awaited arrival of the bomb ships. Cochrane had been eyeing the American land defenses through his spyglass. He could see the breastworks and redoubts on the triangular ridge along the city's northeast, but he told Ross the line could be attacked and "completely turned" because it had no depth.[31]

The first clash was not long in coming. General Smith had deployed more than three thousand men to forward positions. All were under the command of another veteran of Bladensburg, General Stricker. Fortunately, part of the road from Hampstead Hill toward North Point had been repaired and leveled the year before in expectation of having to bear the weight of heavy artillery and masses of militiamen.[32] At dusk on Sunday, Stricker had reached the Methodist Meeting House, seven miles southeast of Baltimore, at the junction of two roads leading from Baltimore to North Point. Nearly everyone camped overnight near the head of Bear Creek, which ran down on their right into the waters of the Patapsco.

The army of citizen soldiers got what sleep they could in the bucolic sweep under the lunar light. By 7 A.M. the camp was all motion. Videttes reined in their horses to give accounts of the landings off the bluff of North Point. Stricker moved his troops into parallel lines of defense. Five hundred and fifty men of the 5th Regiment moved up Long-log Lane until the extreme right stood at the head of a branch of Bear Creek while its left reached up to the main North Point road. Five hundred men of the 27th Regiment marched to the opposite side of the road, in line with the 5th, but its left wing extended toward a branch of the Back River. The two regiments were separated by 75 artillerymen fielding six 4-pounders. This long line was reinforced three hundred yards behind by 450 militiamen of the 39th Regiment, who faced the backs of the 27th, and 700 troops of the 51st in the rear of the 5th. Stricker held 620 combatants of the 6th Regiment in reserve half a mile behind the second line, not far from Cook's Tavern.

Stricker's orders were brief and unambiguous. If, as expected, his front line had to fall back, they should filter through the second line and regroup to the right of the reserve regiment. The riflemen were directed to the fringe of a thick, low pine wood beyond the blacksmith's shop and ordered to use the cover of the trees while taking aim at the advancing enemy.

As the British force marched rapidly up the main road, American cavalrymen turned and rode hard for Stricker's headquarters to report the movement. But the general was in for the first blow of the day. "Imagine my chagrin," he recalled, "when I perceived the whole rifle corps falling back upon my main position, having too credulously listened to groundless information that the enemy was landing on Back river to cut them off."[33]

He immediately bolstered his right flank with riflemen and cavalry, but when videttes rode in to report that a British unit was "enjoying" itself three miles ahead at Gorsuch's farm, Stricker was livid. It was more than a provocation. It seemed that the enemy was deliberately tweaking him. He dispatched about 230 men and a 4-pounder to dislodge them. This would be his way of saying he was prepared to stand and fight, even if the bulk of the land forces appeared.

Ross had ridiculed the American citizen-soldiers, scoffing in a widely quoted remark that he did not care if it "rained militia" as this would create more disorder in their army, making them easier to beat.[34] He and Cockburn had already taken three captives in their first hour on land when they stumbled on an impressive but unfinished trench stretching from the Patapsco to the Back River.[35] The few defenders had scattered, but three horsemen sent to scout the British advance failed to get out in time. Under interrogation they boasted of twenty thousand men being dug in to defend Baltimore, but their captors dismissed the figure as a not unexpected exaggeration and merely a scare tactic.[36]

Meanwhile, Colonel Brooke, second in command to Ross, had decided to challenge the general's orders to stay and supervise the landing of remaining troops at North Point before catching up. Scores of troops were fainting in the broiling heat, and Brooke was desperate to get those who had already landed into the shade of a wooded area. He rode hard to report the change of plans to Ross, whom he found sitting with Cockburn on the steps of a house about a mile and a half higher up the peninsula. They decided that Brooke should advance only when all his troops were united. Ross was anxious to reach a certain point that day so that the following morning he would be well positioned for the final push on Baltimore.[37]

Ross and a number of other officers breakfasted that morning at Gorsuch's farmhouse. As they were about to move out, Gorsuch asked the general if he should prepare supper for the same party on their return. "No," Ross replied. "I shall sup in Baltimore tonight, or in hell!"[38]

A small advance unit with Ross and Cockburn covered more ground in flat and heavily wooded terrain under the intense heat.[39] They had now advanced about five miles since landing but were heading into dangerous terrain.[40] There was no telltale sign that riflemen from Capt. Edward

Aisquith's company of Baltimore sharpshooters lay in wait, among them two tall eighteen-year-old apprentice saddlers, Daniel Wells and Henry McComas.[41] It was midday when shots rang out from behind the trees. The British returned fire. Some of the Americans fell, others bolted. Ross decided to bring up the trailing columns and shouted to Cockburn, "I'll return and order up the light companies."[42] He was cantering to the rear when more shots rang out.[43] Contemporary accounts credit either Wells or McComas with firing the shot that felled Ross. A bullet pierced his uniform, cut through his right arm, and lodged in his breast.[44] The forty-eight-year-old Irish-born general slumped and crumpled. He was bleeding, but his aide-de-camp, already by his side, reached out to cushion his fall.[45] No eyewitness account of the next few moments has survived, but Lieutenant Gleig vividly remembered closing in on the area of gunfire when "another officer came at full speed towards us, with horror and dismay in his countenance, and calling loudly for a surgeon. Every man felt within himself that all was not right, though none was willing to believe the whispers of his own terror. But what at first we would not guess at, because we dreaded it so much, was soon realized; for the aide-de-camp had scarcely passed when the general's horse, without its rider, and with the saddle and housings stained with blood, came plunging onwards."[46]

A soldier had run toward Cockburn, asking if he knew the general had been shot. The admiral was flabbergasted. "It is impossible," he remarked, "I parted with him this moment."[47] Ross was still alive when Cockburn reached his side, but he understood that the end was near. His thoughts were of his devoted wife, who seven months earlier had ridden a mule a hundred miles over snowy mountains to nurse him when he lay gravely wounded from a French bullet.[48] The general had shrugged off that scare lightheartedly, writing, "You will be happy to hear that the hit I got in the chops is likely to prove of mere temporary inconvenience."[49] This time, however, there would be no convalescence. Feebly, he handed Cockburn a locket that had hung from his neck. "Give that to my dear wife and tell her I commend her to my King and my country," gasped the hero of so many battles past.[50]

By the time Gleig and his unit arrived at the scene, Ross was lying by the side of a road under a canopy of blankets. "All eyes were turned upon him as we passed," Gleig wrote, "and a sort of involuntary groan ran from rank to rank, from the front to the rear of the column."[51] The general was apparently in the throes of death. His body was placed in a cart which took the bumpy road back to where the troops had landed. Ross had asked to be covered to hide his identity from troops who might be demoralized by the sight of their fallen leader. However, the grave news spread quickly and his passage back resembled a solemn funeral procession. By the time the cart reached North Point, the major general was already dead. Later, Cockburn confided to John Skinner that Ross might have lived had he been carried gently by litter rather than transported by a cart jolting over the rough road.[52] The commander's body was taken aboard the *Royal Oak* and immersed in a hogshead of rum, there to swish and sway in the dark spirit until his interment at Halifax, Nova Scotia.[53]

Meanwhile, the two young American sharpshooters generally credited with downing the British land commander lay dead on the skirmishing ground. Wells had been shot through the head. Though they lived brief lives, their deeds were immortalized when the city approved a petition of their colleagues to erect a monument to the duo "who fell in the attack on the city of Baltimore in 1814."[54]

Ross's death cast a pall over the forces he commanded. His heroism on the field of battle had time and again won him the affection of his men, who had offered proof of their adulation with the gift of a ceremonial sword.[55] Even his enemies had praised his chivalrous nature. A grieving Cochrane lamented the loss of "one of the brightest ornaments" in the British army.[56] Word filtered through the sorrowful ranks of how the aloof Cockburn had mourned the loss of his colleague with angry bravado. Still in the woods where Ross had fallen, Cockburn spotted an American rifleman taking aim at him from behind a tree. Instead of taking cover or firing back, Cockburn reportedly scared him off by shaking his fist and shouting, "You damned Yankee, I'll give it you!"[57]

Meanwhile, Brooke's remaining troops had disembarked and marched together for only two hundred yards when the assistant quartermaster general galloped out of the distance. He broke the devastating news, telling Brooke that Ross's wound was probably fatal. Brooke did not record his immediate reaction, but later he eulogized the deceased major general as a talented commander "whose only fault, if it may be deemed so, was an excess of gallantry, enterprise and devotion to the service."[58]

Brooke immediately dug in his heels, pushing his horse as fast as it would go to the front. After riding for just two miles, he found that the advance light troops had halted because the Americans were in the woods opposite. Brooke reconnoitered and from a rise in the land saw the strength of the densely packed American lines, part of which were behind a high post and rail fence cutting across the main road. By contrast, the British were exposed in the open fields. At that moment Stricker's artillery opened fire.

Thrust so unexpectedly into command of the land forces, Brooke would later record in a diary his sense of unpreparedness, "knowing nothing of the intentions of the general and without a single person to consult with."[59] But he was quick to respond, ordering his exposed artillery to keep the Americans tied down while he waited for the arrival of his main body of troops.

The colonel estimated his adversary had about six thousand men. Once the British veterans had caught up with Brooke, he placed them in position for a general attack. The light brigade covered the width of the front, supported by elements of the 44th Regiment, the marines, and even blue-jacketed sailors trained in small arms. The 4th Regiment would target the American left. A mix of the 21st Regiment and marines were stationed in columns on the main road, poised to strike at the American right flank the moment an opening looked promising.

Private Winchester, shouldering his musket about thirty yards behind the American front line, saw his countrymen open fire on the left. The sharp snap of musket fire spread down the length of the 250-yard-long front line.[60] Soon the pastoral setting echoed with the thunderous boom of heavy guns. Gleig saw shrapnel scything so many Americans that conspicuous gaps opened in their front line. But he also witnessed the terrible toll the American fieldpieces took on the 21st Regiment and the sailors directly ahead on the main road.

As the artillery roared on both sides, Cockburn rode his white horse at a walk up and down the British line, his gold-laced hat making him an even more conspicuous target. Jokingly, his troops warned each other to keep out of the admiral's way because he drew so much fire. "Look out my lads! Here is the admiral coming! You'll have it directly!"[61]

Brooke had launched Congreve rockets in the opening round, but according to Stricker they streaked overhead, landing harmlessly on his left flank. One of the airborne incendiaries fell short, plummeting into a haystack in a barn and setting off crackling flames and cloudy smoke that spread to a farmhouse, stables, and outhouses.

Not long after the first rockets fell, the American guns grew silent. By ordering a cease-fire, Stricker hoped to draw the foreigners closer, into the range of his canister. But then he realized the British were out to turn his left flank. Instantly, he moved the 39th Regiment and two artillery pieces up into his front line, positioning these 450 men on the outer left flank. Then he raced 700 men of the 51st Regiment to stand at right angles to the outer edge of the 39th. The maneuver, initially misunderstood and botched by the colonel in charge of the 51st, was hurriedly corrected by junior staff officers, but the British continued to pound this flank.

Volleys of shells burst upon the flat farmland for almost three-quarters of an hour, spraying clods of earth and maiming and killing combatants and horses on both sides. Fighting was fiercest on the American right, where the 5th held the British 21st at bay. Casualties here were brutally high. Gleig, who had few words of praise for his foe, admitted the Americans here "seemed to be the flower of the enemy's infantry as well as the main body of their artillery."[62]

However, the tide had already turned. According to Stricker, the 51st on the American left flank had fired only once, "at random," then turned tail and fled. Seeing the rout on their own left, many more deserted the second battalion of the 39th, every fugitive looking out for himself. Stricker looked on in alarm and disgust. He tried to rally the escapees, but it was hopeless. He bristled with rage, every military instinct repelled by such cowardice. The general was unforgiving and in his official report damned them for their "disgraceful example."[63]

Brooke, who had been riding up and down his line making spot assessments, suddenly ordered a forward thrust. Buglers blasted the signal above the roar and din of battle, and the line moved ahead in classic British tradition, impeccably disciplined and unflinching. Without uttering a word the infantry kept measured steps, closing inexorably on the American front. Not a single Briton opened fire as they drew nearer with fixed bayonets. When they were under a hundred yards away, the long American line crackled with musket fire as the militiamen whooped and shouted. Many of the balls found their mark, but the survivors stood resolute. Only then did Brooke give the order to charge "in quick time."[64]

It was all over about an hour after it began.[65] In the stampede to flee, one American turned and leveled his rifle at Lieutenant Scott, then only half a dozen paces away. The ball grazed the left side of Scott's flannel waistcoat, then pierced the chest of a young man standing behind. As the wounded Briton sank to the ground he was slashed dead with the swipe of a saber wielded by an English lieutenant who thought he was shirking combat.[66]

Brooke later reported that the Americans dispersed in every direction, abandoning a considerable number of dead, wounded, and prisoners, as well as two cannons. "Had we but 300 cavalry," he wrote, "scarcely a man should have escaped."[67] Stricker's account gave the impression he calmly and thoughtfully ordered a preemptive withdrawal after his left flank had been dismembered and his right flank looked like it might also be turned.[68] He regrouped half a mile ahead of Smith's entrenchments on the city's eastern fringes.

The long day was far from over. Now the Americans prepared for a likely British attack at night. The hill swarmed with thousands of armed men moving from the western defenses to the eastern hills. General Winder, accompanied by a brigade of Virginia militia and U.S. dragoons, settled in on Stricker's left. A patriotic pull drew more civilian volunteers into the ranks of those already dug in on the hills. One of the newcomers, an aged customs officer, drew admiration from younger soldiers when he came to be by the side of his son, a company sergeant.[69] As the night closed in, all eyes were trained on the main road leading in from North Point.

In the British camp, the men were buoyed by the afternoon's outcome. At the first opportunity he got to write home to his brother in Canterbury, James Sandys gloated how "their skirmishing party of 10,000 men got a very hearty thrashing."[70] But Brooke's men were worn out. They always tired earlier than usual just after getting off the ships because of their lack of exercise. Brooke had won his first victory as commander of British land forces, but it was clearly time to rest. They camped over the vacated American positions, but sleep did not come easily in the heavy post-midnight rain. Instinctively, the soldiers did their best to keep their muskets dry, some wrapping leather around the locks of their guns, others using their bodies to shield the weapons.[71] The wounded of both sides were brought to the Methodist Meeting House, where the groans of dying men filtered through the night air.

While they rested, Cochrane penned a note to his new land commander. "The sad account of the death of General Ross has just reached me," he wrote at 7:30 P.M. aboard the *Surprize*. He wasted no time in bringing Brooke into line. "It is proper for me to mention to you that a system of retaliation was to be proceeded upon in consequence of the barbarities committed in Canada." This was a reference to a recent letter from Canada's governor-general about "disgraceful outrages" by Americans on the Niagara frontier, where he said they had burned villages and destroyed private property. The governor-general had called for "severe retribution" by the admiral's forces.[72] Cochrane let Brooke know that if Ross had seen the letter "he would have destroyed Washington *and* Georgetown [emphasis added]." He told the colonel that Cockburn was well aware of the policy. "A kind of latitude is given, receiving contributions instead of destruction," he noted. But Cochrane left the option to Brooke, saying, "You will best be able to judge what can be attempted."[73]

At daybreak the cold and wet expeditionary force broke camp and slogged toward its damp opponents, leaving behind guards at the Methodist Meeting House to round up and protect the wounded.[74] Along the way they had to stop and clear trees felled and heaved across the road by Stricker's men. Sloshing in the mud, they bypassed farmers and others who remained put in the sprinkling of homes. But the army felt free to ransack and plunder abandoned houses.[75] One group veered down a lane off the main road and occupied the residence of Colonel Sterett, commander of Maryland's 5th Infantry Regiment. Only the servants were home when the officers burst in. Unchallenged, they rifled its contents, forcing open closets and even dining in splendor. One of the officers, claiming to have dined with Mrs. Sterett's father years back, inquired after her and told the servants he regretted she was not at home. Before they left, the soldiers took their spoils of war, carrying out baskets laden with Sterett's fine wines.[76]

By midmorning Brooke was way ahead of his army and reconnoitering at a leisurely pace about two miles distant from the mass of Americans. It would take hours before his extended line of stragglers caught up. They would also have to be resupplied with ammunition and rations of rum shipped to the mainland by boats from HMS *Seahorse.*[77] British intelligence had accurately assessed the American strength at about fifteen thousand men, and as he surveyed their preparations the British commander could not help but be impressed. The best-fortified posts were directly ahead of him on Hampstead Hill, towering over and dominating the city. A frontal attack would be met by superior numbers of men and artillery protected by the chain of palisaded redoubts connected by a small breastwork. But intelligence briefings gave him good reason to believe that defenses in the north and west were weak and unfinished. Brooke decided to hold off his attack until nightfall, when the Americans would not be able to take reliable aim or get a fix on ranges with their larger quantity of artillery.[78]

From his hilltop headquarters, General Forman trained his telescopic glasses on the British. He could see them distinctly as they moved about on the road and in the surrounding countryside. They were too tempting a target for Forman, now giddy with the prospect of winning personal fame and glory. In a candid letter to his wife, he explained the rush of sensations that impelled him to "strike a bold stroke which would serve my country and immortalize my dear little wife's husband." Having secured permission to attack by night, Forman wrote, "My imagination soared into the regions of fame and my darling Martha's approbation."[79] But it was not to be. Clearer heads prevailed when even his own senior officers spoke out against such a rash move, and the plan was quashed.

The fifteen thousand sleepless guardians of Baltimore braced for another chilly night of gloom in the rain and puddles. Poised only to defend, they kept a high state of alert. So little ground separated the two armies that forward sentinels could hear each other distinctly in the dark.[80]

16. Bombs over Baltimore

A squadron of seventeen frigates, sloops, schooners, bomb boats, and a single rocket ship had meanwhile advanced gingerly up the Patapsco River to close in on Baltimore. Fifteen-year-old Robert Barrett, mate of the main deck aboard the frigate *Hebrus*, was in one of the rowboats ahead of the squadron taking depth soundings to warn against hidden shoals. Just in case any of the warships grounded, they had stream and kedge anchors and coiled cables ready to hoist them free. They also carried scaling ladders in the event they were called upon to coordinate with the land army in physically storming the fortifications and the city.[1] But their professionalism did not prevent numerous groundings in the uncharted channel, even though most of the ships followed the lead.[2]

When Lieutenant Newcomb looked south from Fort Covington on the morning of Tuesday, 13 September, he saw that the British warships had taken their stations in a line about two and three-quarter miles from Fort McHenry. It was hazy, with moderate breezes blowing from the south and east.[3] Cochrane was aboard the light frigate *Surprize* taking personal command of the forward naval offensive. Key, Skinner, and Beanes were in their Norfolk packet anchored well back near where the land forces disembarked, but if they stood on deck they could distinctly see the Stars and Stripes flying over Fort McHenry.

As Cochrane watched, fiery projectiles hissed off the lone rocket ship, *Erebus*, rising high above the clutch of frigates and five bomb vessels. Artillerymen scanning the bay from the bastions of Fort McHenry sus-

pected they were nothing more than signals to British forces on the peninsula.[4]

But the rockets were followed almost immediately by shots which
opened up a new battlefront. A pair of frigates opened fire, apparently to
test their range, but seeing their opening volleys fall short they moved
in half a mile. With feline speed, the fort's commander orchestrated a fero-
cious response as he stood atop a parapet. Major Armistead first signaled
a battery of 24-pounders to blast away at the frigates. Then he brought in
the long 42-pounders. Soon every other heavy metal gun was spewing
tons of hot explosives over the water. As their ammunition struck the sta-
tionary ships in several places, jubilant artillerymen cheered and hollered,
their spirits lifted even higher when musicians piped out the jaunty tune
of "Yankee Doodle."

They watched the frigates slink back out of range, but just then the
bomb vessels inched forward—not quite as far as the frigates had gone,
but enough to taunt their rivals and once more gauge the distance. During this initial encounter, young Robert Barrett was in one of two reconnaissance boats about three hundred yards ahead of the *Hebrus* when an
American shot hurtled down into his neighboring craft, struck a man
standing in the center of the boat, and instantly cut him in two.[5] Barrett
and his companion lost no time in reboarding their vessel.

Again the cannons roared in Fort McHenry, but this time their balls
splashed harmlessly into the water. They tried again with half a dozen
mortar rounds, but the barrels were not long enough to propel the shot
all the way to their target. In the quickening trade-off, British gunners
replied with shells weighing over two hundred pounds each.[6] They arced
above the Patapsco and fell with gathering momentum in and around the
massive fort. Satisfied with their aim and range, the mariners could now
fire with absolute impunity. It was 2 P.M. and raining heavily. They
dropped anchor and broadsided with a single-minded purpose—to blud-
geon Fort McHenry into early submission. If they succeeded they would
be able to plant the Union Jack in the heart of the city and trap its defenders between the long-range guns of the warships and the army hovering
on the east.

Inside the fort, men watched with dismal helplessness as they hunkered
down beside their guns. The fort did not have a single bombproof shel-

ter. Armistead watched with mounting concern as the stream of shells screeched down, but not a man flinched or ran from his post, neither regular nor volunteer. When it appeared that the giant flag atop its high flagstaff was acting as a forward marker for British gunners, most of Nicholson's volunteers followed orders to regroup against the walls outside the fort for better protection. They had already taken up new positions when a shell struck the powder magazine but did not explode. Instantly, the artillery volunteers rolled out barrels of powder to safer positions against the walls. Young Mendes Cohen, still eight months shy of his nineteenth birthday, sat on a barrel sealed only with woollen stuffing as the company shared in a basket of food brought down by one of their servants.[7]

At about 2 P.M. a single shell crashed down on the southwest bastion, instantly killing the man in charge, Lt. Levi Claggett, and wounding four others. It also toppled a 24-pounder and shattered its carriage wheel. Even as the wounded bled and winced, another shell burst over the heads of more volunteer artillerymen only twenty-five paces away. A two-inch-thick piece of shrapnel the size of a dollar sliced through Sgt. John Clemm's navel with such velocity that it cut clean through the ground to a depth of two feet. The young sergeant did not survive, but a volunteer by his side, an editor of the *Baltimore Patriot,* was unscathed. In their brief moment together as combat soldiers, the editor had been impressed by his sergeant's "amiable character, gentlemanly manners and real courage."[8]

Three bomb ships immediately weighed anchor and sailed closer—tempted, perhaps, by the obvious disarray of men scrambling to remove the wounded and put the gun back in place. They gave Armistead the opportunity he had been waiting for to strike back. Powder burned and guns crumped as the entire garrison concentrated its fire on the three probing ships. The deafening crescendo held steady for almost half an hour before the trio of bomb vessels had second thoughts and withdrew to their earlier station. Ecstatic, the gunners in Fort McHenry stopped firing and gave themselves three resounding cheers. But the worst was yet to come. No one would cheer again that afternoon, nor even through the rainy night that followed.

The barrage was so intense that, on average, a bomb a minute thundered out of the British barrels for hour after hour. Hoping for a combination of luck and calculation, the crews measured lengths of fuses expected to ignite the powder while the shells were still airborne. A perfectly timed explosion would rip the shell casing apart a few yards above ground, spraying deadly shrapnel in every direction. Messengers scurrying between General Smith's headquarters and the besieged Fort McHenry had nothing but their speed and courage to get them through the firestorm.[9]

Midshipman Robert Stockton thrilled to the danger. The greater the peril, the more he felt challenged. Utterly fearless, he seemed to welcome combat with youthful gusto. Colleagues familiar with Stockton's metamorphosis under fire nicknamed him "Fighting Bob."[10] It was a fitting nom de guerre for Commodore Rodgers's nineteen-year-old aide-de-camp, charged with blocking enemy access to the basin lapping the city's southern fringe. Young Stockton ignored the hail of bombs as his naval unit towed twenty-four sacrificial ships—brigs, schooners, cargo ships, and a sloop—to the mouth of the harbor and sank them in the channel next to Fort McHenry.[11] There was barely time to remove them from the wharves. Nearly all of them went down with their fixtures and fittings still in place. One ship, the *Thomas Wilson*, which normally plied the Indian and South American routes, was ditched with more than two hundred tons of stone ballast on board and plunged beyond the water bed into fifteen feet of mud.[12] Beverly Diggs, who had commanded one of the Chesapeake flotilla barges, towed three vessels so hastily to the scuttling ground that he did not even have time to ask who owned them. His crew sank the last ship by swinging an ax and chopping a hole in her hull. The American mariners worked feverishly, convinced to a man that "the only real preservation" of their city depended on obstruction of the waterway.[13] Stockton the teenager would win fame and honor for this and other daring exploits, which added luster to a family name already notable for his grandfather's signature on the Declaration of Independence.

By nightfall the defenders were tired, hungry, and dripping from the torrential downpour. Pvt. Severn Teackle struggled to keep awake as he manned one of the fort's batteries. He felt the strain of the ordeal, particularly the "rattling and whistlery" of passing bombs and shells. It so unnerved him that long after it was over Teackle would still groan for divine deliverance from those terrible sounds.[14] He was lucky, however, for he survived an explosion while removing powder from a magazine, suffering nothing more than torn and sullied pantaloons.

Even though Fort McHenry had now become the principal target, troops on Hampstead Hill were under strict orders to remain at the ready. When officers strolled off to get their evening meals they were forbidden to stray beyond the sound of a warning drum, and if the drummer signaled a special roll they would have to get back at the double.[15]

The stream of explosives created an awesome sight. Observers clearly saw the trail of sparks from burning fuses stuffed inside the streaking shells. Men, women, and children crammed the roofs of houses to see what one spectator described as "the most awful spectacle of shot and shells and rockets shooting and bursting through the air."[16] Eyewitnesses stood mesmerized. One of them said the roaring cannons shook houses in the city and beyond, reverberating in the hills and valleys. He compared the echoing din to "the most terrible of thunderstorms."[17]

The night sky lit up with such a brilliance of bursting shells and fleeting rockets that observers gasped at its peculiar beauty. It gave Lieutenant Harris something to marvel at as he passed the time in his dugout on the eastern hills. Ahead of him were plenty of redcoats, though still out of musket range, so he looked south to the incandescent shower of burning powder and cascading metal. The grand illumination transfixed the lieutenant. "I think the handsomest sight I ever saw was during the bombarding to see the bombs and rockets flying and the firing from our three forts," he wrote afterwards. "It was much handsomer at night than in the day."[18]

Detonating bombs lit up distant homes. Debbie Cochran, sheltering at the residence of the Spanish consul, a mile beyond her own home, thought "it was like continued flashes of lightning." Agitated and frightened, she swung between despair and composure, though she was convinced they would all die before it was over. She waited impatiently for daybreak. "I thought the hours would never roll around, and then thought if it was but light I would wish to be forty miles off."[19]

But distancing herself from Baltimore would not have calmed her. In Philadelphia, where the rapid fire of six guns in succession would signal the inhabitants they had forty-eight hours to escape an invasion, Phoebe Morris was frantic with worry.[20] She confided her deepest, private fears to her father, Anthony Morris, then U.S. minister to Spain. "My dear Papa," she wrote, "at this moment we are in a state of the most unpleasant suspense, they are fighting in Baltimore. . . . Baltimore was so much better defended than Philadelphia that if they are defeated we shall not attempt a resistance."[21] Her desperation became almost a valedictory in a second letter hours later. "They are making the bravest resistance but a letter has been received by Mr. Dallas which says that Baltimore must fall! . . . Tomorrow I shall be obliged to write the sad account of the defeat of Baltimore."[22]

Terrible rumors had already reached some quarters in Washington. The president of Georgetown College, Father Grassi, noted that night in his diary the reception of "news that Baltimore has been attacked and perhaps has also surrendered."[23]

One traveler who arrived in Washington from Baltimore called at the offices of the *National Intelligencer* to tell the daily newspaper what he had seen. His information was vague and brief but enough to prepare the public for a shocking climax. Wednesday's edition summed it up in a single sentence: "The moment of suspense is awful."[24]

Tension was also mounting in the British encampment on the peninsula. A plan worked out between Colonel Brooke and Admiral Cochrane called for a combined assault in the middle of the night, with Cochrane pushing past the main fort and creating a feint up the Ferry Branch, behind Fort McHenry. This diversionary unit would force the Americans to siphon off defenders from the eastern hills and rush them to check Cochrane's night raiders. That would allow Brooke's army to break through the weakened eastern defenses. British casualties on the eastern hills would be no more than five hundred men, according to Cockburn's estimate to Cochrane. Brooke had already briefed his divisional commanders on the imminent assault. His two-pronged scenario called for a strike against the Americans' weaker left flank by two columns who would then try and crash through to the rear. A third column would make a diversionary push on the American right.[25]

The troops were on alert, geared for battle, when Lieutenant Scott arrived with a letter from Cochrane to Cockburn. George Cockburn was in high spirits. He had just returned with Brooke from surveying the

American fortifications. "Well, Scott," he asked jauntily, "have you delivered my message to the commander-in-chief? We have had an excellent view of their defenses. Before 2 o'clock tomorrow morning all that you now see will be ours. What force is to assist us on the waterside?"[26]

Aware of the letter's contents, Scott could only murmur that he hoped it would not frustrate the admiral's plans. But Cockburn's mood blackened as he read it first, then handed it to the colonel. Brooke was incredulous when he realized that Cochrane was pulling out of the combined attack. "It is impossible for the ships to render you any assistance," Cochrane wrote. He had seen the barrier of scuttled ships at the mouth of the harbor and taken note of armed American gunboats drawn up behind them. He did not think he could breach this obstacle, seeing it was also defended on both sides by Fort McHenry and the Lazaretto. Cooperation from the naval force was therefore out of the question, and he did not recommend that Brooke go it alone. "The town is so far retired within the forts it is for Col. Brooke to consider under such circumstances whether he has force sufficient to defeat so large a number as it is said the enemy has collected, say twenty thousand strong," wrote Cochrane. "It will be only throwing the men's lives away." Pointedly, he warned, "As the enemy is daily gaining strength, his loss, let it be ever so great, cannot be equally felt."[27]

Cochrane would later report to his superiors in London that he was confident of success. He did not, however, think that capturing the city would compensate for the huge numbers of anticipated British casualties. Above all, he reminded the Admiralty, he had to keep in mind "the ulterior operations of this force."[28] It was a coded reference to the far more significant assault on New Orleans from the Gulf of Mexico which Cochrane was scheduled to command toward the end of the year.[29] Every available fighting man would be needed for that climactic battle to gain control of the Mississippi River and its rich commercial traffic, and the admiral could not afford to cut his troop strength through massive losses in Baltimore.

Brooke was devastated. Calling off the assault would be a crushing blow to his ambitions. This was a singular opportunity to prove himself and perhaps win legendary status among his countrymen. Like General Forman on the American side, he, too, had dreamed of fame and glory. "All my hopes were in a moment blasted," Brooke regretted in his private diary. "If I took the place I should have been the greatest man in England. If I lost, my military character was gone for ever."[30]

Characteristically, Cockburn still wanted to launch the land assault, but he stood alone. Brooke had only just assumed overall command and had neither a flair for the unorthodox nor the boundless self-confidence of his naval compatriot. He summoned his senior officers to mull over the dramatic turn of events. After lengthy deliberation, a majority sided with Cochrane.[31] Storming the city without help from the navy was not worth the risk of heavy losses. The army would have to preserve its strength for major battles yet to come.[32] At midnight Brooke prepared a brief reply to Cochrane. He announced cancellation of an all-out assault he had planned for 3 A.M. "I have therefore ordered the retreat to take place tomorrow morning."[33] He expected to return within two days to the place where they had disembarked from landing craft.

As Brooke made preparations to pull back, the ships' guns fell silent and a thick darkness cloaked the adversaries. Tired men huddled in the open under pouring rain in an unseasonably cold night.[34] But unknown to Brooke and to the Americans, an elite force of about twelve hundred British marines and seamen was already gliding silently up the Patapsco River, rowing barges with muffled oars and accompanied by a rocket ship, five launches, two pinnaces, and a gig.[35] Cochrane had not been able to abort the diversionary raid past Fort McHenry and up the Ferry Branch. Midnight had arrived and he had not yet heard whether Brooke would abandon the plan or go it alone. Bound by the earlier agreement for this western feint to be launched in the dead of night, Cochrane had no choice but to give the go-ahead.[36]

The British commander in chief had taken an acutely personal interest in planning the mission. He told Lieutenant Napier, commander of the ghostly squadron, to make sure the oars of the gunboats were muffled before rowing abreast of the bomb ship *Meteor*. Then he was to keep close to shore until the force rounded the point of the Patapsco River. Cochrane's plan called for the night raiders to row up the Patapsco no more than a mile and a half before ceasing all movement and keeping "perfectly quiet." At precisely 1 A.M. on Wednesday, 14 September, the rocket and bomb ships would resume a heavy bombardment of Fort McHenry. Simultaneously, Napier's force would open fire on the opposite side of the river. Occasionally they were to fire only blank cartridges because their sole purpose was to deceive and distract the Americans on the eastern hills. With all eyes on the west, Cochrane expected Brooke to pounce upon the defenders facing him. Hopefully he would make a quick breakthrough.[37]

But the lull in firing brought a quick end to the bright illumination and the return of an opaque darkness. As the waterborne marines and seamen veered west into the Ferry Branch, eleven of the boats lost their bearings in the downpour and continued north toward the blocked channel. They were saved from possible calamity only because they saw lights ahead in Baltimore, realized their error, and quickly turned back toward the frigates and bomb vessels.[38] The remaining nine boats, including the rocket ship, made stealthy headway, passing Fort McHenry undetected.

A week earlier Napier had been wounded in the neck by a musket ball during the embattled descent down the Potomac. Now he faced a potentially graver encounter. He had steered the force to a point about a mile west of Fort McHenry when sailing master John Webster, lying on his blanket atop a four-foot-high earthen breastwork at the six-gun Battery Babcock, distinctly heard something splash. Webster was sure it sounded like oars on a barge. So did the thirty men under his command, all of whom were now aroused and alert. The Americans spotted tiny glimmers of light about two to three hundred yards offshore, some winking closer to Fort Covington, but all looking like matches aboard barges. From his perch on the eastern hills, James Piper saw a rocket zoom above the location of the squadron, shedding a blue glare through the thick haze.[39]

Whether the rocket was intended as a signal or as a flare to scan the land, American reaction was rapid. Webster leapt off the breastwork to check the wet guns' priming mechanisms. Fortunately he had loaded the heavy French guns an hour earlier with 18-pound balls and grape shot, carried from a protective hole dug into the side of a hill about sixty feet back. Using the twinkling lights as his only guide, Webster took aim and fired. The splashing stopped and the barges bobbed in place. As the wooden craft returned fire, Webster took aim at the flash of their guns.

The artillery of the circular battery half a mile behind Webster joined with those from Fort Covington, five hundred yards further west. During the pause when weapons were loaded, the shrieks of wounded Britons filtered across to Battery Babcock. So, too, did the cries of others, who screamed in their distress, "By George, they'll blow us out of the water!"[40] By contrast, Napier's munitions fell wide of the mark. Even the schooner's matching 18-pounders proved innocuous in the blackness, with at least twenty shots plopping in front of the breastwork or thudding into the hill behind.

Webster detailed a midshipman to hurry to the battery behind and return with thirty men loaned the evening before to help mount cannons. But neither the midshipman nor the absent artillerymen would reappear that night. The midshipman ran on into the city, proclaiming the British had landed and that Webster had abandoned his post. Lt. George Budd, commanding the circular battery, refused to release the thirty men because he wanted them to help cover Webster's expected retreat.

Short of manpower and angry that his orders were ignored, Webster pitched in to handle the weighty ammunition. It took a severe toll on his physical well-being. He dislocated his right shoulder, and a handspike broke one of his bones, leaving him permanently handicapped and in constant pain, unable to move his right hand to his opposite hip or to the top of his head.[41] One of his subordinates, a midshipman who was a native Englishman, switched sides during the exchange of fire and slinked off to lay a trail of powder to the magazine in the rear. When Webster discovered the treachery he floored the sailor with a swing of a handspike and left him for dead, but the defector came to and crawled out of sight through the corn and cabbage fields.[42]

Lieutenant Newcomb, whom Commodore Rodgers had placed in command of eighty seamen at Fort Covington, later maintained that his had been the first of the batteries to open fire. He, too, had trouble identifying the squadron, but he was certain it included a bomb vessel and a schooner. His artillerists concentrated their fire on the foremost light craft, directly in front, which responded by lobbing 12-, 18-, and 24-pound shot. Some of the British shells sailed over Fort Covington, wounding a man in the new works going up on the top of the hill. Other shells and rockets drifted well off target beyond the fort.[43]

About 2 A.M. Napier decided to quit and fired rockets to signal his own superiors that he was on his way back.[44] As they passed by Fort McHenry their outlines were vaguely visible, and they had to endure a barrage from the lower water battery. Armistead's artillerists trained their weaponry in the direction of the flashing guns and blazing rockets, but the British were too far out and managed to slip by without further apparent injury or damage.[45]

On the eastern hills, the opposing armies were so close to each other that the men on Hampstead Hill could see the British grouped around their campfires. At about 1 or 2 A.M. the American forward pickets opened fire, perhaps startled by imagined movement in the darkness. Some of the pickets returned to base, triggering a high state of alert that lasted throughout the night.[46]

The slowed tempo of salvos was a welcome relief to Baltimoreans. Women and children at the home of Rev. Baxley had been close to hysteria ever since the American guns had targeted Napier's force. The noise had been so deafening that it had awakened the Methodist preacher and kept him on edge for several hours. "Such a terrible roar of cannon and mortars I never heard before and never wish to hear again," Baxley wrote in his journal.[47] Fearful of what might come next, he had prepared his family for instant flight should the British set fire to the city.

Daybreak revealed the macabre aftermath as British corpses floated aimlessly in the Patapsco. They drifted in the currents, some wrapped in shrouds, others in waterlogged uniforms, their open wounds washed clean by the flowing water.[48] Webster pulled in two empty barges with shattered sides.[49] Armistead reported the grotesque discovery of two dead men in a sunken barge.[50] Grim reminders continued to surface. Two weeks after the clash, the body of a British naval officer washed ashore at Fort McHenry, his rank determined by the two epaulettes still in place on his uniform.[51]

Stymied by the stoic holdout at Fort McHenry and its neighboring batteries, Cochrane decided to quit and lead his squadron back to the rest of the idling fleet. The last shots were fired shortly after 7 A.M., at which point a stillness spread over the wide waters. Aboard the bomb ship *Volcano*, pennants were hoisted to signal compliance with the cease-fire. It was a welcome relief for a crew exhausted from firing twenty-eight 13-inch shells and thirty-three 10-inch shells during the intense bombardment after 1 A.M.[52]

At 9:30 A.M. that Wednesday, 14 September, the squadron sailed downriver, but the departure led to sullen discontent among many of the officers and men aboard the warships.[53] "It was a galling spectacle for British seamen to behold," thought the teenager Robert Barrett aboard the *Hebrus*.[54] The Americans, for good measure, fired off a parting shot which rang as a cheeky rebuke from improbable survivors. Seamen in Fort Covington so relished the scrap that their commanding officer reported they were "extremely indignant that the enemy fought no longer."[55]

The pounding had gone on for twenty-five hours, broken only by two brief periods when the guns were stilled. Armistead guessed they had thrown between fifteen hundred and eighteen hundred shells at his stubborn fortress. A few had fallen short, but a large proportion had burst overhead, showering the fort with jagged shrapnel. Many of the lethal explosives had screeched over the fort, but about four hundred had been right on target, seriously damaging two buildings and slightly scarring others. Armistead reported a remarkably low number of casualties—"wonderful as it may appear"—amounting to four dead and twenty-four wounded. "Every officer and soldier under my command did their duty to my entire satisfaction," he attested.[56] Rev. Baxley was a welcome sight when he visited the fort with coffee and refreshments an hour after the guns fell silent.[57] The warm drink meant a lot to the troops who had been standing in the mud and puddles for hours. Armistead, however, was so overcome by the rigors of sleepless command outside in the rain that it would be almost two weeks before he rose from his sickbed to summarize an official report.

Up on Hampstead Hill, Lt. Peter Hedges, a company commander in the 51st Regiment, could no longer bear the cold and the damp. His thin cotton pantaloons were wet and torn. He felt sick and wretched but had neither a blanket nor a great coat to keep himself warm. Like others in his company, Hedges had hardly slept since marching down the peninsula two days earlier. Now, at about the same time Fort McHenry fired its parting shot at the retreating warships, Lt. Col. Henry Amey denied Hedges's request for permission to go home for a change of clothing. The colonel had turned down others and would not make an exception, especially since the 51st Regiment was drawn up to block the British, whom he erroneously thought were then camped near Murray's Tavern on the Philadelphia road. Damning the consequences, Lieutenant Hedges stole off home instead of going back to his post. His absence might have gone unnoticed had orders not come down less than an hour later for the regiment to march into town for a dismissal ceremony at 2 P.M. He was a marked man, and at his court-martial eight weeks later he was found guilty of disobeying orders and summarily cashiered.[58]

Hedges was not the only officer to fall prey to the brutalizing effects of cold sleepless nights on the wet earth, with scant food and inadequate clothing. Like most of the men on Hampstead Hill, Joshua Turner, a newly commissioned lieutenant, was unused to the hardships of front-line warfare and quick to succumb to the challenge. About noon on Tuesday, 13 September, Turner had returned to his battalion of the 1st Regiment after a volunteer stint as forward picket. He felt queasy, chilled to the bone, and physically drained. Turner was so fixated with the need to go home and slump on his bed, then shave, change into clean clothing, and eat a good meal that even though given permission to hurry off for a short while to his boardinghouse a quarter of a mile away, he stretched it out until the following morning. A night of good sleep cost him a lifetime of shame when a court-martial sentenced him to be stripped of his rank and thrown out of the military for disobeying orders.[59]

Civilians were also bleary-eyed and worn out on the morning of Wednesday, 14 September. Debbie Cochran had not slept since midnight and hoped she would never again have to go through the horrors she had just survived. She was tired and feeling "badly" until she looked out toward the beleaguered forts and saw the Stars and Stripes still flying above each of them. It boosted her spirits to such heights that at breakfast she overrode objections and insisted on going into Baltimore to visit relatives and friends.[60]

17. The Birth of an Anthem

*J*ohn Skinner and Francis Scott Key had spent the night on the deck of their ship trying to guess at possible damage to Fort McHenry. They monitored shells by listening raptly after each firing to hear whether it was followed by an explosion. So long as the bombardment continued, they knew the fort had not fallen. The exhausting vigil held hour after hour. But when the shelling slackened in the darkness before dawn, they did not know whether Fort McHenry had surrendered or whether the bombardment had been abandoned. Nervously pacing the wet deck and constantly looking at their watches to see how long they had to wait for daylight, the two men futilely trained their glasses on the darkened fort to see whose flag flew above the ramparts. Then the light quickened, and as the breeze cleared away the mist, Key marveled. A gigantic star-spangled banner flew conspicuously above the fort. "Our flag was still there!" he later told Roger Taney, his brother-in-law.[1]

The night had been calamitous for the British. They had been punished and beaten back. Americans, by contrast, could hold their heads high as the new day dawned. They had refused to yield, heroically withstanding a full day and long night of sustained terror and frightening blasts without protective cover. The flag flew triumphantly over the fort, fluttering with a new sheen to its glory. Never before had Francis Scott Key looked with such reverence upon the symbol of his country. The patriot within him swelled with pride. He was overcome by a profound need to pay tribute to the gallant defenders. As Key focused on the red, white, and blue cloth, words and phrases tumbled through his mind. He took a letter out of his pocket and began to scribble on the back. Under the sway of an inner compulsion, he tried to record instant sensations, fearful that he might never recapture their intensity once the historic moment had passed. He jotted down lines of poetry and notes that would help him recall his fervor.[2]

There would be time enough to craft and polish, because the enemy would not release Key and his compatriots until the British troops had reembarked and the fleet was ready to sail out of the Patapsco and down the bay. This would not take place until Friday, 16 September. When Key and Skinner trained their spyglasses on the rowboats closing in on the anchored fleet during the next two days, they saw a dreadful cargo of wounded men, gory evidence of a crushing toll exacted on the would-be conquerors. The British now focused attention on their returning land army. Brooke had led his expeditionary force cautiously back to North Point. When they had broken camp about 3 A.M. on Wednesday, 14 September, it was still raining and so dark that General Smith did not even notice until daylight that they had pulled out.[3] By the time they got to the previous day's battlefield, it had stopped raining and the moon shone brightly out of a clear sky. Here they rested, some inside the Methodist Meeting House, while others picked up blankets they had discarded to lighten their load on the way up to Baltimore.[4]

The dead lay strewn over soaked fields, their stench not yet appalling. Lieutenant Gleig saw several American corpses stuck in the branches of trees. During the battle they had apparently climbed up for better aim and to avoid capture, but once discovered, they had been picked off like birds on perches and left to rot where they died.[5]

Brooke expected the Americans to follow hard on his heels and attack or at least harass, but there was only one notable incident when the buglers sounded an alarm and the infantry and artillery did a smart about-face. It was over very quickly when the band of American cavalrymen on reconnaissance snatched two prisoners before a single artillery shell landed.[6] Toward evening Brooke moved his troops up another three and a half miles and camped overnight, but it was only later the following morning that he covered the final stretch back to North Point, convinced the Americans would not pursue. The defenders, however, were not lacking in courage. The last few days had sapped their energy, and Smith had concluded they were "so worn out with continued watching, and with being under arms during three days and nights, exposed the greater part of the time to very inclement weather," that it was useless to do any more than pick up a few British stragglers.[7]

As the last elements of the land army boarded the idling fleet, the most comfortable and preferred quarters were prepared for the wounded. Once the men were all aboard, there was no escaping the swift enforcement of military justice. Those who had flouted the law would now face stern retribution, if not the ultimate punishment. At 8 A.M. on Saturday, a court-martial assembled on board HMS *Albion* to determine whether two seamen would live or die. James Crosby and Michael Welch were charged with attempting to desert to the enemy. At 10 A.M. the ship weighed anchor and sailed down the Chesapeake to Kent Island, the fate of the men still unknown. But at noon the evidence was in and the verdict pronounced. Both men were found guilty. They would hang until they were dead, and then their bodies would be discarded in the foreign waters. Two days later, before a sober mix of crew and combatants, the seamen dangled from a yardarm.[8]

The last of the lingering British ships cleared the Patapsco River four days after the guns fell silent.[9] Their departure did not still preparations for another round. Every American military commander on the scene expected them to return. A flurry of orders from military headquarters warned that "the enemy have retired—not departed."[10]

Contempt and even hatred for the British were slow to disappear, particularly in Baltimore, the so-called "mob town" where ruffian undercurrents were so strong. Many days after Brooke's army clashed with Stricker's defenders, some ghoulish locals dug up the decomposing body of an English soldier, set it against a fence, and rammed it through with a pointed rail. Other men brought the rotting cadavers of American dead to Hampstead Hill, where horrified relatives and fellow combatants could do no better than try and identify them by their clothing.[11]

As British warships distanced themselves from Baltimore, the marine guard left Key's captive sloop. The three Americans were now free to sail for Baltimore. While they crossed the watery stretch, Key worked on his poem as if driven, combining notes with memory. By the time they landed it was evening and he was done.[12] There were thirty-two lines, eight to each of the four stanzas. Key went directly to a hotel at the corner of Hanover and Market Streets, took lodgings for the night, and wrote out the completed version with minimal changes.[13] It had no title, but was to be sung to the tune of a very popular old English drinking song, "To Anacreon in Heaven."

The following morning, Saturday, 17 September, Key asked his brother-in-law Joseph Nicholson what he thought of the poem. The judge was so impressed that he took it to a printer, arranging to have copies run off like a handbill.[14] Within an hour, single-sheet copies were distributed throughout the city to a receptive public. Everyone stationed at Fort McHenry received his own copy of the new song.[15] More than six decades later, Mendes Cohen, a volunteer artilleryman at Fort McHenry during the bombardment, said Key landed at the fort with a rough copy of the "Star-Spangled Banner," where it was copied by a number of men who "all amused themselves trying to find a tune for it."[16] When Skinner called on Key that morning, he, too, read the handwritten version and thought it perfectly described "the period of anxiety to all, but never of despair."[17] Skinner took it to the offices of a local newspaper, the *Baltimore Patriot*, which published the poem the following Tuesday. Navy Secretary Jones was so impressed he sent a copy to his wife, noting, "He is a Federalist, but with such Federalists I can have but a common feeling."[18] One hundred and sixteen years later it became the official national anthem.[19]

News of the sensational outcome spread quickly to other parts of the country. In Philadelphia an ecstatic Phoebe Morris could not wait to get word to her father in Spain. The day after the barrage stopped she wrote, "My dear Papa. What a change from despair to joy. The British are defeated! General Ross is killed! About noon we heard a loud huzza in the streets and throwing open the windows heard the glad, the unexpected shout of victory! Victory! Ross is killed! The enemy are driven to their ships!"[20]

On Sunday, September 18, just four days after the bomb ships sailed away from Baltimore, the sound of artillery once more boomed across the city's hills and shores in a federal salute to the stunning American naval victory over the British, a week earlier, on Lake Champlain at Plattsburgh,

New York.[21] This time around the port city rejoiced. It was the Sabbath, and the citizens gathered to offer up a collective prayer of thanks for their very visible salvation.

Palpable relief spread across the country, and a new optimism took hold. The British were no longer invincible. They had been held at bay. The stand at Baltimore gave Phoebe Morris new heart. She was now able to tell her father with stronger conviction, "We may yet be able to repulse the enemy and not, as I have heard the Federalists say, be obliged in less than three months to take the oath of allegiance to Great Britain."[22]

The tide had turned, and Americans girded themselves with a new confidence. But it was otherwise for the British. As Admiral Malcolm set sail with the mournful task of ferrying away the lifeless body of General Ross, he vented a feeling of disgust toward the stubborn foe. "These Americans are a vile race," he wrote to his sister. "Be assured that it is not an enviable country to live in."[23] Yet he took heart from the projected winter campaign to capture New Orleans and gain control over the rich Mississippi River trade. "So soon as a force can be sent to that quarter, which will be the case when the sickly season is past, they will find another thorn in their sides," he boasted in a long letter home. "We are now in earnest and will bring the Americans to their senses."[24]

The bravado, however, rang hollow. Britain's finest had been blocked and blunted at Baltimore. Wearily, Malcolm scrawled a joyless three-page letter to his wife, Clementina. His eyes were failing, and as it was now difficult for him to read by candlelight, he asked her to send him a pair of spectacles. Wistfully, he shared with his spouse his innermost longing. "If the question is ever put to you whether I should have any objections to return home—say no. On the contrary, he will be well pleased to be recalled. I foresee I shall tire of the war if it continues long."[25]

Epilogue

*W*ith the U.S. House and Senate in ruins, influential Washingtonians acted frantically to prevent the capital from being moved to another city. Prosperous businessmen, fearing Washington would be reduced to a ghost town, promised to build a temporary legislature while the Capitol was restored.[1]

When Congress reconvened on Monday, 19 September, it met in the Patent Office building, spared from the British torch by Dr. Thornton's personal intervention. Though carpenters had been hastily released from the military to spruce up the interior, the legislative chamber was not big enough to seat every congressman, even though the furniture was packed tight all the way up to the fireplaces and windows. The only advantage in the cramped quarters was that legislators no longer had to shout to make themselves heard.[2]

Two years of war had failed to still partisan passions, and members came to blows even before debate got under way. Congressmen had to step in and pull scufflers apart after Rep. Willis Alston of North Carolina shoved the virulently antigovernment newspaper publisher Alexander Contee Hanson, who reacted by slapping the southerner's face.[3]

When the House of Representatives debated whether to move the capital temporarily to Philadelphia, the geographic split was as deep as it had been on the vote for war twenty-seven months earlier. Connecticut, New Hampshire, Rhode Island, and New Jersey voted solidly for removal. But not a man flinched in fierce opposition from Georgia, Maryland, Tennessee, and Virginia. Just one man broke North Carolina ranks to vote with the New Englanders, while only two of the twenty-two Massachusetts congressmen favored staying put. The final outcome rested with the sharply split blocs from New York, Pennsylvania, and Kentucky.

"I would rather sit under canvas in the city than remove one mile out of it to a palace," fumed Rep. Samuel Farrow of South Carolina. "Shall we go off in a panic from a place not even menaced by the enemy?" asked Rep. Joseph Pearson of North Carolina. "To do so would be ten times more degrading than the result of the late incursion of the enemy."[4] Rep. Joseph Hawkins of Kentucky declared he was "unwilling to add one disgrace to another by flying now from that enemy who has so precipitately fled from us."[5]

As the debate raged on into mid-October, Rep. Robert Wright of Maryland called for a quick vote to spare Washingtonians further agony. He was no longer willing "to suspend the people of the city by the eyelids. Even the savages destroy their victim the same day they begin to inflict the deathly tortures on him."[6] Southerners were wary of any relocation, even if limited in time. "If the seat of government is once set on wheels, there is no saying where it will stop," warned Rep. Nathaniel Macon of North Carolina.[7]

Their opponents were equally persuasive. Suitable accommodation, already available elsewhere, would save the country untold dollars in restoration work. Besides, said Rep. Richard Stockton of New Jersey, the presence of congressmen would tempt the British to return. "The dispersion or capture of the members of Congress would gratify the pride and resentment of the English nation more than any other operation their army on the coast could perform."[8] The man who initiated the debate, Rep. Jonathan Fisk of New York, demanded they move more than a hundred miles north of Washington to be in closer touch with events on the more important Canadian war front and to restore confidence in government by northern and eastern creditors.[9]

On October 6 the New Englanders and their allies won a cliffhanger vote by 72 to 71 on a nonbinding resolution to leave Washington. Then a formal bill was drawn up, calling for temporary removal to Philadelphia within twenty days of approval. A vote on the first reading passed with 79 in favor and 76 against. But when the votes were called for a decisive third and final reading, the room was jammed with slightly more members. Their votes tipped the balance in favor of the southerners and their allies, who triumphed by 83 to 74.[10] If just five of them had voted the other way, the northerners would have won. But the measure was never taken up in the Senate, and even if both houses of Congress had voted to reassemble in Philadelphia they would not have been able to muster the necessary two-thirds majority to override an expected presidential veto.[11] Washington, though charred and humbled, had won a reprieve from the people's representatives. It would remain the seat of government, even during the lowest point of its esteem.

At 4 P.M. on Christmas Eve 1814, five American peace commissioners arrived at the splendidly refurbished living quarters of a former Carthusian monastery in the Belgian city of Ghent. They were greeted stiffly by Adm. Lord Gambier and the other two British delegates to the peace talks, begun in the medieval seaport almost five months earlier. John Quincy Adams, the American leader, together with Henry Clay, Albert Gallatin, James Bayard, and Jonathan Russell, listened intently as the three-thousand-word peace treaty was read aloud to make sure the text was identical in each side's set of triplicate copies. After minor corrections, the eight men put their signatures to a "Treaty of Peace and Amity" between their countries and shook hands.

After two and a half years, the war was over. All that was missing was the approval of their governments and the signatures of the Prince Regent and President Madison—mere formalities in the war-weary countries burdened by costly hostilities.

The men who had bargained hard during rocky negotiations exchanged copies of the treaty. Adams, who would emulate his father in being elected president of the United States a decade later, hoped it would be the last peace treaty between the two great English-speaking countries. A carriage stood by in the yard outside, waiting to whisk British delegation secretary Anthony St. John Baker to a ship standing by at Ostend. The historic event was to remain secret until he had notified his government in London.

At 6:30 P.M. the Americans returned for the last time to the Lovendeghem House, their rented mansion at the corner of the Veldstraat and the Voldersstraat, about two-thirds of a mile south of the British quarters. The clocks had not yet chimed in Christmas Day when the forty-seven-year-old Adams went to bed, having thanked God for the peace and prayed hard that it would be in the best interests of his country.[12]

It would take almost a month for the first hint of peace to filter across the Atlantic, and almost two months for the arrival of official confirmation. When the rumors aired in Washington, the *National Intelligencer* warned its readers to be distrustful, especially since the British army was known to be poised in the Gulf of Mexico for an assault on New Orleans.[13]

But Washingtonians were just as ignorant of military movements near the Mississippi River as they were of political events abroad. An exceptionally heavy snowfall, followed by the coldest snap in memory, had cut off the capital from the south and the west. Bridges were down, roads blocked, and mail deliveries suspended over the rough and mountainous routes.[14] For weeks there was no way of communicating with American fighting forces in the South.

By the time the snow cleared and battlefield dispatches arrived in Washington, it was already mid-February. Piecemeal reports, however, pointed to an epic outcome more than a month before, the likes of which had not been recorded since England's King Henry V battled the French at Agincourt. At New Orleans one side had been almost wiped out in a battlefield left sticky with blood and heavy with corpses. The victors, barely scratched, were stunned by the lopsided result.

Yet the combatants had squared off needlessly and the vanquished had died in vain. Neither friend nor foe had known of the peaceful handshakes in Ghent. The battle should never have been fought.

Guided by American traitors who knew the terrain well, the British had sneaked up to the banks of the Mississippi River, about nine miles below New Orleans, just one day before the ceremonial signing in Ghent.[15] Their arrival was a triumph of stealth and stamina, and their confidence was fully restored. Admiral Codrington had written home one week earlier boasting of "the folly of resistance."[16]

There was good cause to feel cocky. A retired British seaman had escaped from New Orleans, and would vouch that the city "must inevitably fall" based on the mismatch of opposing forces.[17] As sixteen hundred men from advance British units took positions on the stubble of sugarcane fields between the river and parallel cypress woods less than a mile east, twenty-four hundred reinforcements were catching up, shuttling in from the east across Lake Borgne and paddling and wading through malarial and alligator-infested swamps, where the heat of the day gave way to such cold at night that it left ice an inch thick in their washtubs.[18] The final stretch of the grueling eighty-four-mile incursion would take them fourteen miles down the bayous and across plantation fields to the makeshift base by the banks of the Mississippi.[19] Staying alive had required as much caution as endurance, and those who did not keep their wits about them flailed helplessly in the bogs before being sucked under.[20]

The defenders, by contrast, were a hodgepodge of regulars, untrained militiamen, volunteers, and even foreigners randomly rounded up on the streets.[21] Crackshot troops racing down from Tennessee had reached the vicinity of New Orleans three days before the British, but reinforcements from Kentucky would not show until the end of the month.[22] The overall commander, Maj. Gen. Andrew Jackson, was so feebled with dysentery that he would request a replacement to take command "when I shall be unable to do justice to it."[23]

But Jackson's own presence would energize his motley army. Fortune had slipped the boldest and ablest American field commander into position at the critical moment. Fearless and earthy, the forty-seven-year-old Tennessean was revered by his troops. Like many of them, he had been raised in a humble home on the untamed frontier, where the best education was learning how to survive. The scar on his forehead was a reminder of the day when a British officer had struck the fourteen-year-old Jackson with a sword after the boy refused to clean his boots. And the frontiersman still carried a bullet in his lung, eight years after dueling with and killing a man for insulting Jackson's wife.

The general acted decisively after learning at noon on Friday, 23 December, of the surprise British breakthrough past sentinels, captured at the mouth of the bayous before they could sound the alarm. Expecting a two-pronged assault from the north and south he sent Tennessean and New Orleans militiamen to cover the approaches above the city while he marched south at 5 P.M. with a ragtag force of fifteen hundred.[24]

As darkness closed in and Britons cooked dinner by campfires, the American schooner *Caroline* slipped quietly down the Mississippi. Careful to stay out of musket range, the schooner dropped anchor opposite the puzzled enemy, who thought it might be a harmless merchantman or even one of their own. But at precisely 7:30 P.M. a voice boomed across the water: "Give them this for the honor of America!" and instantly the ship's guns blazed in a signal for a simultaneous attack by Jackson's land forces.[25] Caught off guard, the British hastily turned to their erratic rockets, which fell predictably wide of the mark. In the darkening confusion so many weapons were fired that a pall of smoke hovered overhead. At least thirty New Orleans notables fell dead or wounded when their volunteer rifle company found itself trapped and surrounded. Other Americans fell to the friendly fire of novices mistaking their own for the enemy.[26] Elsewhere, clusters of men grappled in fierce hand-to-hand combat.

But Jackson was buoyed, confident he would be able to destroy or at least capture the startled foe. Within the hour, however, he reversed action swiftly as thick fog mingled with dense gunpowder smoke. Fearful the haze would undermine the performance of his men acting together for the first time, he disengaged, and in the predawn chill fell back two miles closer to New Orleans.[27] Acutely aware of the mostly amateur makeup of his forces, Jackson could not risk prolonged offensive movements in such open country against the sizable and disciplined foe. He would have to sit tight and cut down the British when they rose up to storm his line.[28]

In the days that followed, the *Caroline* and another U.S. warship, the *Louisiana*, kept the British pinned down and off balance as Jackson strengthened his position. The Christmas Day arrival of the new British field commander, Maj. Gen. Sir Edward Pakenham, gave new heart to troops skeptical of the abilities of the untested Maj. Gen. John Keane, who had been in temporary command since the unexpected death of General Ross near Baltimore. General staff officers were ebullient, rating Pakenham second only to the redoubtable Duke of Wellington.[29]

Pakenham's immediate priority was to silence flanking fire from the guns of the *Caroline*. Feverishly, the British assembled a battery of five artillery pieces by the riverbank and on 27 December targeted the schooner as she lay idle, unable to escape in the windless dawn. The second shot, a flaming hot ball of metal, punched through the ship's main hold under her cables. Successive fiery rounds knocked down the bulwarks and lodged in the cabin and the gunpowder storage room, sparking fires that forced the crew to abandon ship. They had barely swum to the opposite bank when the

Caroline blew up.[30] Elated, Admiral Codrington thought it "exploded beautifully."[31]

Attempting at first to penetrate the American flanks, Pakenham withdrew from the flat fields in the face of more accurate artillery and small arms fire. What the Americans lacked in infantry training they more than made up for as sharpshooters and expert gunners. Billowing flames sent blinding, choking smoke among the British ranks when Americans scored direct hits on scattered plantation houses and outbuildings they had earlier stuffed with flammable materials.

Determined to breach the American line, the British labored throughout the last night of 1814, lugging thirty pieces of heavy cannon through the slippery mud during a drenching downpour. By 4 A.M. they had put together six batteries a mere three hundred yards from Jackson's defenses. Then they waited.

As the early-morning mist cleared on New Year's Day 1815, British expeditionary troops could clearly see festive Americans dressed in civilian clothes, apparently celebrating with musicians below colorful floating streamers. But when the guns boomed the British once again failed to intimidate or blast their way through. Their vaunted artillerymen wasted most rounds by firing too high.[32] By contrast, the Americans found their targets with impeccable range. With his forces also under bombardment from the *Louisiana's* long guns firing from the furthest bank of the Mississippi, Pakenham had little option but to fall back again.

Five days later the British were revitalized, their numbers swollen by the anticipated arrival of Maj. Gen. Sir John Lambert at the head of sixteen hundred reinforcements from the 7th and 43rd Regiments. Pakenham's purposeful wait was at an end. On 7 January he gave the go-ahead for a plan so bold and innovative that if all went well the Union Jack might fly above New Orleans by sunset the following day.

Success depended on whether they could widen the canal leading across a neck of land from the bayou to the Mississippi, allowing boats to be physically hauled down to the river, to ferry fourteen hundred men across to the other side. Their goal would be to capture the American guns and turn them on Jackson's right flank while Pakenham's main force overran the distracted front line. In a rare departure from his habit of standing aside and giving free rein to the army's field commanders, Admiral Cochrane personally suggested carving the channel broad enough to drag the boats through.[33]

It was a herculean undertaking. Four companies of soldiers and seamen dug by day and by night, shoveling with backbreaking effort. American reconnaissance, however, spotted the unusual activity, and when Commodore Daniel Patterson focused his own spyglass on the scene he immediately asked Jackson for emergency backup forces to meet the new threat to his side of the Mississippi. Jackson's response was swift, and four hundred newly arrived Kentucky militiamen, though tired and poorly armed and equipped, arrived on the west bank of the river about 5 A.M. on 8 January.[34]

At that hour, on that day, the British should already have crossed the river, overcome opposition, and been ready to open fire on Jackson's right flank. But the wet clay on the edges of the canal made it difficult to get footholds to pull the fifty boats, most of which grounded stubbornly in only eighteen inches of water.[35] The leader of the expedition, Colonel Thornton, now recovered from severe wounds suffered at the battle of Bladensburg five months earlier, crossed over eight hours later than scheduled and with only six hundred of the available fourteen hundred men because not enough boats had made it through the canal. Strong currents delayed Thornton further as crews struggled to keep the craft from separating and landing far from one another. The colonel, who had planned on crossing the Mississippi soon after dark, was delayed so long that it was already daybreak before he disembarked. As his soldiers, sailors, and marines clambered out of the boats they saw British guns open fire across the river. The frontal assault had begun, while Thornton and his men had yet to tackle their own target four miles off. General staff officers would later murmur among themselves that Pakenham had been recklessly impatient and should not have launched his attack until Thornton was securely in position.[36]

The main army on the east bank now stretched out on the plantation field, prepared to charge the thousand-yard-long defenses. Their most formidable obstacle would be the four-foot-deep Rodriguez canal running the length of the American line.[37] Units of the 44th Regiment had been singled out to carry the ladders and fascines with which the army hoped to ford the canal and scale the ramparts packed with wood, mud, and bales of cotton. But somehow they had botched the order and forgotten the vital equipment. Pakenham, surveying his line of battle, was flabbergasted. Galloping up in the nick of time, he roared at the 44th's regimental colonel to halt his men until they had gone back for the ladders and fascines. Though the omission was corrected, valuable momentum had been lost. For the second time that fateful morning, the British had stumbled at the start.

They unleashed a heavy shower of bombs and Congreve rockets, but now they were visible and vulnerable themselves in the breaking light. The American line, a little more than two hundred yards distant, rumbled and snapped in a thick volley of heavy and small arms fire.[38] Scores of Englishmen fell in the headlong dash toward the wall of lethal fire. Unprotected in the open, level field, they could not even dash for momentary cover. Many on the right were picked off easily as they grappled without ladders to storm the makeshift parapet. Others climbing on their colleagues' shoulders were shot or taken prisoner. Yet more, slowed by wounds, floundered and drowned in the canal, now filling up as a pool of uniformed corpses. Close to the river, Lt. Col. Robert Renny had the calf ripped off one of his legs as he stormed the three-gun battery, but he pressed on with a pistol in each hand and shot dead a sergeant and a corporal before a rifleman from New Orleans took aim and brought him down. Undaunted, men from the same 21st Regiment tried crossing a single plank over the canal before heavy casualties forced them back and even out of the hard-won battery.[39]

Pakenham, who had ridden to the front in a conspicuous show of leadership, was urging his men forward from the crest of a glacis, just fifty paces from the Americans, when a bullet tore into his knee. Another pierced his body, and he slumped dead into the arms of his aide-de-camp.[40] At almost the same moment a bullet felled Maj. Gen. Samuel Gibbs, whose columns made four successive thrusts to try and dent Jackson's weakest point on the marshy left beside the woods.[41] Each time they were repulsed with heavy loss of life by the volunteers from Tennessee and the militia from Kentucky.[42] Mortally wounded, Gibbs was carried off the field. Not long after, the survivors fled in confusion, leaving behind their groaning wounded and silent dead.

General Keane was saved from certain death by the fluke content of his clothing. A single ball, which cut holes in his underpants and shirt as it drove deep into his groin, was bounced outwards by the elasticity of the thick worsted waistband of his pantaloons.[43]

Exhilarated by the performance of his army, Jackson raced along the line crying out, "Give it to them, my boys! Let's finish the business today!"[44] But even as he saw the day was his, he could not but marvel at the enemy's courage. Though bloodied and bludgeoned, they continued to regroup to charge again. Hundreds nearest the American entrenchments begged for their lives and were taken prisoner. Others, in the finest tradition of the professional military, were unyielding. But when they rallied further back they became even surer targets for the grape and canister shot of the unrelenting artillery.[45] Intrepid survivors bore multiple wounds from repeated sorties.[46]

There was now no doubt in Jackson's mind that he could destroy the entire British army. It was inevitable, as he would later recount to his troops.[47] But he had hardly begun to savor the moment when word arrived in midmorning of a dramatic setback on the opposite bank of the Mississippi.

The Kentucky militiamen who had crossed over at daybreak fled in disarray after a brief exchange of fire and as soon as Thornton's amphibious force charged behind a shower of rockets. Their panic spread to New Orleans militiamen stationed close by, and they, too, turned tail and scattered past protesting officers. Among the sixteen pieces of ordnance left behind and seized by the British was a 10-inch brass howitzer bearing the inscription, "Taken at the surrender of York Town, 1781."[48]

The rout sealed the fate of Commodore Patterson's thirty-man battery at the edge of the river. They had swiveled their guns from Pakenham to Thornton but had to stand by uselessly as hordes of fleeing militiamen blocked their line of fire. Looking on with dismay and fury, Patterson would later accuse them of "flying in a most shameful and dastardly manner,"[49] but a military court of inquiry would absolve them of misconduct because they were poorly armed and spread too thin behind scant defenses.[50] With his flanking cover gone and Thornton's overwhelming force moving up, Patterson felt "inexpressible pain" as he hurriedly destroyed his powder and spiked the guns.[51] While he moved to join militia units regrouping at a sawmill canal two miles higher up, three gunboats rowed by men of the Royal Navy covered Thornton's advance.

The silencing of Patterson's guns was of small comfort to the remnants of the British army, now in ragged disarray. But Jackson worried that his gains might be in jeopardy from the resurgent British force on the west bank. His fears were short-lived. General Lambert, who had assumed field command on Pakenham's death, ordered the severely wounded Thornton and his entire force moved to the east bank because he could not spare the minimum two thousand support troops which intelligence suggested would be necessary to hold the position. The new field commander was also quick to tell Cochrane they should call off the frontal attack.[52] Thornton no sooner left than the American militiamen reoccupied his vacated battery.

In the afternoon the British asked for a cease-fire to recover their casualties. Americans began lifting the bodies of hundreds of enemy dead, dying, and wounded, carrying them to the line of demarcation six hundred yards distant along a high ridge of grass, beyond which neither side was allowed to cross. The macabre processions took so long that Jackson stretched the lull in hostilities from noon until 4 P.M. the following day.[53]

American casualties in the main action on the east bank that day could almost be counted on two hands, with just 6 dead and 7 wounded.[54] By their own account, British losses numbered 2,037 with 291 killed, 484 missing, and 1,262 wounded.[55] The victors also held some 500 prisoners, many with mortal wounds, and an impressive pile of about a thousand captured weapons. "Such a disproportion in loss," Jackson reported to the secretary of war, "must excite astonishment."[56]

With a sternness proper to combatants holding the strong upper hand, Jackson forbade the British from even trying to penetrate the swamps or woods on his left, or from sending reinforcements across the river, where he was adamant the cease-fire would not apply.[57] He relished the predicament of the new English commander, telling an acquaintance, "To advance he cannot—to retreat is shameful. Reduced to this unhappy dilemma, I believe he is disposed to encounter disgrace rather than ruin."[58]

In the postmortem hunt for scapegoats, many Englishmen openly shunned survivors of two of their own regiments, whom they accused of poor discipline and bad leadership. "We have a very sad story to relate in return for all our laborious exertions," mused Admiral Codrington. "There never was a more complete failure."[59]

Three days after the bloodbath, as both sides met under a flag of truce to exchange more prisoners, the Americans passed on a wild rumor of peace between the two countries. It seemed far-fetched, but Codrington was ecstatic. "God send it may be so!" he wrote his wife with an unabashed yearning to go home.[60]

With the dead laid to rest and the wounded recovered, the shriek and whine of war again pierced the quiet of the plantations. Mercilessly, the Americans renewed their shelling, even from across the Mississippi, where Patterson moved a 9-pounder brass fieldpiece two miles closer to pound the enemy camp by day and by night.[61]

The American victor had guessed correctly that the British would depart in ignominy. Cochrane personally began the extended retreat six days after the catastrophic loss, leading a pathetic line of sick and wounded, and dismal men who dragged light artillery, military equipment, medical provisions, and food supplies that had dwindled to the point where even the bread allowance had been cut in half.[62] In his earliest dispatch to London, Cochrane appeared to duck responsibility for his nation's deep humiliation, avoiding any detailed account of the conflict or reason for defeat, and pointedly noting that it was Lambert who had made the decisions to pull back from the west and quit the main battlefield.[63]

Jackson allowed the melancholy Englishmen to trudge away without serious harassment. It would have been too great a risk to stalk the foe over such forbidding terrain, with its swamps, canals, redoubts, and entrenchments.[64] Besides, he no longer feared the imperial army. "Louisiana is now clear of its enemy," he advised the secretary of war—even before the last of the Britons were out of sight.[65]

The British would never be so humiliated on the field of battle. Now the weary losers struggled to stay alive in the treacherous marshes. This was an army still smarting from the stalemate at Baltimore, which expected to capture New Orleans to redeem its reputation. These veterans of glorious campaigns were to have blackened the eyes of the troublesome Americans. Instead, the battle they had just lost would forever stain their country's enviable record.

Andrew Jackson could confidently claim that the army he had trounced "is too much crippled to meditate anything serious."[66] He had won the hearts of all and become the toast of the country. It was only a matter of time before his election to the highest office in the land.

Rumors of peace electrified Americans even before the courier arrived in Washington with a copy of the treaty on Valentine's Day, 14 February. Commodity prices instantly plummeted, especially foreign imports which had been hard to come by during the war. Sugar plunged from $26.00 to $12.50 per hundredweight and tea from $2.25 to $1.00. Investments soared and Treasury notes climbed 13 percent. Marine insurance stock jumped 30 percent in the expectation of a return to freedom of shipping on the high seas.[67] The nation was euphoric and poised to applaud.

On 15 February the U.S. Senate met in traditional secret session for its constitutional duty of voting up or down on every treaty. The scribes were ejected and the doors fastened shut as senators reviewed a mass of documents which had passed between the government and the envoys of both sides at Ghent.

Proof that America and Britain had tired of the costly war was transparent. None of the fundamental causes of the war was addressed. There was no word on sailors' rights and free trade, nor of impressment and the British claim to lifelong allegiance of its nationals, even those who became naturalized Americans. Instead, the treaty demanded they both return land seized during the conflict. Disputed ownership of a few islands would be determined by a third party, if necessary. They agreed to end hostilities against Indians and to return all captured possessions. The signatories also committed themselves to work toward abolition of the slave trade, a practice denounced as "irreconcilable with the principles of humanity."[68]

Yet the war had not been in vain. America now stood taller in its own eyes and in the estimation of the European powers. One British naval officer declared, "Though you may have acquired no territory by the war, you have greatly gained by it. You have acquired a character by the exploits of your army and navy, which alone is worth more than all it has cost you."[69]

The following day, Thursday, 16 February, senators representing the Union's eighteen states prepared for the historic vote as the question was put: "Will the Senate advise and consent to the ratification of this treaty?" All thirty-five present voted for approval.[70] The lone absentee was from North Carolina, where a vacancy still existed following a senator's resignation.[71]

Attention then shifted to the Octagon, the elegant home of wealthy plantation owner Col. John Tayloe, who had given it over temporarily to French minister Serurier during the British occupation. For the past six months it had been the living quarters of James and Dolley Madison as plans evolved to rebuild the President's House a few hundred yards east.

On Friday, 17 February, Madison walked into his study, an exquisite wood-paneled circular room over the entrance hall. He crossed the pine floor and sat down before a delicate mahogany desk, its round top covered by dark green leather stamped with gold. With characteristic precision and formality, Madison put his signature to the "Treaty of Peace and Amity."

The president and his cabinet repressed their obvious happiness with dignified demeanor, but others in the precious brick building had few inhibitions. Paul Jennings, the president's teenage slave, recalled how they went "crazy with joy." Dolley Madison's cousin Sally Coles cried out from the top of the stairs, "Peace! Peace!" and instructed the butler to fill the wineglasses for everyone, servants included. French John, the patrician head of the household staff, drank so heavily that he and a few others were drunk for two days. Jennings contributed to the merriment by playing "The President's March" on his violin.[72]

Throughout the day, Washingtonians gathered for festivities and the capital decked itself in patriotic splendor. Outside city hall the Stars and Stripes flew beside the Union Jack. At 7 P.M. a gun salute boomed across the capital and the darkened city instantly twinkled with the synchronized illumination of homes by the light of candles and oil lamps. Orchestrated by Mayor James Blake as a "rational demonstration of joy," the celebration was set to last two hours. But, fearful that revelers might get out of hand, the mayor put police officers on high alert.[73]

It was a sign that life was returning to normal.

The second war of independence was over.

Notes

ABBREVIATIONS

ACP   Alexander Cochrane Papers, Library of Congress

ASP   *American State Papers*

BCVS   Baltimore Committee of Vigilance and Safety, War of 1812 Collection, Maryland Historical Society, Baltimore

DCP   Daniel Carroll Papers, Library of Congress

DHC   Dumbarton House Collection, Headquarters of The National Society of The Colonial Dames of America, Washington, D.C.

DMP   Dolley Madison Papers, Library of Congress

FAPC   Foreign Affairs, Political Correspondence, Paris–United States, Library of Congress

FM   Fort McHenry National Monument and Historic Shrine, Baltimore

GCP   George Cockburn Papers, Library of Congress

GL   The Gelman Library, Special Manuscripts, George Washington University, Washington, D.C.

GUL   Georgetown University Library, Special Collections, Washington, D.C.

HL   Hollingsworth Letters, Maryland Historical Society

HP   Howard Papers, Maryland Historical Society

HSP   Historical Society of Pennsylvania, Philadelphia

HSW   Historical Society of Washington, Washington, D.C.

JMP   James Madison Papers, Library of Congress

JWP   James Winchester Papers, Tennessee Historical Society Collection, Tennessee State Library and Archives, Nashville

LC   Library of Congress, Washington, D.C.

MAHS   Massachusetts Historical Society, Boston
MBSP   Margaret Bayard Smith Papers, Library of Congress
MDHS   Maryland Historical Society, Baltimore
NA   National Archives, Washington, D.C.
NFP   Nourse Family Papers, Special Collections Department, University of Virginia Library, Charlottesville
NHFC   Naval Historical Foundation Collection
NYHS   New York Historical Society, New York
PMP   Pulteney Malcolm Papers, William L. Clements Library, University of Michigan, Ann Arbor
RFP   Rodgers Family Papers, Library of Congress
RG   Record Group
RRP   Richard Rush Papers, Library of Congress
SMP   Samuel Miller Papers, Marine Corps History and Museums Division, Washington, D.C.
SSP   Samuel Smith Papers, Library of Congress
UCSC   Uselma Clarke Smith Collection, William Jones Correspondence, Historical Society of Pennsylvania, Philadelphia
WC   War of 1812 Collection, Maryland Historical Society

CHAPTER 1. WAR

1. "Thou Has Done a Deed, Whereas Valor Will Weep," *Federal Republican and Commercial Gazette* (Georgetown), 20 June 1812 (hereafter cited as *Federal Republican*).
2. *National Intelligencer* (Washington, D.C.), 25, 30 June 1812; *Report of the Committee of Grievances and Courts of Justice, House of Delegates, Maryland, on the Subject of the Recent Mobs and Riots in the City of Baltimore*, 2–3 (hereafter cited as *Committee of Grievances*).
3. *Federal Republican*, 26 July 1812.
4. H. Lee, *Correct Account*, 2.
5. Henry Gaither deposition, *Committee of Grievances*, 193.
6. Quoted in Royster, *Light-Horse Harry Lee*, 155.
7. Edward Johnson deposition, *Committee of Grievances*, 165.
8. R. Lee, *Memoirs of the War*, 16.
9. H. Lee, *Correct Account*, 6–7.
10. Elijah Warfield and Middleton Magruder depositions, *Committee of Grievances*, 227, 304.

11. H. Lee, *Correct Account*, 8.
12. Elijah Warfield deposition, *Committee of Grievances*, 227.
13. Barney to Stricker, 26 Aug. 1812, in *National Intelligencer*, 24 Sept. 1812.
14. Henry Gaither deposition, *Committee of Grievances*, 193.
15. Cassell, "Great Baltimore Riot," 250, quoting *Maryland Gazette*, 29 Oct. 1812.
16. William Barney deposition, *Committee of Grievances*, 263–64.
17. H. Lee, *Correct Account*, 9.
18. William Jessop and William Merryman depositions, *Committee of Grievances*, 93, 112.
19. John Worthington deposition, ibid., 49.
20. Nicholas Brice deposition, ibid., 252.
21. John Howard Payne deposition, ibid., 16.
22. Elijah Warfield and William Barney depositions, ibid., 228, 273.
23. Hanson et al. affidavit, 12 Aug. 1812, in Scharf, *History of Maryland*, 3:12.
24. Stricker to Governor of Maryland, 29 Aug. 1812, in *National Intelligencer*, 24 Sept. 1812.
25. *Frederick-Town Herald*, 5 Sept. 1812.
26. William Barney deposition, *Committee of Grievances*, 272.
27. John Thompson narrative, 6 Aug. 1812, in Scharf, *History of Maryland*, 3:22.
28. Edward Johnson deposition, *Committee of Grievances*, 167.
29. Hanson et al. affidavit, 12 Aug. 1812, in Scharf, *History of Maryland*, 3:14.
30. Edward Johnson deposition, *Committee of Grievances*, 169–70.
31. Hanson et al. affidavit, 12 Aug. 1812, in Scharf, *History of Maryland*, 3:15.
32. H. Lee, *Correct Account*, 13.
33. James Biays Jr., deposition, *Committee of Grievances*, 145.
34. Hanson et al. affidavit, 12 Aug. 1812, in Scharf, *History of Maryland*, 3:17.
35. *Annals of Congress*, 6th Cong., 1310.
36. John Thompson narrative, 6 Aug. 1812, in Scharf, *History of Maryland*, 3:23.
37. John Owen deposition, *Committee of Grievances*, 295.
38. Ibid.
39. Cassell, "Great Baltimore Riot," 257, quoting James Boyd to James McHenry, 2 Aug. 1812.
40. Gerson, *Light-Horse Harry*, 241–44.
41. Carey, *The Olive Branch*, Abstract, Returns to State Department.
42. *London Gazette*, 17 Oct. 1807, in *National Intelligencer*, 14 Dec. 1807.
43. Foster to Mother, 1 Feb. 1806, in Parr, "Augustus John Foster," 183.
44. Dyer, *Great Senators*, 223.
45. Unedited memoirs, Isaac Bassett Papers, U.S. Senate Collection.

46. Watson, *In Memoriam*, 221.
47. Ibid., 218.
48. Ibid., 221.
49. Robertson, *Sketches of Public Characters*, 47–48; Foster to Mother, 10 Mar. 1806, in Parr, "Augustus John Foster," 190.
50. *Annals of Congress*, 12th Cong., 1st sess., 452.
51. Dyer, *Great Senators*, 148.
52. *Annals of Congress*, 12th Cong., 1st sess., 482–83.
53. Rhees, *The Smithsonian Institution*, 1:139, 173–74.
54. *Annals of Congress*, 12th Cong., 1st sess., 487.
55. Ibid., 457.
56. Ibid., 601–2.
57. Ibid., 1461.
58. Ibid., 288, 291–92.
59. Recalled by President John Tyler, then a Virginia state legislator, and recounted by Wise in *Seven Decades of Union*, 52–53.
60. "Hon. John Randolph," *Federal Republican*, 7 Sept. 1814.
61. Sarah Young to Maria Nourse, 28 Aug. 1812, NFP.

Chapter 2. Target Washington

1. Armstrong letter, 17 Oct. 1814, Jones letter, 31 Oct. 1814, and Rush letter, 15 Oct. 1814, *ASP*, Mil. 16, 1:538, 540–41.
2. William Jones to Eleanor Jones, 7 Sept. 1814, UCSC.
3. Dutton, *Oliver Hazard Perry*, 70.
4. Summary, Congressional Inquiry, *ASP*, Mil. 16, 1:535.
5. Jones letter, 31 Oct. 1814, ibid., 540.
6. George Prevost to Cochrane, 11 May 1814, ADM 1/506, No. 173, Public Record Office, London.
7. Summary, Congressional Inquiry, *ASP*, Mil. 16, 1:524.
8. Monroe to Jefferson, 21 Dec. 1814, in *Writings of James Monroe*, 5:303.
9. James Burr to Charles Nourse, 5 July 1814, NFP.
10. John Van Ness statement, 23 Nov. 1814, *ASP*, Mil. 16, 1:581.
11. Cochrane to Bathurst, 14 July 1814, War Office 1: Secretary at War, LC.
12. Cochrane to Cockburn, 1 July 1814, ACP.
13. "Too Much British," *Niles' Weekly Register*, 21 Aug. 1813.
14. Cockburn to Cochrane, 17 July 1814, ibid.

15. Cochrane to Monroe, 18 Aug. 1814, in *National Intelligencer*, 10 Sept. 1814.
16. John Strachan to Thomas Jefferson, 30 Jan. 1815, in Coffin, *1812; The War and Its Moral*, Appendix 1; Prevost to Cochrane, 3 Aug. 1814, ACP.
17. Nourse to Cockburn, 23 July 1814, GCP.
18. Nourse to Cochrane, 17 Sept. 1814, ACP.
19. Nourse to Cockburn, 23 July 1814, GCP.
20. FitzRoy Somerset to Robert Ross, 14 May 1814, Ross Collection, GL.
21. Pack, *The Man Who Burned the White House*, 45.
22. *Extract from a Diary of Rear-Admiral Sir George Cockburn*, 42.
23. *Buonaparte's Voyage to St. Helena*, 25.
24. James, *Naval History of Britain*, 5:264.
25. Barrett, "Naval Recollections," Part 1, 457.

Chapter 3. A Village for a Capital

1. Abigail Adams to Abby Smith, 21 Nov. 1800, in *Letters of Mrs. Adams*, 433.
2. Green, *Secret City*, 33.
3. Hines, *Early Recollections*, 45.
4. J. Smith, *Correspondence and Miscellanies*, 204.
5. Varnum, *Washington Sketch Book*, 92.
6. J. Smith, *Correspondence and Miscellanies*, 206.
7. Washington to Alexander White, 11 Jan. 1798, in *Writings of Washington*, 36:124.
8. Janson, *Stranger in America*, 217, 223 n. 17.
9. Ibid., 209–10.
10. Foster to Mother, 8–15 Feb. 1805, in Parr, "Augustus John Foster," 100.
11. Ibid., 2 June 1805, 114.
12. Ibid., 27 Mar. 1806, 201.
13. Ibid., 30 Dec. 1804, 97.
14. Janson, *Stranger in America*, 210.
15. Foster to Mother, 1 Dec. 1805, in Parr, "Augustus John Foster," 167–68.
16. Ibid., 30 June 1805, 121–22.
17. Ibid., 8 Feb. 1805, 102.
18. Pitch, *Congressional Chronicles*, 56.
19. Fearon, *Sketches of America*, 314–15.
20. *America Visited*, 103.
21. Hamilton, *Men and Manners*, 224.

22. Seaton, *William Winston Seaton,* 113.

23. Quoted in Wharton, *Social Life,* 163.

24. Hines, *Early Recollections,* 14; Jennings, *Colored Man's Reminiscences,* 19.

25. Diary of Lord Francis Jeffrey, typescript copy, Office of the Curator, the White House.

26. Phoebe Morris to Anthony Morris, 17 Feb. 1812, DHC.

27. Latrobe to Joel Barlow, 12 Aug. 1812, in *Correspondence of Latrobe,* 3:360.

28. Latrobe to Stephen Row Bradley, ca. 13–21 Dec. 1808, ibid., 2:686.

29. Gerry, *Diary,* 180.

30. Ibid., 180–81.

31. Richard Rush to John Adams, 5 Sept. 1814, RRP.

32. Warden, *Description of District of Columbia,* 25–26; Green, *Secret City,* 33.

33. Seaton, *William Winston Seaton,* 113–14.

Chapter 4. Invasion

1. Bourchier, *Memoir of Codrington,* 1:314–18.

2. Barrett, "Naval Recollections," Part 1, 456–58.

3. Logs HMS *Albion,* 19 Aug. 1814, GCP.

4. J. Brown et al., *Charles County Maryland,* 60.

5. [Gleig], *A Subaltern,* 6– 8, 99.

6. H. Smith, *Autobiography,* 198.

7. Monroe to Madison, 20 Aug. 1814, ASP, Mil. 16, 1:537.

8. Barney to Jones, 19 Aug. 1814, Select Committee Papers and Reports (HR13A-D15-3), RG 233, NA.

9. Jones to Barney, 19 Aug. 1814, ibid.

10. Barney to Jones, 20 Aug. 1814, ibid.

11. Jones to Barney, 20 Aug. 1814, ibid.

12. Jones to Porter, 19 Aug. 1814, ibid.

13. Jones to Rodgers, 19 Aug. 1814, ibid.

14. Rodgers to Jones, 23 Aug. 1814, with footnote by Jones, ibid.

15. Hines, *Early Recollections,* 15.

16. Monroe to Madison, 20 Aug. 1814, ASP, Mil. 16, 1:524, 537.

17. [Gleig], *A Subaltern,* 22.

18. Barrett, "Naval Recollections," Part 1, 458.

19. Gleig, *Campaigns,* 53–54.

20. H. Smith, *Autobiography,* 203.

21. Monroe to Madison, 21 Aug. 1814, *ASP,* Mil. 16, 1:537.
22. Samuel Davies to Mother, 31 Aug. 1814, in Burnett, *Rise and Fall,* 224.
23. Tuckerman, *Life of Kennedy,* 75.
24. Ibid., 71–72.
25. Monroe to Madison, 21 Aug. 1814, *ASP,* Mil. 16, 1:537.
26. Burrows, *The Essex Regiment,* 68.
27. Monroe letter, 13 Nov. 1814, Winder narrative, 26 Sept. 1814, and Smith statement, 6 Oct. 1814, *ASP,* Mil. 16, 1:536, 555, 563.
28. Gordon to Cochrane, 9 Sept. 1814, ACP.
29. Statement by British deserter James Curran, 5 Sept. 1814, M625, Area 7, roll 77, Correspondence Relating to Exchange and Release of Prisoners of War, American-British, June–Oct. 1814, RG 45, NA.
30. Gordon to Cochrane, 9 Sept. 1814, ACP.
31. Green, *Secret City,* 33.
32. Alexandria Committee of Council, 7 Sept. 1814, *ASP,* Mil. 16, 1:590.
33. Charles Simms report, 28 Sept. 1814, ibid., 589.
34. Alexandria Committee of Council, 7 Sept. 1814, ibid., 590.
35. Ibid.

CHAPTER 5. PANDEMONIUM

1. Van Ness statement, 23 Nov. 1814, *ASP,* Mil. 16, 1:581.
2. Van Ness to Armstrong, 20 Aug. 1814, ibid., 583.
3. Van Ness statement, 23 Nov. 1814, ibid., 582.
4. Stephen Pleasonton to Winder, 7 Aug. 1848, in Hildt, "Letters Relating to Capture," 65.
5. Wadsworth to Winder, 19 Aug. 1814, Correspondence 1812–89, vol. 2, NM-26E-3, RG 156, NA.
6. Wadsworth to James Calhoun Jr., 19 Aug. 1814, ibid.
7. Wadsworth to Daniel Carroll, 12 Nov. 1814, DCP.
8. Notice signed by Superintendent Peter Lenox, *National Intelligencer,* 20 Aug. 1814.
9. Blake letter to Editor, ibid., 10 Sept. 1814.
10. Pendleton Heronimus advertisement, *Federal Republican,* 7 Sept. 1814.
11. Pontius Stelle to Jonathan Rhea, 22 July 1814, Wright Collection, GL.
12. Joseph Nourse Ledger, 1811–25, NFP.
13. Key to Mother, 22 Aug. 1814, and Key to Randolph, 5 Oct. 1814, HP.

14. Jefferson to Caesar Rodney, 24 June 1802, in *Works of Jefferson*, 9:377.

15. Buckner Thruston Diary, 22 Aug. 1814, HSW.

16. Booth to Tingey, 10 Sept. 1814, Reports on the Removal of Powder from the Navy Yard at the Time of the British Invasion of Washington 1814, RG 45/350, NA.

17. Lewis D. Cook Research Collection, 1931, MS 253, HSW.

18. Patrick Magruder to House Speaker, 17 Dec. 1814, *ASP,* Misc. 38, 2:258.

19. *1812 Catalogue*, xv–xvi.

20. Benjamin Burch certificate, 15 Dec. 1814, *ASP,* Misc. 38, 2:259.

21. Harvey Bestor, undated certificate, ibid., 260.

22. Samuel Burch and J. T. Frost to Patrick Magruder, 15 Sept. 1814, ibid., 245.

23. Machen, *Letters*, 10.

24. Lewis Machen to unnamed, 15 Aug. 1814, Machen Papers, LC.

25. Lewis Machen to William Rives, 12 Sept. 1836, Rives Papers, LC.

26. Ibid.

27. John Gardiner letter, 5 Nov. 1814, *ASP,* Misc. 38, 2:255.

28. Benjamin Homans letter, 5 Nov. 1814, ibid.

29. Margaret Smith to Mrs. Kirkpatrick, [?] Aug. 1814, MBSP.

30. Sarah Young to Maria Nourse, 28 Aug. 1814, NFP.

31. Pleasonton to Winder, 7 Aug. 1848, in Hildt, "Letters Relating to Capture," 65; Pleasonton to James Buchanan, 7 Feb. 1853, Buchanan Papers, LC.

32. Estate of Stephen Pleasonton, District of Columbia, Probate Court, Old Series Administration Case Files, 1801–78, no. 3562, RG 21, NA.

33. Mason to Washington Boyd, 20 Aug. 1814, Commissary General of Prisoners, Letter Books, 1814, vol. 1, RG 217, NA.

34. Mason to Deputy Marshal of Maryland, 23 Aug. 1814, ibid.

35. Blake letter to Editor, *National Intelligencer,* 10 Sept. 1814.

36. Jones to Dolley Madison, 23 Aug. 1814, in *Memoirs of Dolly Madison*, 105–6.

37. Dolley Madison to Anna Cutts, 23 Aug. 1814, DMP.

38. Dolley Madison to Mary Latrobe, 3 Dec. 1814, quoted in Clark, *Life and Letters*, 166. The author has been unable to locate the original or a handwritten copy of this much-quoted letter.

39. Dolley Madison to Anna Cutts, 23 Aug. 1814, DMP; John Morton report, *ASP,* Mil. 16, 1:587.

40. McCormick, "First Master of Ceremonies," 175–77.

41. Dolley Madison to Anna Cutts, 23 Aug. 1814, DMP.

CHAPTER 6. THE JUGGERNAUT ROLLS ON

1. Cockburn to Cochrane, 22 Aug. 1814, GCP; Scott, *Recollections*, 3:277–78; Barrett, "Naval Recollections," Part 1, 459.
2. Davies to Mother, 31 Aug. 1814, in Burnett, *Rise and Fall*, 224.
3. Barney to Jones, 21, 22 Aug. 1814, Select Committee Papers and Reports (HR13A-D15-3), RG 233, NA.
4. Jones to Barney, 20 Aug. 1814, ibid.; Barney, n.d., to *National Intelligencer*, in Barney, *Biographical Memoir*, Appendix, 320.
5. Scott, *Recollections*, 3:278–79.
6. Cockburn to Cochrane, 22 Aug. 1814, GCP.
7. Hanson Catlett statement, n.d., *ASP,* Mil. 16, 1:584.
8. Lavall statement, 31 Oct. 1814, ibid., 570.
9. Stansbury report, 15 Nov. 1814, ibid., 560.
10. Walter Smith statement, 6 Oct. 1814, ibid., 563.
11. Sterett statement, 22 Nov. 1814, ibid., 568.
12. Winder narrative, 26 Sept. 1814, ibid., 555–56.
13. Smith statement, 6 Oct. 1814, ibid., 563.
14. Col. Arthur Brooke, Diary, 163, Ulster-American Folk Park, Omagh, Northern Ireland (hereafter cited as Brooke, Diary).
15. [Gleig], *A Subaltern*, 44–46.
16. Cockburn to Cochrane, 27 Aug. 1814, GCP; Scott, *Recollections*, 3:280; Roger Taney to Charles Howard, 17 Mar. 1856, in Key Poems, MDHS.
17. Cockburn to Cochrane, 27 Aug. 1814, GCP.
18. Cockburn to Cochrane, 23 Aug. 1814, ACP.
19. John Croker to Cochrane, 10 Aug. 1814, and Lord Melville to Cochrane, 29 July 1814, ibid.
20. Cochrane to Croker, 20 June 1814, and Cochrane to Bathurst, 14 July 1814, War Office 1: Secretary at War, LC.
21. Scott, *Recollections*, 3:283.
22. J. S. Skinner letter to Editor, *National Intelligencer*, 4 June 1849.
23. Scott, *Recollections*, 3:284.
24. Davies to Mother, 31 Aug. 1814, in Burnett, *Rise and Fall*, 224.
25. George Peter to John Williams, 24 May 1854, in Williams, *History of Invasion*, 360–61.
26. William Tatham to Armstrong, 2 July 1814, M221, roll 66, Letters Received by Secretary of War, Registered Series 1801–1860, RG 107, NA.
27. Winder narrative, 26 Sept. 1814, *ASP,* Mil. 16, 1:556.

28. Monroe to Madison, 23 Aug. 1814, ibid., 538.
29. Hanson Catlett statement, n.d., ibid., 584.
30. John Law statement, 10 Nov. 1814, ibid., 585.
31. Burch statement, 12 Oct. 1814, ibid., 574.
32. Lavall statement, 31 Oct. 1814, ibid., 570.
33. Barney to Jones, 29 Aug. 1814, ibid., 579.
34. Stansbury report, 15 Nov. 1814, ibid., 560.
35. William Tatham to Armstrong, 2 July 1814, M221, roll 66, Letters Received by Secretary of War, Registered Series 1801–1860, RG 107, NA.
36. Burch statement, 12 Oct. 1814, *ASP,* Mil. 16, 1:574.
37. Ibid.
38. Peter to Williams, 24 May 1854, in Williams, *History of Invasion,* 362.
39. Winder narrative, 26 Sept. 1814, and Jones report, 3 Oct. 1814, *ASP,* Mil. 16, 1:557, 576.
40. George Hoffman to John Hoffman, 9 Sept. 1814, WC.
41. Tuckerman, *Life of Kennedy,* 77–78.
42. Monroe letter, 13 Nov. 1814, *ASP,* Mil. 16, 1:536.
43. Sterett statement, 22 Nov. 1814, ibid., 568.
44. Tuckerman, *Life of Kennedy,* 78–79.
45. Stansbury report, 15 Nov. 1814, *ASP,* Mil. 16, 1:561.
46. William Pinkney statement, 16 Nov. 1814, ibid., 572.
47. Tuckerman, *Life of Kennedy,* 78.
48. George Hoffman to John Hoffman, 9 Sept. 1814, WC.
49. Minor statement, 30 Oct. 1814, *ASP,* Mil. 16, 1:569.
50. Carbery statement, 16 Dec. 1814, ibid., 597.
51. Minor statement, 30 Oct. 1814, ibid., 568–69.
52. Wadsworth to Daniel Carroll, 6 Nov. 1814, DCP.
53. Catlett statement, n.d., *ASP,* Mil. 16, 1:584.
54. McClane, "Journal of the Campaign," 234–35.
55. Campbell letter, 7 Dec. 1814, *ASP,* Mil. 16, 1:599. After incorporation of Fredericktown in 1817 the name was changed to its present form of Frederick.
56. Law statement, 10 Nov. 1814, and Jones report, 3 Oct. 1814, ibid., 585, 576.
57. Jones to Creighton, 24 Aug. 1814, Select Committee Papers and Reports (HR13A-D15-3), RG 233, NA.
58. Richard Rush letter, 15 Oct. 1814, *ASP,* Mil. 16, 1:542.
59. Memorandum by James Madison, 24 Aug. 1814, JMP.
60. H. Adams, *History of the United States,* 1018.
61. Campbell letter, 7 Dec. 1814, *ASP,* Mil. 16, 1:598–99.

62. Armstrong letter, 17 Oct. 1814, ibid., 539.
63. Lavall statement, 31 Oct. 1814, ibid., 570.
64. Law statement, 10 Nov. 1814, ibid., 586.
65. Burch statement, 12 Oct. 1814, ibid., 574.
66. [Gleig], *A Subaltern*, 67.
67. John Webster to Brantz Mayer, 22 July 1853, WC.
68. Barney to Jones, 29 Aug. 1814, *ASP*, Mil. 16, 1:579.
69. List of Marines at Bladensburg, and Miller to David Henshaw, 24 Dec. 1843, SMP.
70. *Narrative of the Battle of Bladensburg*, 5.
71. George Hoffman to John Hoffman, 9 Sept. 1814, WC.
72. Smith statement, 6 Oct. 1814, William Beall statement, 22 Nov. 1814, and Winder narrative, 26 Sept. 1814, *ASP*, Mil. 16, 1:564–65, 571, 557.
73. *National Intelligencer*, 7 July, 20 Sept. 1814; Madison to Simmons, 6 July 1814, in *Federal Republican*, 8 July 1814.
74. *National Intelligencer*, 8 July 1814; "Labor Lost," *National Intelligencer*, 18 July 1814; Simmons to *Federal Republican*, 8, 11, 18 July 1814.
75. Simmons letter, 28 Nov. 1814, *ASP*, Mil. 16, 1:596–97.

Chapter 7. The Battle of Bladensburg

1. Catlett statement, n.d., *ASP*, Mil. 16, 1:585; H. Smith, *Autobiography*, 199.
2. [Gleig], *A Subaltern*, 66.
3. Winder to Armstrong, 27 Aug 1814, *ASP*, Mil. 16, 1:548.
4. Sir Duncan MacDougall letter to Editor, *Times* (London), May 1861, Ross Collection, GL.
5. Wright, *Port O'Bladensburg*, 2, 21, 23, 27.
6. Robert Kyle, "Dueling Pols: How Washington Settled Its Earliest Scores," *Washington Post*, 9 May 1993.
7. The Maryland–National Capital Park and Planning Commission plaque.
8. Ross to Bathurst, 30 Aug. 1814, in James, *Military Occurrences*, 2:496–97.
9. H. Smith, *Autobiography*, 199.
10. Brooke, Diary, 164.
11. Stansbury report, 15 Nov. 1814, *ASP*, Mil. 16, 1:562.
12. Rush to Williams, 10 July 1855, in Williams, *History of Invasion*, 279; Catlett statement, n.d., *ASP*, Mil. 16, 1:584.
13. "Naval," *Niles' Weekly Register*, 2 Apr. 1814.

14. Graves, *Congreve and the Rocket's Red Glare*, 9.

15. H. Smith, *Autobiography*, 199.

16. Scott, *Recollections*, 3:286.

17. William Elliott to William Thornton, 11 Mar. 1815, William Thornton Papers, LC.

18. [Gleig], *A Subaltern*, 71.

19. "The Triumphant Mob . . . Victorious British Army," *Federal Republican*, 2 Sept. 1814.

20. H. Smith, *Autobiography*, 199.

21. Elting, *Military Uniforms*, 2:68.

22. Knox letter to unidentified recipient, 23 Nov. 1814, in [Gubbins], *85th King's*, 153.

23. *Narrative of the Battle of Bladensburg*, 8.

24. Henry Fulford, 26 Aug. 1814, in Marine, *British Invasion of Maryland*, 114.

25. Pinkney statement, 16 Nov. 1814, *ASP*, Mil. 16, 1:573.

26. Doughty to Pinkney, 14 Jan. 1815, in *National Intelligencer*, 2 Feb. 1815.

27. Winder narrative, 26 Sept. 1814, *ASP*, Mil. 16, 1:558.

28. Burch statement, 12 Oct. 1814, ibid., 574.

29. Law statement, 10 Nov. 1814, ibid., 586.

30. Metcalf and Martin, *Marriages and Deaths*, 56.

31. Lavall statement, 31 Oct. 1814, *ASP*, Mil. 16, 1:571.

32. Monroe letter, 13 Nov. 1814, ibid., 537.

33. Stansbury report, 15 Nov. 1814, ibid., 562.

34. George Hoffman to John Hoffman, 9 Sept. 1814, WC.

35. Ibid.

36. Winder to Armstrong, 27 Aug. 1814, *ASP*, Mil. 16, 1:548; List of American prisoners, 25 Aug. 1814, Rolls and Lists of Prisoner of War A-C, RG 45, NA.

37. George Hoffman to John Hoffman, 9 Sept. 1814, WC.

38. Tuckerman, *Life of Kennedy*, 79–80.

39. Henry Fulford, 26 Aug. 1814, in Marine, *British Invasion of Maryland*, 114.

40. Sterett statement, 22 Nov. 1814, *ASP*, Mil. 16, 1:568.

41. Stansbury report, 15 Nov. 1814, ibid., 562.

42. Winder narrative, 26 Sept. 1814, ibid., 558.

43. *Narrative of the Battle of Bladensburg*, 7.

44. William Brent to Smith, 5 Oct. 1814, Select Committee Papers and Reports (HR13A-D15-3), RG 233, NA.

45. [Gleig], *A Subaltern*, 73.

46. Bourchier, *Memoir of Codrington*, 1:318.

47. Davies to Mother, 31 Aug. 1814, in Burnett, *Rise and Fall*, 225; Brooke, Diary, 165.
48. H. Smith, *Autobiography*, 199–200.
49. Scott, *Recollections*, 3:289.
50. Winder narrative, 26 Sept. 1814, *ASP*, Mil. 16, 1:558.
51. Ball, *Slavery in the United States*, 362.
52. Barney to Jones, 29 Aug. 1814, *ASP*, Mil. 16, 1:579.
53. Thompson to Smith, 5 Oct. 1814, Select Committee Papers and Reports (HR13A-D15-3), RG 233, NA.
54. John Webster to Brantz Mayer, 22 July 1853, WC.
55. Scott, *Recollections*, 3:287; [Gleig], *A Subaltern*, 75; Barrett, "Naval Recollections," Part 1, 459.
56. Barney, n.d., to *National Intelligencer*, in Barney, *Biographical Memoir*, Appendix, 321.
57. Miller to David Henshaw, 24 Dec. 1843, SMP.
58. Ball, *Slavery in the United States*, 362.
59. "The Triumphant Mob . . . Victorious British Army," *Federal Republican*, 2 Sept. 1814.
60. John Webster to Brantz Mayer, 22 July 1853, WC.
61. Barney to Jones, 7 Sept. 1814, UCSC.
62. Gleig, *Campaigns*, 67; *Historical Record of the Fourth*, 119.
63. Davies to Mother, 31 Aug. 1814, in Burnett, *Rise and Fall*, 224–25.
64. John Webster to Brantz Mayer, 22 July 1853, WC.
65. Scott, *Recollections*, 3:291.
66. Barney to Jones, 29 Aug. 1814, *ASP*, Mil. 16, 1:580.
67. Bourchier, *Memoir of Codrington*, 1:317.
68. Margaret Smith to Mrs. Kirkpatrick, 11 Sept. 1814, MBSP.
69. Lt. F. Williams report, 30 Aug. 1814, in *Federal Republican*, 6 Dec. 1814.
70. Catlett report, n.d., *ASP*, Mil. 16, 1:584–85.
71. Winder to Armstrong, 27 Aug. 1814, ibid., 548.

CHAPTER 8. THE CAPITAL ABANDONED

1. Dolley Madison to Anna Cutts, 24 Aug. 1814, DMP.
2. Jennings, *Colored Man's Reminiscences*, 10.
3. Latrobe to Dolley Madison, 22 Mar. 1809, in *Correspondence of Latrobe*, 2:708.
4. Jennings, *Colored Man's Reminiscences*, 11.
5. Dolley Madison to Anna Cutts, 24 Aug. 1814, DMP; Daniel Carroll letter to Editor, *New York Herald*, 31 Jan. 1848.

6. Copy of Bill of Sale, 5 July 1800, Office of the Curator, the White House.

7. Ingersoll, *Historical Sketch*, 2:206.

8. Oral statement, Barker to Lossing, Apr. 1861, in Lossing, *Pictorial Fieldbook*, 935; Robert DePeyster to Dolley Madison, 3 Feb. 1848, DMP.

9. Mecklenburg and Wimsatt, *White House Portrait*, 10.

10. Dolley Madison to Robert DePeyster, 11 Feb. 1848, in McCormick, "First Master of Ceremonies," 183.

11. Lossing, *Pictorial Fieldbook*, 936.

12. Dolley Madison to Anna Cutts, 24 Aug. 1814, DMP.

13. Jones memorandum, n.d., UCSC.

14. Weller, "Unwelcome Visitors," 87.

15. Ewell, *Planter's and Mariner's*, 633.

16. Ibid.

17. Minor statement, 30 Oct. 1814, *ASP*, Mil. 16, 1:569.

18. Summary of House report, ibid., 530; Monroe letter, 13 Nov. 1814, ibid., 537; Winder narrative, 26 Sept. 1814, ibid., 558–59.

19. George Hoffman to John Hoffman, 9 Sept. 1814, WC.

20. John Webster to Brantz Mayer, 22 July 1853, ibid.; Webster to Mayer, 10 Aug. 1853, in *Baltimore Sun*, 23 Sept. 1928.

21. Booth to Tingey, 10 Sept. 1814, Reports on the Removal of Powder from the Navy Yard at the Time of the British Invasion of Washington 1814, RG 45/350, NA.

22. Smith statement, 6 Oct. 1814, *ASP*, Mil. 16, 1:565.

23. Booth to Tingey, 10 Sept. 1814, RG 45/350, NA.

24. Tingey to Jones, 27 Aug. 1814, *ASP*, Mil. 16, 1:578.

25. Hackett, "Capt. Thomas Tingey," 120–22; Lewis D. Cook Research Collection, 1931, MS 253, HSW.

26. "Died," *National Intelligencer*, 29 Apr. 1814.

27. Jones, 3 Oct. 1814, *ASP*, Mil. 16, 1:577.

28. Tingey to Jones, 27 Aug. 1814, ibid., 578.

29. Booth to Tingey, 10 Sept. 1814, RG 45/350, NA.

30. Anna Maria Thornton Diaries, 24 Aug. 1814, LC (hereafter cited as Thornton, Diaries).

31. Clark, "James Heighe Blake," 144.

32. Thornton, Diaries, 24 Aug. 1814, LC.

33. John Hugh's advertisement, *Federal Republican*, 30 Sept. 1814.

34. Jones memorandum, n.d., UCSC.

35. Jones report, 3 Oct. 1814, *ASP*, Mil. 16, 1:577.

36. H. Adams, *History of the United States*, 1018.
37. Serurier to Talleyrand, 27 Aug. 1814, FAPC.
38. Jones memorandum, n.d., UCSC; Ingersoll, *Historical Sketch*, 2:207; Jennings, *Colored Man's Reminiscences*, 12.
39. Advertisement, "New Public House," *National Intelligencer*, 19 Aug. 1814; Simmons letter, 28 Nov. 1814, *ASP*, Mil. 16, 1:597.
40. Lavall statement, 31 Oct. 1814, *ASP*, Mil. 16, 1:571.
41. Catlett statement, n.d., ibid., 584.
42. Jennings, *Colored Man's Reminiscences*, 11.
43. Shiner, Diary, 5–7, LC.

CHAPTER 9. WASHINGTON IN FLAMES

1. Ross to Bathurst, 30 Aug. 1814, in *Federal Republican*, 6 Dec. 1814; Brooke, Diary, 165.
2. *Federal Republican*, 2 Sept. 1814; Burnett, *Rise and Fall*, 225; Chester Bailey letter to *Poulson's Paper* (Philadelphia), 29 Aug. 1814, in *Times* (London), 29 Sept. 1814.
3. Scott, *Recollections*, 3:298–300.
4. Martha Peter to Timothy Pickering, 28 Aug. 1814, Pickering Papers, MAHS.
5. Louisa to Eliza, 31 Aug. 1814, RFP (NHFC).
6. Booth to Tingey, 10 Sept. 1814, Reports on the Removal of Powder from the Navy Yard at the Time of the British Invasion of Washington 1814, RG 45/350, NA.
7. Tingey to Jones, 27 Aug. 1814, *ASP*, Mil. 16, 1:578.
8. Jones report, 3 Oct. 1814, ibid., 577.
9. Peck, *Round-Shot to Rockets*, 31.
10. Advertisements, Jesse Marrell and John Caldwell, *National Intelligencer*, 7, 9 Sept. 1814.
11. Jones report, 3 Oct. 1814, *ASP*, Mil. 16, 1:577.
12. Tingey to Jones, 18 Oct. 1814, ibid., 578.
13. Jones report, 3 Oct. 1814, ibid., 577.
14. Booth to Tingey, 10 Sept. 1814, RG 45/350, NA.
15. Jones letters, 31 Oct., 12 Nov. 1814, *ASP*, Mil. 16, 1:540, 541.
16. Booth to Tingey, 10 Sept. 1814, RG 45/350, NA.
17. Tingey to Jones, 27 Aug. 1814, *ASP*, Mil. 16, 1:579.
18. Scott, *Recollections*, 3:300.
19. H. Smith, *Autobiography*, 200.

20. Hazelton, *The National Capitol*, 32.

21. Latrobe to Dolley Madison, 21 Apr. 1809, in *Correspondence of Latrobe*, 2:711.

22. Seale, *The President's House*, 1:39; Latrobe to Philip Mazzei, 29 May 1806, in *Correspondence of Latrobe*, 2:228.

23. Latrobe letter to Editor, *National Intelligencer*, 30 Nov. 1807.

24. Latrobe to Samuel Hazlehurst, 24 March 1805, in *Correspondence of Latrobe*, 2:32.

25. Latrobe letter to Editor, *National Intelligencer*, 30 Nov. 1807.

26. McElroy, "Recollections," 13, Maryland Province Archives, GUL.

27. McElroy, Diary, 39, ibid.

28. Latrobe letter to Editor, *National Intelligencer*, 30 Nov. 1807.

29. Latrobe to Peale, 18 Apr. 1806, in *Correspondence of Latrobe*, 2:215.

30. Peale to Latrobe, 21 Apr. 1806, ibid., 218 and n. 1.

31. Latrobe to Jefferson, 27 Aug. 1806, ibid., 270.

32. Scott, *Recollections*, 3:301.

33. Latrobe to D.C. Commissioners, 19 Apr. 1815, Records of D.C. Commissioners and of Offices Concerned with Public Buildings, Letters Received 1791–1861, M371, Roll 18, RG 42, NA.

34. Latrobe to Jefferson, 12 July 1815, in *Correspondence of Latrobe*, 3:670.

35. Latrobe to D.C. Commissioners, 19 Apr. 1815, RG 42, NA; Latrobe letter to Editor, *National Intelligencer*, 30 Nov. 1807.

36. Latrobe to Jefferson, 12 July 1815, in *Correspondence of Latrobe*, 3:670.

37. *Documentary History of the Construction and Development of the United States Capitol Building and Grounds*, 158 (hereafter cited as *Documentary History of the Capitol*).

38. Rare book dealer Dr. A. S. W. Rosenbach donated the book to the Library of Congress in 1940 after authenticating Cockburn's handwriting.

39. Burch and Frost to Patrick Magruder, 15 Sept. 1814, and Washington Bowie certificate, 15 Dec. 1814, *ASP*, Misc. 38, 2:245, 261.

40. Latrobe to Jefferson, 12 July 1815, in *Correspondence of Latrobe*, 3:670.

41. Latrobe to Jefferson, 18 Nov. 1808, in *Documentary History of the Capitol*, 146–47; Allen, *United States Capitol*, 8.

42. Latrobe to Madison, 28 Dec. 1810, in *Documentary History of the Capitol*, 164.

43. Latrobe to Thruston, 18 Feb. 1809, ibid., 154.

44. G. Brown, *History of the Capitol*, 44; *1812 Catalogue*, xii–xiii.

45. *1812 Catalogue*, xxi.

46. *The Senate Chamber*, 3.

47. "Some Unknown Foreigner," *Inchiquin*, 52.

48. Latrobe to Madison, 3 Jan. 1811, in *Documentary History of the Capitol*, 162.

49. Latrobe to Commissioner of Public Buildings, 28 Nov. 1816, ibid., 192; Latrobe to Jefferson, 12 July 1815, in *Correspondence of Latrobe*, 3:671.

50. Latrobe to Jefferson, 18 Nov. 1808, in *Documentary History of the Capitol*, 147; Allen, *United States Capitol*, 7–8.

51. Latrobe to Jefferson, 11 Sept. 1808, in *Correspondence of Latrobe*, 2:660 n. 3; *Documentary History of the Capitol*, 135.

52. Latrobe to Jefferson, 28 Aug. 1809, in Frary, *They Built the Capitol*, 80; Castiello, "Italian Sculptors," 33.

53. McElroy, Diary, 39, GUL.

54. Thornton, Diaries, 24 Aug. 1814, LC; Thornton letter to Editor, *National Intelligencer*, 7 Sept. 1814.

55. Latrobe to Mary Elizabeth Latrobe, 17 Apr. 1815, in *Correspondence of Latrobe*, 3:644.

56. Ewell, *Planter's and Mariner's*, 637–40.

57. Scott, *Recollections*, 3:302; *Annals of Congress*, 13th Cong., 3rd sess., 1100.

58. Wadsworth to Daniel Carroll, 12 Nov. 1814, DCP.

59. Serurier to Talleyrand, 27 Aug. 1814, FAPC.

60. William Gardner letter to Editor, *Federal Republican*, 16 Sept. 1814.

61. Ibid.

62. Chester Bailey letter to *Poulson's Paper* (Philadelphia), 29 Aug. 1814, in *Times* (London), 29 Sept. 1814; Margaret Smith to Mrs. Kirkpatrick, 30 Aug. 1814, MBSP.

63. Proof the two women remained in the city: Seth Pease to anonymous "Dear Sir," 1 Sept. 1814, Individual Manuscripts Collection, GL.

64. Varnum, *Washington Sketch Book*, 240ff.

65. Mary Stockton Hunter to Susan Stockton Cuthbert, 30 Aug. 1814, Miscellaneous Hunter Manuscripts, NYHS.

66. Ibid.

67. Chester Bailey quoted in *Baltimore Patriot*, 26 Aug. 1814, in *Times* (London), 29 Sept. 1814; Davies to Mother, 31 Aug. 1814, in Burnett, *Rise and Fall*, 224.

68. Seaton, *William Winston Seaton*, 117–18.

69. Chester Bailey quoted in *Baltimore Patriot*, 26 Aug. 1814, in *Times* (London), 29 Sept. 1814.

70. William Gardner letter to Editor, *Federal Republican*, 16 Sept. 1814.

71. Advertisement in *National Intelligencer*, 14 July 1814.

72. Survey maps Square 226, 22 Feb. 1817, Squares 1–816, Real Estate Assessment and Related Plats, Maps, and Directories for Washington, D.C., to 1934, Roll

1, 1874, in Real Estate Directory, Washingtoniana Division, District of Columbia Public Library, Washington, D.C.; Thomas Herty estate, *National Intelligencer,* 2, 6 June 1814, 15 Mar. 1815.

73. Ingersoll, *Historical Sketch,* 2:186; Estate of Isabella Suter, District of Columbia, Probate Court, Old Series Administration Case Files, 1801–78, no. 3562, RG 21, NA.

74. Ingersoll, *Historical Sketch,* 2:186.

75. Scott, *Recollections,* 3:304.

76. Ross to Ned, n.d., in "Memoir of Major-General Robert Ross," 414–15; Buchan, *History of Royal Scots,* 171.

77. Martha Peter to Timothy Pickering, 28 Aug. 1814, Pickering Papers, MAHS.

78. Metcalf and Martin, *Marriages and Deaths,* 60.

79. Copy of deed of sale, John Jackson to Bank of the Metropolis, 16 Apr. 1814, liber A.G. 32, folio 295, D.C. Land Records, The History Factory, Chantilly, Virginia.

80. Margaret Smith to Mrs. Kirkpatrick, 30 Aug. 1814, MBSP.

81. Scott, *Recollections,* 3:304.

82. Louisa to Eliza, 31 Aug. 1814, RFP (NHFC).

83. Gerry, *Diary,* 180.

84. Phoebe Morris to Anthony Morris, 14 Sept. 1814, DHC.

85. Archibald Kains returned it, saying his grandfather, Thomas Kains, paymaster, HMS *Devastation,* stole it (Archibald Kains to President Franklin D. Roosevelt, 20 Apr. 1939, FDR Papers, PPF 5888, Franklin Delano Roosevelt Library, Hyde Park, N.Y.). But *Devastation* crew never landed in Washington.

86. *Morning Post* (London), 5 Oct. 1814; W025/776 Fol. 392, Map Room, Public Record Office, Richmond, England; Obituary, *Aberdeen Journal* (Scotland), 9 Oct. 1861.

87. Tayloe, *Neighbors on Lafayette Square,* 14.

88. Mrs. Serurier to Mrs. Thornton, 20 Aug. 1814, William Thornton Papers, LC.

89. Serurier to Talleyrand, 27 Aug. 1814, FAPC.

90. Kimball, "Original Furnishings," 483, 485–86.

91. Latrobe to George Harrison, 20 June 1809, in *Correspondence of Latrobe,* 2:731.

92. Klapthor, "Benjamin Latrobe," 158–59.

93. Gerry, *Diary,* 182.

94. Burnett, *Rise and Fall,* 11–12, 225.

95. H. Smith, *Autobiography,* 200.

96. *Correspondence of Latrobe,* editorial note, 2:707.

97. Gerry, *Diary,* 180.

98. Klapthor, "Benjamin Latrobe," 157.
99. Gerry, *Diary*, 180.
100. James Monroe to Senate and House of Representatives, 10 Feb. 1818, *Compilation of the Messages and Papers of the Presidents*, 2:595.
101. Margaret Smith to Mrs. Kirkpatrick, 30 Aug. 1814, MBSP.
102. *Report of the Commission on the Renovation of the Executive Mansion*, 26–28.
103. Proceedings, 16–20 Dec. 1793, Records of D.C. Commissioners and of Offices Concerned with Public Buildings, Proceedings 1791–1798, M371 Roll 1, RG 42, NA.
104. Seale, *The President's House*, 1:50ff.
105. Ibid., 27, 31.
106. George Hadfield to D.C. Commissioners, 13 Oct. 1814, Records of D.C. Commissioners and of Offices Concerned with Public Buildings, Letters Received 1791–1861, M371 Roll 18, RG 42, NA.
107. Buchan, *History of Royal Scots*, 171.
108. "Reminiscences of Washington by an Old Inhabitant," *Washington Evening Star*, 13 Dec. 1879.
109. Washington to D.C. Commissioners, 21 Oct. 1796, in *Writings of Washington*, 35:250; Washington to Alexander White, 25 Mar. 1798, ibid., 36:190.
110. Margaret Smith to Mrs. Kirkpatrick, 30 Aug. 1814, MBSP.
111. Scott, *Recollections*, 3:305.
112. Jos. Stretch report, 26 Oct. 1814, *ASP*, Misc. 38, 2:250.
113. *National Metropolitan Bank*, 12.
114. Copy of deed of sale, John Jackson to Bank of the Metropolis, 16 Apr. 1814, liber A.G. 32, folio 295, D.C. Land Records, The History Factory, Chantilly, Virginia.
115. Minute Book, Bank of the Metropolis, 24 Aug. 1814, The History Factory, Chantilly, Virginia.
116. *National Intelligencer*, 3 Apr. 1815.
117. Minute Book, Bank of the Metropolis, 15, 29 Mar. 1815, The History Factory, Chantilly, Virginia.
118. Chester Bailey, letter to *Poulson's Paper* (Philadelphia), 29 Aug. 1814, in *Times* (London), 29 Sept. 1814.
119. Brooke, Diary, 166.
120. Gleig, *Campaigns*, 70.
121. Mary Stockton Hunter to Susan Stockton Cuthbert, 30 Aug. 1814, Miscellaneous Hunter Manuscripts, NYHS.
122. *Memoirs of Dolly Madison*, 108.

123. C. Lee, *Lee Chronicle*, 291.

124. Rush to Williams, 10 July 1855, in Williams, *History of Invasion*, 275.

125. Jennings, *Colored Man's Reminiscences*, 12.

126. Booth to Tingey, 10 Sept. 1814, RG 45/350, NA.

127. Ibid.; Steadman, *Falls Church*, 463.

128. Inventory form for Salona, *Historic American Buildings, Survey*, published by the Fairfax County Office of Comprehensive Planning, 1970; Anderson, *Salona, Fairfax County*, 14–15.

129. *Alexandria Gazette*, 18 Nov. 1811.

130. Jennings, *Colored Man's Reminiscences*, 12–13.

131. Ibid., preface.

132. Daniel Sheldon Jr. to Dr. Daniel Sheldon, 26 Aug. 1814, in Lamb, ed., "Burning of Washington, 1814," 467.

133. Stephen Pleasonton to Winder, 7 Aug. 1848, in Hildt, "Letters Relating to Capture," 65–66.

134. Daniel Sheldon Jr. to Dr. Daniel Sheldon, 26 Aug. 1814, in Lamb, ed., "Burning of Washington, 1814," 468.

135. David Winchester to James Winchester, 25 Aug. 1814, JWP.

136. Booth to Tingey, 10 Sept. 1814, RG 45/350, NA.

137. Ibid.

138. Jennings, *Colored Man's Reminiscences*, 13.

139. Ingersoll, *Historical Sketch*, 2:208.

140. Robert Young statement, 3 Oct. 1814, *ASP*, Mil. 16, 1:567.

141. Jennings, *Colored Man's Reminiscences*, 13.

142. Matilda Sayrs, "Reminiscences," Alexandria Library, Special Collections, Alexandria, Virginia.

143. C. Lee, *Lee Chronicle*, 291.

144. Young statement, 3 Oct. 1814, *ASP*, Mil. 16, 1:567.

145. Madison to Monroe, 26 Aug. 1814, JMP.

CHAPTER 10. A LIGHTNING OCCUPATION

1. Ewell, *Planter's and Mariner's*, 641.

2. Chester Bailey quoted in *Baltimore Patriot*, 26 Aug. 1814, in *Times* (London), 29 Sept. 1814; Margaret Smith to Mrs. Kirkpatrick, 30 Aug. 1814, MBSP.

3. Martha Peter to Timothy Pickering, 28 Aug. 1814, Pickering Papers, MAHS; Grassi, Diary, 25 Aug. 1814, GUL.

4. Thornton letter to Editor, *National Intelligencer,* 7 Sept. 1814.
5. Richard Cutts to Thomas Cutts, 16 July 1813, Key-Cutts-Turner Family Papers, University of Virginia Library, Charlottesville.
6. Monroe report, 9 Nov. 1814, *ASP,* Misc. 38, 2:251.
7. Tobias Lear report, 27 Oct. 1814, ibid., 251.
8. John Bell report, 26 Oct. 1814, ibid., 252.
9. John Morton report, 27 Oct. 1814, and Monroe report, 14 Nov. 1814, ibid.
10. Thornton letter to Editor, *National Intelligencer,* 7 Sept. 1814.
11. Warden, *Description of District of Columbia,* 37.
12. Brown, Lyon, Hadfield, and Nicholson letter to Editor, *National Intelligencer,* 24 Sept. 1814.
13. Chester Bailey quoted in *Baltimore Patriot,* 26 Aug. 1814, in *Times* (London), 29 Sept. 1814.
14. Mary Stockton Hunter to Susan Stockton Cuthbert, 30 Aug. 1814, Miscellaneous Hunter Manuscripts, NYHS.
15. Martha Peter to Timothy Pickering, 28 Aug. 1814, Pickering Papers, MAHS; *Federal Republican,* 2 Sept. 1814; Margaret Smith to Mrs. Kirkpatrick, 30 Aug. 1814, MBSP.
16. "Joe and His Types," *Federal Republican,* 26 Sept. 1814.
17. Anonymous naval officer, letter to unnamed recipient, 31 Aug. 1814, in *Morning Post* (London), 3 Oct. 1814.
18. Ames, *History of the "National Intelligencer,"* 99–100.
19. "Notice to Subscribers," *National Intelligencer,* 1 Sept. 1814.
20. Seaton, *William Winston Seaton,* 117; *National Intelligencer,* 1 Sept. 1814.
21. Ewell, *Planter's and Mariner's,* 655.
22. Martha Peter to Timothy Pickering, 28 Aug. 1814, Pickering Papers, MAHS.
23. Ibid.
24. Thornton letter to Editor, *National Intelligencer,* 22 Sept. 1814.
25. "Early Washington: An Old Resident's Recollections of the War of 1812," *Washington Evening Star,* 31 Mar. 1888.
26. Cockburn to Cochrane, 27 Aug. 1814, GCP.
27. Tingey to Jones, 27 Aug. 1814, *ASP,* Mil. 16, 1:579.
28. William Gardner letter to Editor, *Federal Republican,* 16 Sept. 1814.
29. Ewell, *Planter's and Mariner's,* 646.
30. Scott, *Recollections,* 3:312; *National Intelligencer,* 31 Aug. 1814; Cockburn to Cochrane, 27 Aug. 1814, GCP.
31. Ewell, *Planter's and Mariner's,* 646.
32. Gleig, *Campaigns,* 69–70.

33. Heiskell letter, *Salem Gazette*, 27 Sept. 1814.

34. *National Intelligencer*, 20 Sept. 1814.

35. Anonymous officer, letter to unnamed recipient, 30 Aug. 1814, in *Morning Post* (London), 7 Oct. 1814.

36. Heiskell letter, *Salem Gazette*, 27 Sept. 1814.

37. Moore, "Reminiscences of Washington," 103.

38. McElroy, Diary, 40, GUL.

39. McElroy, "Recollections," 13–14, ibid.

40. Ewell, *Planter's and Mariner's*, 649.

41. Ewell letter to Editor, *National Intelligencer*, 12 Sept. 1814.

42. Seth Pease to anonymous "Dear Sir," 1 Sept. 1814, Individual Manuscripts Collection, GL.

43. Wadsworth to Daniel Carroll, 12 Nov. 1814, DCP.

44. Thornton, Diaries, 29 Aug. 1814, LC; Moore, "Reminiscences of Washington," 102–3; Margaret Smith to Mrs. Kirkpatrick, 25, 27 Aug. 1814, MBSP; Gleig, *Campaigns*, 75–76; Scott, *Recollections*, 3:313.

45. Shiner, Diary, 8, LC.

46. Wharton, *Social Life*, 174.

47. Barrett, "Naval Recollections," Part 1, 460; Logs HMS *Albion*, 25 Aug. 1814, GCP; Logs HMS *Tonnant*, 25 Aug. 1814, WC.

48. Ewell, *Planter's and Mariner's*, 645.

49. Affidavit, Edward Lee et al., 6 July 1815, ACP.

50. Ibid.

51. Ewell, *Planter's and Mariner's*, 645–46.

52. Wadsworth to Daniel Carroll, 12 Nov. 1814, DCP.

53. Bourchier, *Memoir of Codrington*, 1:317–18.

54. Norton, Journal, 46, MAHS; Varnum, *Washington Sketch Book*, 242–43; Ingersoll, *Historical Sketch*, 2:188; John A. Washington, chart, *Augustine Washington's Descendants*, library, Mt. Vernon Ladies Association, Mt. Vernon, Va.

55. "Early Washington: An Old Resident's Recollections of the War of 1812," *Washington Evening Star*, 31 Mar. 1888.

56. Ewell, *Planter's and Mariner's*, 650.

57. Brooke, Diary, 172.

58. H. Smith, *Autobiography*, 201.

59. McElroy, "Recollections," 14, GUL; Gleig, *Campaigns*, 77–78; Shiner, Diary, 9, LC; Catlett statement, n.d., *ASP*, Mil. 16, 1:584.

60. David Winchester to James Winchester, 28 Aug. 1814, JWP.

61. Logs HMS *Albion*, 25 Aug. 1814, GCP.
62. Margaret Smith to Mrs. Kirkpatrick, 30 Aug. 1814, MBSP.
63. Calvert, *Autobiographic Study*, 77.
64. H. Smith, *Autobiography*, 203–4.
65. Miller to David Henshaw, 24 Dec. 1843, SMP.
66. Catlett statement, n.d., *ASP*, Mil. 16, 1:584.
67. Roger Taney to Charles Howard, 17 Mar. 1856, Key Poems, MDHS.
68. John Mason to Ross, 2 Sept. 1814, Commissary General of Prisoners, Correspondence on Prisoner Exchanges, RG 45, NA; Gleig, *Campaigns*, 80.
69. Levin Winder to Ross, 31 Aug. 1814, in Marine, *British Invasion of Maryland*, 190.
70. Ross to Mason, 7 Sept. 1814, Commissary General of Prisoners, Correspondence on Prisoner Exchanges, RG 45, NA.
71. Levin Winder to Ross, 31 Aug. 1814, in Marine, *British Invasion of Maryland*, 189.
72. Roger Taney to Charles Howard, 17 Mar. 1856, Key Poems, MDHS.
73. Cochrane to Bathurst, 14 July 1814, War Office I: Secretary at War, LC.
74. Brooke, Diary, 167.
75. Cochrane to Gloucester, 3 Sept. 1814, ACP.
76. Pulteney Malcolm to Nancy Malcolm, 1 Sept. 1814, PMP.
77. Pulteney Malcolm to Clementina Malcolm, 2 Sept. 1814, ibid.
78. William Kirke to Charles Kirke, 13 Nov. 1814, DD.MM43, Nottinghamshire Archives Office, England.
79. Davies to Mother, 31 Aug. 1814, in Burnett, *Rise and Fall*, 225.
80. H. Smith, *Autobiography*, 206–7.
81. *Times* (London), 27 Sept. 1814.
82. H. Smith, *Autobiography*, 213–15.
83. Sarah Young to Maria Nourse, 28 Aug. 1814, NFP.
84. Clarke to Jones, 27 Aug. 1814, UCSC.
85. George Hadfield to D.C. Commissioners, 13 Oct. 1814, Records of D.C. Commissioners and of Offices Concerned with Public Buildings, Letters Received 1791–1861, M371, Roll 18, RG 42, NA.
86. Thornton letter to Editor, *National Intelligencer*, 7 Sept. 1814.
87. Editorial footnote to Thornton letter to Editor, ibid., 13 Sept. 1814.
88. Thornton letter to Editor, ibid., 7 Sept. 1814.
89. Blake letter to Editor, ibid., 10 Sept. 1814.
90. Thornton letter to Editor, ibid., 13 Sept. 1814.
91. Blake letter to Editor, ibid., 10 Sept. 1814.
92. Ibid.

CHAPTER 11. A FLAG FURLED IN DARKNESS

1. Maj. Ferdinando Marsteller to R. H. Winder, 1 Nov. 1814, U.S. vs. Dyson, 98, Court-Martial Case Files, 1809–94, RG 153, NA.
2. Lt. Thomas Harrison testimony, ibid., 58–59.
3. Maj. Robert Hite testimony, ibid., 34, 37.
4. Wadsworth to Armstrong, 28 May 1813, Select Committee Papers and Reports (HR13A-D15-3), RG 233, NA.
5. Lt. James Edwards testimony, 72, and Judge Advocate General Maj. R. H. Winder summation, 140, U.S. vs. Dyson.
6. Edwards testimony, ibid., 68.
7. Dr. William Fitzgerald testimony, ibid., 80–81.
8. Lt. Walter Berryman testimony, ibid., 20.
9. Capt. Samuel Dyson testimony, ibid., 106.
10. Ibid., 115–16.
11. Ibid., 114.
12. Berryman testimony, ibid., 18–19.
13. Winder summation, ibid., 141–42.
14. Harrison testimony, ibid., 49.
15. Dr. William Marshall testimony, ibid., 25.
16. Edwards testimony, ibid., 46, 69.
17. Napier, *Life and Correspondence,* 1:80; Edwards testimony, U.S. vs. Dyson, 68–69.
18. Berryman testimony, U.S. vs. Dyson, 14.
19. Marshall testimony, ibid., 23.
20. Berryman testimony, ibid., 19.
21. Ibid.
22. Dr. John O'Conner testimony, ibid., 43.
23. Edwards testimony, ibid., 78.
24. Gordon to Cochrane, 9 Sept. 1814, ACP.
25. Berryman testimony, 14, and Harrison testimony, 60(a), U.S. vs. Dyson; Gordon to Cochrane, 9 Sept. 1814, ACP.
26. Gordon to Cochrane, 9 Sept. 1814, ACP.
27. Digges to Madison, 30 Aug. 1814, JMP.
28. Tingey to Jones, 27 Aug. 1814, *ASP,* Mil. 16, 1:579.
29. Napier, *Life and Correspondence,* 1:80.
30. Berryman testimony, 14, Harrison testimony, 53, and Edwards testimony, 69, U.S. vs. Dyson.
31. Dyson testimony, ibid., 102.

32. O'Conner testimony, ibid., 44.
33. Dyson testimony, ibid., 116.
34. Winder summation, ibid., 142, 144.
35. Digges to Madison, 30 Aug. 1814, JMP.

CHAPTER 12. REFUGE AMONG PACIFISTS

1. Margaret Smith to Mrs. Kirkpatrick, 27 Aug. 1814, MBSP.
2. *Transactions and Proceedings of the 75th Anniversary of the Medical Society of the District of Columbia, Feb. 16, 1894*, 30–31.
3. Anna Maria Mason to Richard Rush, 5 Sept. 1814, RRP.
4. Madison to Jones, 27 Aug. 1814, UCSC.
5. Margaret Smith to Mrs. Kirkpatrick, 25 Aug. 1814, MBSP.
6. Ibid.
7. Madison to Monroe, 26 Aug. 1814, JMP.
8. Madison to Jones, 27 Aug. 1814, UCSC.
9. James Madison to Dolley Madison, 27 Aug. 1814, JMP.
10. "J.M.'s notes respecting the burning city in 1814," ibid.
11. Watson, *In Memoriam*, 151.
12. Rush to Jared Ingersoll, 8 Sept. 1814, RRP.
13. Rush to Adams, 5 Sept. 1814, ibid.
14. Robert Brown to William Brown, 21 Sept. 1814, Dreer Collection, HSP.
15. Fearon, *Sketches of America*, 284–85.
16. Jennings, *Colored Man's Reminiscences*, 13.
17. Thornton, Diaries, 5 Sept. 1814, LC.
18. Thornton letter to Editor, *National Intelligencer*, 7 Sept. 1814.
19. Beall Account Book, 27 Aug. 1814, MDHS.
20. Monroe to Jefferson, 21 Dec. 1814, in *Writings of James Monroe*, 5:304.
21. Thornton letter to Editor, *National Intelligencer*, 7 Sept. 1814.
22. "J.M.'s notes respecting the burning city in 1814," JMP.
23. James Madison to Dolley Madison, n.d., but indisputably 28 Aug. 1814 because of his reference to a letter sent the day before, 27 Aug. 1814. Quoted in Clark, *Life and Letters*, 172.
24. Ingersoll, *Historical Sketch*, 2:208–9.
25. Dolley Madison to Mary Latrobe, 3 Dec. 1814, quoted in Clark, *Life and Letters*, 166.
26. Margaret Smith to Mrs. Kirkpatrick, 30 Aug. 1814, MBSP.

27. Thornton, Diaries, 28 Aug. 1814, LC.
28. Ibid.
29. Eleanor Jones to William Jones, 1 Sept. 1814, UCSC.
30. William Jones to Eleanor Jones, 7 Sept. 1814, ibid.
31. Ibid.
32. Rush to Monroe, Washington, 28 Aug. 1814, Rush Letters, HSP.
33. James Madison proclamation, *National Intelligencer,* 3 Sept. 1814.
34. Robert Young statement, 3 Oct. 1814, *ASP,* Mil. 16, 1:567.
35. Thornton, Diaries, 29 Aug. 1814, LC.
36. James Madison memorandum, 29 Aug. 1814, JMP.
37. Margaret Smith to Mrs. Kirkpatrick, 30 Aug. 1814, MBSP.
38. James Madison memorandum, 29 Aug. 1814, JMP.
39. Armstrong letter to *Baltimore Patriot,* 3 Sept. 1814, in *National Intelligencer,* 8 Sept. 1814.

CHAPTER 13. ALEXANDRIA SURRENDERS

1. Martha Peter to Timothy Pickering, 28 Aug. 1814, Pickering Papers, MAHS.
2. Gordon to Cochrane, [?] Feb. 1816, ACP.
3. Resolution of Common Council Alexandria, 29 Aug. 1814, *ASP,* Mil. 16, 1:592.
4. Heiskell letter to *Winchester Gazette,* 30 Aug. 1814, in *Salem Gazette,* 27 Sept. 1814.
5. Booth to Tingey, 10 Sept. 1814, Reports on the Removal of Powder from the Navy Yard at the Time of the British Invasion of Washington 1814, RG 45/350, NA.
6. R. I. Taylor statement, 20 Nov. 1814, *ASP,* Mil. 16, 1:593.
7. Heiskell letter to *Winchester Gazette,* 1 Sept. 1814, in *Salem Gazette,* 27 Sept. 1814.
8. Napier, *Life and Correspondence,* 1:83; Thomas Brown, "An Account of the Lineage of the Brown Family," 2:4–6, Ambler-Brown Family Papers, Duke University, Durham (hereafter cited as Brown, "Account of Lineage"); Gordon to Admiralty, 14 Sept. 1814, ACP.
9. Israel Thompson certified report, 6 Oct. 1814, *ASP,* Mil. 16, 1:592.
10. Napier, *Life and Correspondence,* 1:82, 86.
11. Gordon to Cochrane, 9 Sept. 1814, ACP.
12. Brown, "Account of Lineage," 2:4–5; *Federal Republican,* 6 Sept. 1814.
13. Booth to Tingey, 10 Sept. 1814, RG 45/350, NA.
14. James Hillyar to Admiral Brown, Valparaiso Bay, 30 May 1814, in *Federal Republican,* 7 Sept. 1814.

15. Porter, *Memoir*, 254.
16. Porter to Jones, 7 Sept. 1814, in *Niles' Weekly Register*, 1 Oct. 1814.
17. Porter to Hungerford, 19 Dec. 1814, in *National Intelligencer*, 6 Feb. 1815.
18. Brown, "Account of Lineage," 2:8–9; Napier, *Life and Correspondence*, 1:84.
19. "Minerva Rodgers Memoir," 14, typescript, RFP (NHFC).
20. Rodgers to Minerva Rodgers, 23 Apr. 1814, ibid.
21. Report on Rodgers, *National Intelligencer*, 2 July 1812.
22. Rodgers to Jones, 9 Sept. 1814, in *National Intelligencer*, 14 Sept. 1814.
23. Brown, "Account of Lineage," 2:15.
24. Ibid., 12.
25. Grassi, Diary, 5 Sept. 1814, GUL.
26. Norton, Journal, 33, MAHS.
27. John Gallaher to Williams, 5 Sept. 1856, in Williams, *History of Invasion*, 370; Porter to Jones, 7 Sept. 1814, in *National Intelligencer*, 12 Sept. 1814.
28. Perry to Jones, 9 Sept. 1814, in *Niles' Weekly Register*, 1 Oct. 1814.
29. Napier, *Life and Correspondence*, 1:85.
30. "Another Failure," *Federal Republican*, 7 Sept. 1814.
31. Charles Nourse to Maria Nourse, 5 Sept. 1814, NFP.
32. Thornton, Diaries, 29 Aug. 1814, LC.

Chapter 14. Baltimore Defiant

1. "Attack upon Baltimore," *Niles' Weekly Register*, 24 Sept. 1814.
2. A. Robinson to James McHenry, 20 Feb. 1813, WC.
3. Porter to Jones, 27 Aug. 1814, Select Committee Papers and Reports (HR13A-D15-3), RG 233, NA; John Harris to William Harris, 27 Sept. 1814, WC.
4. Nicholson to Jones, 28 Aug. 1814, UCSC.
5. David Winchester to James Winchester, 25 Aug. 1814, JWP.
6. John Harris to William Harris, 27 Sept. 1814, WC.
7. Jones to Rodgers, 23 Aug. 1814, RFP.
8. Jones to Rodgers, 28 Aug. 1814, Select Committee Papers and Reports (HR13A-D15-3), RG 233, NA.
9. Porter to Jones, 27 Aug. 1814, ibid.
10. Rodgers to Minerva Rodgers, 28 Aug. 1814, RFP.
11. Rodgers to Jones, 29 Aug. 1814, RFP (NHFC).
12. Smith to Stockton, 31 Aug. 1814, SSP; Jones to Rodgers, 29 Aug. 1814, Select Committee Papers and Reports (HR13A-D15-3), RG 233, NA.

13. George Hoffman to John Hoffman, 9 Sept. 1814, WC.

14. Thomas Forman to Martha Forman, 29 Aug. 1814, ibid.

15. Smith to Forman, 19 Sept. 1814, SSP.

16. Mrs. M. B. Forman, Diary, typescript, MDHS.

17. Thomas Forman to Martha Forman, 29 Aug. 1814, WC.

18. Minutes, 25 Aug. 1814, BCVS.

19. *Dictionary of American Biography*, 9:341.

20. Minutes, 26 Aug. 1814, BCVS.

21. Ibid., 1 Sept. 1814.

22. Ibid., 10 Sept. 1814.

23. Ibid., 31 Aug. 1814.

24. Smith to Monroe, 1 Sept. 1814, SSP.

25. Curtis, *Life of James Buchanan*, 1:8.

26. Smith to Monroe, 3, 4 Sept. 1814, SSP.

27. Minutes, 2 Sept. 1814, BCVS.

28. Smith to Baltimore Committee of Vigilance and Safety, 3 Sept. 1814, SSP.

29. Minutes, 5 Sept. 1814, BCVS.

30. Ibid., 1 Sept. 1814.

31. Ibid., 31 Aug. 1814.

32. Order Book, 3rd Brigade Maryland Militia, 31 Aug. 1814, WC.

33. Smith to Monroe, 9 Sept. 1814, SSP.

34. Severn Teackle to Phillip Wallis, 23 Sept. 1814, and Order Book, 3rd Brigade Maryland Militia, 31 Aug. 1814, WC.

35. Smith to Stockton, 31 Aug. 1814, and Smith to Monroe, 1 Sept. 1814, SSP.

36. Jones to Rodgers, 3 Sept. 1814, M149, Roll 11, Letters Sent by Navy Secretary to Officers, 1798–1868, RG 45, NA.

37. Rodgers to Jones, 23 Sept. 1814, RFP.

38. John Webster to Brantz Mayer, 22 July 1853, WC.

39. Order Book, 3rd Brigade Maryland Militia, 5 Sept. 1814, ibid.

40. Cochrane to Croker, 17 Sept. 1814, in James, *Military Occurrences*, 2:515; Scharf, *History of Maryland*, 3:100.

41. Smith to Monroe, 19 Sept. 1814, SSP.

42. Smith to Baltimore Committee of Vigilance and Safety, 17 Sept. 1814, SSP.

43. "Attack upon Baltimore," *Niles' Weekly Register*, 24 Sept. 1814.

44. Armistead to Monroe, 24 Sept. 1814, in *Niles' Weekly Register*, 1 Oct. 1814.

45. George Armistead to Louisa Armistead, 10 Sept. 1814, WC.

46. Armistead to Monroe, 24 Sept. 1814, in *Niles' Weekly Register*, 1 Oct. 1814.

47. Minutes, 11 Sept. 1814, BCVS.
48. Rutter to Rodgers, 11 Sept. 1814, RFP.
49. "Minerva Rodgers Memoir," 44, typescript, RFP (NHFC).

CHAPTER 15. THE BATTLE OF NORTH POINT

1. Scott, *Recollections*, 3:326–27.
2. Joseph Nourse to Maria Nourse, 10 Sept. 1814, NFP.
3. Gleig, *Campaigns*, 90–91.
4. Plan of the Island of Tangier, Alexander Cochrane Papers, National Library of Scotland, Edinburgh.
5. Wallace, *Parson of the Islands*, 145–47.
6. Parker to Cochrane, 19 Aug. 1814, ACP.
7. Parker to Cochrane, 30 Aug. 1814, ibid.
8. Skinner to John Mason, 5 Sept. 1814, Correspondence, Exchange and Release of Prisoners, RG 45, NA; Logs HMS *Tonnant*, 7 Sept. 1814, WC.
9. Roger Taney to Charles Howard, 17 Mar. 1856, Key Poems, MDHS.
10. Skinner letter to Editor of *Baltimore Patriot*, in *National Intelligencer*, 4 June 1849.
11. Roger Taney to Charles Howard, 17 Mar. 1856, Key Poems, MDHS.
12. Logs HMS *Surprize*, 8 Sept. 1814, WC.
13. Key to Randolph, 5 Oct. 1814, HP.
14. Ibid.
15. Skinner letter to Editor of *Baltimore Patriot*, in *National Intelligencer*, 4 June 1849.
16. Logs HMS *Albion*, 11 Sept. 1814, GCP.
17. James, *Naval History of Britain*, 6:320.
18. Logs HMS *Tonnant*, 12 Sept. 1814, WC.
19. Gleig, *Campaigns*, 91–93.
20. Logs HMS *Tonnant* and *Surprize*, 12 Sept. 1814, WC.
21. Editor *Baltimore Patriot* to Friend, *Salem Gazette*, 27 Sept. 1814.
22. "Reminiscences of the Bombardment of Fort McHenry," MDHS.
23. Minutes, 11 Sept. 1814, BCVS.
24. Anonymous letter, *National Intelligencer*, 14 Sept. 1814.
25. Phoebe Morris to Anthony Morris, 14 Sept. 1814, DHC.
26. Anonymous letter, *National Intelligencer*, 14 Sept. 1814.
27. David Winchester to James Winchester, 11 Sept. 1814, JWP.
28. Hawkins, *Life of John Hawkins*, 11.

29. John Hewes to Edward Hewes, 12 Sept. 1814, WC.
30. Newcomb to Rodgers, 18 Sept. 1814, RFP.
31. Cochrane to Ross, 12 Sept. 1814, ACP.
32. Cry and Hetzer invoice, 17 Apr. 1813, WC.
33. Stricker to Smith, 15 Sept. 1814, in *Niles' Weekly Register,* 24 Sept. 1814.
34. Phoebe Morris to Anthony Morris, 14 Sept. 1814, DHC; *Niles' Weekly Register,* 24 Sept. 1814; James Piper to Brantz Mayer, 17 Apr. 1854, WC.
35. Brooke, Diary, 181.
36. Gleig, *Campaigns,* 94.
37. Brooke, Diary, 181–82.
38. Hawkins, *Life of John Hawkins,* 9.
39. James Piper to Brantz Mayer, 17 Apr. 1854, WC.
40. Cockburn to Cochrane, 15 Sept. 1814, GCP.
41. Scharf, *History of Maryland,* 3:110 n. 2.
42. Quoted in James, *Naval History of Britain,* 6:318.
43. Ralfe, *Naval Biography of Britain,* 3:301.
44. James, *Naval History of Britain,* 6:318.
45. Skinner letter to Editor of *Baltimore Patriot,* in *National Intelligencer,* 4 June 1849.
46. Gleig, *Campaigns,* 95.
47. Skinner letter to Editor of *Baltimore Patriot,* in *National Intelligencer,* 4 June 1849.
48. Ross, "Ross of Bladensburg," 444.
49. *Dictionary of National Biography,* 17:275.
50. Skinner letter to Editor of *Baltimore Patriot,* in *National Intelligencer,* 4 June 1849.
51. Gleig, *Campaigns,* 96.
52. Skinner letter to Editor of *Baltimore Patriot,* in *National Intelligencer,* 4 June 1849.
53. Anonymous American released prisoner, letter to unnamed recipient, 21 Sept. 1814, in *Boston Yankee,* 30 Sept. 1814; Pulteney Malcolm to Mina Malcolm, 17 Sept. 1814, PMP.
54. Petition, First Baltimore Sharpshooters to City Council, typescript, 25 Mar. 1850, WC.
55. *Morning Post* (London), 6 Oct. 1814.
56. Cochrane to Croker, 17 Sept. 1814, ACP.
57. Gleig, *Campaigns,* 100.
58. Brooke to Bathurst, 17 Sept. 1814, in *Niles' Weekly Register,* 3 Dec. 1814.
59. Brooke, Diary, 182–83.
60. David Winchester to James Winchester, 18 Sept. 1814, JWP.
61. Scott, *Recollections,* 3:337.
62. Gleig, *Campaigns,* 99.

63. Stricker to Smith, 15 Sept. 1814, in *Niles' Weekly Register*, 24 Sept. 1814.
64. Brooke, Diary, 184.
65. David Winchester to James Winchester, 18 Sept. 1814, JWP.
66. Scott, *Recollections*, 3:339–40.
67. Brooke to Bathurst, 17 Sept. 1814, Brooke, Diary, 193.
68. Stricker to Smith, 15 Sept. 1814, in *Niles' Weekly Register*, 24 Sept. 1814.
69. James Piper to Brantz Mayer, 17 Apr. 1854, WC.
70. James Sandys to Charles Sandys, 2 Oct. 1814, ibid.
71. Gleig, *Campaigns*, 101.
72. George Prevost to Cochrane, 3 Aug. 1814, ACP.
73. Cochrane to Brooke, 12 Sept. 1814, ibid.
74. Cockburn to Cochrane, 15 Sept. 1814, GCP.
75. Gleig, *Campaigns*, 102.
76. Lydia Hollingsworth to Ruth Hollingsworth, 30 Sept. 1814, HL.
77. Logs HMS *Seahorse*, 13 Sept. 1814, FM.
78. Brooke to Bathurst, 17 Sept. 1814, in *Niles' Weekly Register*, 3 Dec. 1814.
79. Thomas Forman to Martha Forman, 14 Sept. 1814, WC.
80. Lydia Hollingsworth to Ruth Hollingsworth, 30 Sept. 1814, HL.

CHAPTER 16. BOMBS OVER BALTIMORE

1. Logs *Royal Oak*, 13 Sept. 1814, PMP.
2. Barrett, "Naval Recollections," Part 1, 462.
3. Newcomb to Rodgers, 18 Sept. 1814, RFP.
4. Editor of *Baltimore Patriot* to Friend, *Salem Gazette*, 27 Sept. 1814.
5. Barrett, "Naval Recollections," Part 1, 463.
6. "Attack upon Baltimore," *Niles' Weekly Register*, 24 Sept. 1814.
7. "Reminiscences of the Bombardment of Fort McHenry," MDHS.
8. Editor of *Baltimore Patriot* to Friend, *Salem Gazette*, 27 Sept. 1814.
9. James Piper to Brantz Mayer, 17 Apr. 1854, WC.
10. "A Sketch of the Life of Robert Field Stockton," ibid.
11. Treasury Auditor, 24 Jan. 1838, 1835 and 1838 Claims for Defense of Baltimore, Vertical File, War of 1812, MDHS; Brooke to Bathurst, 17 Sept. 1814, in *Niles' Weekly Register*, 3 Dec. 1814.
12. William Graham, 29 Sept. 1830, and John Barney, 18 Nov. 1830, Claims of State of Maryland Relating to War of 1812, Defense of Baltimore, Vessels Sunk in Harbor, RG 217, NA.

13. Beverly Diggs deposition, 9 Aug. 1832, ibid.
14. Severn Teackle to Phillip Wallis, 23 Sept. 1814, WC.
15. U.S. vs. Lt. William Sellman, 6 Oct. 1814, Court-Martial Case Files, 1809–94, RG 153, NA.
16. Anonymous letter from Baltimore, *Salem Gazette*, 27 Sept. 1814.
17. Ibid.
18. John Harris to William Harris, 27 Sept. 1814, WC.
19. Debbie Cochran to Ruth Tobin, 15 Sept. 1814, HL.
20. Phoebe Morris to Anthony Morris, 6 Sept. 1814, DHC.
21. Phoebe Morris to Anthony Morris, 14 Sept. 1814, ibid.
22. Ibid.
23. Grassi, Diary, 13 Sept. 1814, GUL.
24. "From Baltimore," *National Intelligencer*, 14 Sept. 1814.
25. Brooke, Diary, 185.
26. Scott, *Recollections*, 3:345.
27. Cochrane to Cockburn, 13 Sept. 1814, ACP.
28. Cochrane to Croker, 17 Sept. 1814, in *Niles' Weekly Register*, 3 Dec. 1814.
29. Cochrane to Croker, 20 June 1814, and Cochrane to Bathurst, 14 July 1814, War Office 1: Secretary at War, LC; Croker to Cochrane, 10 Aug. 1814, ACP.
30. Brooke, Diary, 186.
31. Scott, *Recollections*, 3:345.
32. Cochrane to Croker, 17 Sept. 1814, and Brooke to Bathurst, 17 Sept. 1814, both in *Niles' Weekly Register*, 3 Dec. 1814.
33. Brooke to Cochrane, 13 Sept. 1814, ACP.
34. John Webster to Brantz Mayer, 10 Aug. 1853, in *Baltimore Sun*, 23 Sept. 1928.
35. James, *Naval History of Britain*, 6:320; Severn Teackle to Phillip Wallis, 23 Sept. 1814, WC.
36. Skinner letter to Editor of *Baltimore Patriot*, in *National Intelligencer*, 4 June 1849.
37. Cochrane to Napier, 13 Sept. 1814, ACP.
38. James, *Naval History of Britain*, 6:320.
39. James Piper to Brantz Mayer, 17 Apr. 1854, WC; Newcomb to Rodgers, 18 Sept. 1814, RFP.
40. Severn Teackle to Phillip Wallis, 23 Sept. 1814, WC.
41. John Webster to Brantz Mayer, 22 July 1853, ibid.
42. John Webster to Brantz Mayer, 10 Aug. 1853, in *Baltimore Sun*, 23 Sept. 1928.
43. Newcomb to Rodgers, 18 Sept. 1814, RFP.
44. Anonymous letter from Baltimore, *Salem Gazette*, 27 Sept. 1814.

45. John Webster to Brantz Mayer, 22 July 1853, and Severn Teackle to Phillip Wallis, 23 Sept. 1814, WC.

46. U.S. vs. Lt. William Sellman, 6 Oct. 1814, Court-Martial Case Files, 1809–94, RG 153, NA.

47. Hawkins, *Life of John Hawkins*, 13.

48. Severn Teackle to Phillip Wallis, 23 Sept. 1814, WC.

49. John Webster to Brantz Mayer, 22 July 1853, ibid.

50. Armistead to Monroe, 24 Sept. 1814, in *Niles' Weekly Register*, 1 Oct. 1814.

51. *Boston Yankee*, 30 Sept. 1814.

52. Logs HMS *Volcano*, 14 Sept. 1814, FM.

53. Logs HMS *Erebus*, 14 Sept. 1814, ibid.

54. Barrett, "Naval Recollections," Part 1, 464.

55. Newcomb to Rodgers, 18 Sept. 1814, RFP.

56. Armistead to Monroe, 24 Sept. 1814, in *Niles' Weekly Register*, 1 Oct. 1814.

57. Hawkins, *Life of John Hawkins*, 14.

58. U.S. vs. Lt. Peter Hedges, 10 Nov. 1814, Court-Martial Case Files, 1809–94, RG 153, NA.

59. U.S. vs. Lt. Joshua Turner, 2 Oct. 1814, ibid.

60. Debbie Cochran to Ruth Tobin, 15 Sept. 1814, HL.

CHAPTER 17. THE BIRTH OF AN ANTHEM

1. Roger Taney to Charles Howard, 17 Mar. 1856, Key Poems, MDHS.

2. Ibid.

3. Smith to Monroe, 19 Sept. 1814, in *Niles' Weekly Register*, 24 Sept. 1814.

4. Cockburn to Cochrane, 15 Sept. 1814, GCP.

5. Gleig, *Campaigns*, 106.

6. Ibid., 106–7.

7. Smith to Monroe, 19 Sept. 1814, in *Niles' Weekly Register*, 24 Sept. 1814.

8. Logs HMS *Albion*, 17, 19 Sept. 1814, GCP; Barrett, "Naval Recollections," Part 1, 466.

9. Rodgers to Jones, 18 Sept. 1814, RFP (NHFC).

10. Order Book, 3rd Brigade Maryland Militia, 14 Sept. 1814, WC.

11. John Bell to Thomas Bell, 14 Nov. 1814, ibid.

12. Filby and Howard, *Star-Spangled Books*, 45.

13. Skinner letter to Editor of *Baltimore Patriot*, in *National Intelligencer*, 4 June 1849.

14. Roger Taney to Charles Howard, 17 Mar. 1856, Key Poems, MDHS.
15. Severn Teackle to Phillip Wallis, 23 Sept. 1814, WC.
16. "Reminiscences of the Bombardment of Fort McHenry," MDHS.
17. Skinner letter to Editor of *Baltimore Patriot*, in *National Intelligencer*, 4 June 1849.
18. William Jones to Eleanor Jones, 30 Sept. 1814, UCSC.
19. President Herbert Hoover approved 3 Mar. 1931.
20. Phoebe Morris to Anthony Morris, 15 Sept. 1814, DHC.
21. Order Book, 3rd Brigade Maryland Militia, 18 Sept. 1814, WC.
22. Phoebe Morris to Anthony Morris, 15 Sept. 1814, DHC.
23. Pulteney Malcolm to Mina Malcolm, 17 Sept. 1814, PMP.
24. Pulteney Malcolm to Nancy Malcolm, 1 Sept. 1814, ibid.
25. Pulteney Malcolm to Clementina Malcolm, 17 Sept. 1814, ibid.

EPILOGUE

1. Jennings, *Colored Man's Reminiscences*, 14.
2. *Annals of Congress*, 13th Cong., 3rd sess., 353–54, 392.
3. "Anticipated Meeting of Congress," *Federal Republican*, 20 Sept. 1814, and *National Intelligencer*, 9 Sept. 1814.
4. *Annals of Congress*, 13th Cong., 3rd sess., 316.
5. Ibid., 320.
6. Ibid., 391.
7. Ibid., 313.
8. Ibid., 354.
9. Ibid., 311, 389.
10. Ibid., 376, 395–96.
11. "The Seat of Government," *National Intelligencer*, 27 Sept. 1814.
12. *Memoirs of John Quincy Adams*, 3:126–27.
13. Editorial, *National Intelligencer*, 2 Feb. 1815.
14. *National Intelligencer*, 28, 31 Jan. 1815.
15. Gleig, *Campaigns*, 148.
16. Codrington to Wife, 16 Dec. 1814, in Bourchier, *Memoir of Codrington*, 1:331.
17. G. Guin to Cochrane, Havannah, 21 Jan. 1815, ACP.
18. Codrington to Wife, 23 Dec. 1814, in Bourchier, *Memoir of Codrington*, 1:332.
19. Lambert to Bathurst, 28 Jan. 1815, and Maj. C. Forrest journal entry, both in War Office 1: Secretary at War, LC; Cochrane to Croker, 18 Jan. 1815, in James, *Military Occurrences*, 2:551.

20. Gleig, *Campaigns*, 188.
21. Patterson to Navy Secretary, 29 Dec. 1814, in *National Intelligencer*, 14 Feb. 1815.
22. William Carroll to William Blount, 6 Mar. 1815, in *National Intelligencer*, 6 May 1815.
23. Jackson to Monroe, 29 Dec. 1814, in *Papers of Jackson*, 3:224.
24. Jackson to Monroe, 26, 27 Dec. 1814, in *National Intelligencer*, 30 Jan. 1815.
25. Gleig, *Campaigns*, 153; Codrington to Wife, 27 Dec. 1814, in Bourchier, *Memoir of Codrington*, 1:333.
26. John Johnson letter in Louisiana *Time Piece*, 30 Dec. 1814, in *National Intelligencer*, 4 Feb. 1815.
27. Jackson to Monroe, 26, 27 Dec. 1814, in *National Intelligencer*, 30 Jan. 1815.
28. Jackson to Monroe, 9 Jan. 1815, in James, *Military Occurrences*, 2:557.
29. Codrington to Wife, 2 Feb. 1815, in Bourchier, *Memoir of Codrington*, 1:339.
30. Henley to Patterson, 28 Dec. 1814, in *National Intelligencer*, 14 Feb. 1815.
31. Codrington to Wife, 27 Dec. 1814, in Bourchier, *Memoir of Codrington*, 1:333.
32. Codrington to Wife, 4 Jan. 1815, ibid., 334.
33. Lambert to Bathurst, 28 Jan. 1815, War Office 1: Secretary at War, LC.
34. Patterson to Navy Secretary, 13 Jan. 1815, in *National Intelligencer*, 14 Feb. 1815.
35. Lambert to Bathurst, 28 Jan. 1815, War Office 1: Secretary at War, LC.
36. Codrington to Wife, 9 Jan. 1815, in Bourchier, *Memoir of Codrington*, 1:337.
37. Gleig, *Campaigns*, 169.
38. Lambert to Bathurst, 10 Jan. 1815, War Office 1: Secretary at War, LC.
39. Gleig, *Campaigns*, 178–79; Anonymous letter, 12 Jan. 1815, in *National Intelligencer*, 6 Feb. 1815; Fred Stovin, n.d., in James, *Military Ocurrences*, 2:554–57.
40. Lambert to Bathurst, 10 Jan. 1815, War Office 1: Secretary at War, LC.
41. U.S. Adjutant General's Office, General Orders, 21 Jan. 1815, in *National Intelligencer*, 27 Feb. 1815.
42. Jackson to Citizens, 21 Jan. 1815, in *National Intelligencer*, 27 Feb. 1815.
43. Codrington to Wife, 28 Jan. 1815, in Bourchier, *Memoir of Codrington*, 1:339.
44. Anonymous letter, 12 Jan. 1815, in *National Intelligencer*, 6 Feb. 1815.
45. Jackson to Citizens, 21 Jan. 1815, in *National Intelligencer*, 27 Feb. 1815.
46. Anonymous letter, 12 Jan. 1815, in *National Intelligencer*, 6 Feb. 1815.
47. Jackson to Citizens, 21 Jan. 1815, in *National Intelligencer*, 27 Feb. 1815.
48. Maj. J. Mitchell, Return of Ordnance, 8 Jan. 1815, in James, *Military Occurrences*, 2:549.
49. Patterson to Navy Secretary, 13 Jan. 1815, in *National Intelligencer*, 14 Feb. 1815.
50. Orders, Adjutant General's Office, 9 Feb. 1815, in *National Intelligencer*, 13 Apr. 1815.

51. Patterson to Navy Secretary, 13 Jan. 1815, in *National Intelligencer,* 14 Feb. 1815.

52. Lambert to Bathurst, 10 Jan. 1815, War Office 1: Secretary at War, LC.

53. Anonymous letter, 13 Jan. 1815, in *National Intelligencer,* 6 Feb. 1815.

54. Adj. Gen. Robert Butler, Report, "Action on Both Sides the River 8 Jan. 1815," *National Intelligencer,* 13 Feb. 1815. Total American casualties that day, including a sortie after the main clash and statistics from action on the west bank, amounted to 13 killed, 19 missing, and 39 wounded.

55. Deputy Adj. Gen. Lt. Col. Fred Stovin, "Return of Casualties on 8 Jan. 1815," n.d., in James, *Military Occurrences,* 2:554–57.

56. Jackson to Monroe, 13 Jan. 1815, in *National Intelligencer,* 6 Feb. 1815.

57. Jackson to Lambert, 8 Jan. 1815, in *Papers of Jackson,* 3:236.

58. Jackson to David Holmes, 18 Jan. 1815, ibid., 249.

59. Codrington to Wife, 9 Jan. 1815, in Bourchier, *Memoir of Codrington,* 1:183.

60. Codrington to Wife, 11 Jan. 1815, ibid., 337.

61. Patterson to Navy Secretary, 20 Jan. 1815, in *National Intelligencer,* 14 Feb. 1815.

62. Codrington to Wife, 11 Jan. 1815, in Bourchier, *Memoir of Codrington,* 1:338.

63. Cochrane to Croker, 18 Jan. 1815, in James, *Military Occurrences,* 2:553.

64. Jackson to Monroe, 19 Jan. 1815, in *Papers of Jackson,* 3:250.

65. Jackson to Monroe, 19 Jan. 1815, in *National Intelligencer,* 13 Feb. 1815.

66. Jackson to James Winchester, 31 Jan. 1815, in *Papers of Jackson,* 3:262.

67. *National Intelligencer,* 22 Feb. 1815.

68. *Annals of Congress,* 13th Cong., 3rd sess., 1409–15.

69. Editorial, *National Intelligencer,* 10 May 1815.

70. *Journal of the Executive Proceedings of the Senate,* 2:620.

71. *Biographical Directory of the American Congress, 1774–1989.* Bicentennial Edition. Senate Document No. 100-34 (Washington, D.C.: Government Printing Office, 1989), 84.

72. Jennings, *Colored Man's Reminiscences,* 15–16.

73. Mayor Blake proclamation, *National Intelligencer,* 20 Feb. 1815.

Selected Bibliography

MANUSCRIPTS

Alexandria Library, Special Collections, Alexandria, Va.
  Sayrs, Matilda Roberts, "Reminiscences" (ca. 1892), typescript, Eleanor Lee
  Templeman Manuscript Collection, Sayrs Family
District of Columbia Public Library, Washingtoniana Division, Washington, D.C.
  Rimensnyder, Nelson. "Rhodes Tavern and the History of the Planning, Devel-
  opment, and Institutions of the Nation's Capital, 1799–1981." Paper presented
  at annual Washington, D.C., history conference, 2 Feb. 1982
  Squares 1–816, Real Estate Assessment and Related Plats, Maps, and Directo-
  ries for Washington, D.C., to 1934, in Real Estate Directory
Duke University, Special Collections Library, Durham, N.C.
  Brown, Thomas, "An Account of the Lineage of the Brown Family," Ambler-
  Brown Family Papers, 1936, typescript, vol. 2
Dumbarton House Collection, Headquarters of The National Society of The Colo-
  nial Dames of America, Washington, D.C.
Fort McHenry National Monument and Historic Shrine, Baltimore
  Logs HMS *Tonnant, Erebus, Seahorse, Volcano, Surprize*
Franklin Delano Roosevelt Library, Hyde Park, N.Y.
  Roosevelt (Franklin Delano) Papers
Gelman Library, Special Collections, George Washington University, Washington,
  D.C.
  Individual Manuscripts Collection
  Ross (Robert) Collection
  Wright (W. Lloyd) Collection

Georgetown University Library, Special Collections, Washington, D.C.
    Grassi (Father Giovanni) Diary (1814), in Catholic Historical Manuscript Collection
    McElroy, Rev. John, S.J., "Recollections," in Maryland Province Archives
    McElroy (Rev. John, S.J.) Papers, Diary (1813–21)
Historical Society of Pennsylvania, Philadelphia
    Clarke Smith (Uselma) Collection, 1378A
        Jones (William) Correspondence
        Jones (William) and Loxley (Benjamin) Papers
    Dreer Collection
    Rush (Richard) Letters, AM13520
Historical Society of Washington, D.C.
    Cook (Lewis D.) Research Collection, 1931, MS 253
    Thruston (Buckner) Diary, 1810–1843, MS 251
The History Factory, Chantilly, Va.
    D.C. Land Records
    Minute Book, Bank of the Metropolis
Library of Congress, Manuscripts Division, Washington, D.C.
    Carroll (Daniel) Papers
    Cochrane (Sir Alexander) Papers
    Cockburn (Sir George) Papers
    Foreign Affairs, Political Correspondence Paris–United States
    Machen (Lewis) Papers
    Madison (Dolley) Papers
    Madison (James) Papers
    Rives (William) Papers
    Rodgers Family Papers
        Naval Historical Foundation Collection
    Rush (Richard) Papers
    Shiner (Michael) Diary
    Smith (Margaret Bayard) Papers
    Smith (Samuel) Papers
    Thornton (Anna Maria) Diaries
    Thornton (William) Papers
    War Office 1: Secretary at War, in-letters, vols. 141–42
Marine Corps History and Museums Division, Personal Papers Collection, Washington, D.C.
    Miller (Samuel) Papers, including List of Marines at Bladensburg
Maryland Historical Society Library, Baltimore

Beall (Thomas) Account Book, MS 112

Forman (Mrs. M. B.) Diary, typescript, MS 1779

Hollingsworth Letters, 1802–1837, MS 1849

Howard Papers, MS 469

Key (Francis Scott) Poems (includes letter, Roger Taney to Charles Howard, 17 Mar. 1856), MS 511

"Reminiscences of the Bombardment of Fort McHenry 'The Star Fort' in Sept. 1814," narrated by Col. M. I. Cohen, and handwritten by Benjamin Cohen, 21 Nov. 1897, Mendes Cohen Letters, MS 251.3

Vertical File, War of 1812

War of 1812 Collection, MS 1846

Massachusetts Historical Society, Boston

Norton, Richard C., Journal, 1811–21, in Jacob Norton Papers

Pickering Papers

National Archives, Washington, D.C.

Record Group 21, District Courts of the United States

Record Group 42, Offices of Public Buildings and Public Parks of the National Capital

Record Group 45, Office of Naval Records and Library

Record Group 107, Office of the Secretary of War

Record Group 153, Office of the Judge Advocate General (Army)

Record Group 156, Office of the Chief of Ordnance

Record Group 217, Accounting Officers of the Department of the Treasury

Record Group 233, U.S. House of Representatives

National Library of Scotland, Edinburgh

Plan of the Island of Tangier in Chesapeake Bay, ca. 1812, MS 2608, Alexander Cochrane Papers

New York Historical Society, New York, N.Y.

Hunter (Mary S.), Miscellaneous Manuscripts

Nottinghamshire Archives Office, Nottingham, England

Pvt. William Kirke to Charles Kirke, 13 Nov. 1814, DD.MM43

Tennessee Historical Society Collection, Tennessee State Library and Archives, Nashville

Winchester (James) Papers

Ulster-American Folk Park, Omagh, Northern Ireland

Brooke (Col. Arthur) Diary, D3004/D/2

University of Virginia Library, Special Collections Department, Charlottesville

Key-Cutts-Turner Family Papers

Nourse Family Papers (#3490-A)

U.S. Senate Collection, U.S. Senate Curator's Office, Washington, D.C.
    Isaac Bassett Papers
William L. Clements Library, Manuscripts Division, University of Michigan
    Malcolm (Pulteney) Papers

NEWSPAPERS

Aberdeen Journal (Scotland)
Alexandria Gazette
Baltimore Patriot
Baltimore Sun
Boston Yankee
Federal Republican and Commercial Gazette (Georgetown)
Frederick-Town (Md.) *Herald*
Morning Post (London)
National Intelligencer (Washington, D.C.)
New York Herald
Niles' Weekly Register (Baltimore)
Poulson's Paper (Philadelphia)
Salem (Mass.) *Gazette*
Times (London)
Washington Evening Star

BOOKS, ARTICLES, AND DISSERTATIONS

Adams, Abigail. *Letters of Mrs. Adams, the Wife of John Adams.* Ed. Charles Francis Adams. Boston: Little & Brown, 1840.
Adams, Henry. *History of the United States of America during the Administrations of James Madison.* New York: Scribner, 1891.
Adams, John Quincy. *Memoirs of John Quincy Adams.* Ed. Charles Francis Adams. Vol. 3. Philadelphia: Lippincott, 1874.
Allen, William C. *The United States Capitol: A Brief Architectural History.* Washington, D.C.: Government Printing Office, 1990.
America Visited. Arranged by Edith I. Coombs. New York: The Book League of America, n.d.

American State Papers: Class 5, Military Affairs. Serial 16, vol. 1. Washington, D.C.: Gales & Season, 1832.

American State Papers: Class 10, Miscellaneous. Serial 38, vol. 2. Washington, D.C.: Gales & Season, 1834.

Ames, William E. *A History of the "National Intelligencer."* Chapel Hill: University of North Carolina Press, 1972.

Anderson, Ellen. *Salona, Fairfax County, Virginia.* Fairfax: Fairfax County Office of Comprehensive Planning, 1979.

Annals of the Congress of the United States, 1789–1824: Debates and Proceedings in the Congress of the United States. 42 vols. Washington, D.C.: Gales & Seaton, 1834–56.

Anthony, Katharine. *Dolly Madison: Her Life and Times.* New York: Doubleday, 1949.

Architect of the Capitol. *Compilation of Works of Art and Other Objects in the United States Capitol.* Washington, D.C.: Government Printing Office, 1965.

Arnett, Ethel Stephens. *Mrs. James Madison: The Incomparable Dolley.* Greensboro, N.C.: Piedmont Press, 1972.

Ball, Charles. *Slavery in the United States: A Narrative of the Life and Adventures of Charles Ball, a Black Man.* 1836. Reprint, Detroit, Mich.: Negro History Press, 1970.

Barney, Mary, ed. *A Biographical Memoir of the Late Commodore Joshua Barney.* Boston: Gray & Bowen, 1832.

[Barrett, Robert J.]. "Naval Recollections of the Late American War." *United Service Journal and Naval and Military Magazine,* Part 1 (April 1841): 455–67; Part 2 (May 1841): 13–23.

Bourchier, Lady, ed. *Memoir of the Life of Admiral Sir Edward Codrington.* 2 vols. London: Longmans, Green, 1873.

Brant, Irving. *James Madison, Commander in Chief, 1812–1836.* New York: Bobbs-Merrill, 1961.

Brown, Glenn. *History of the United States Capitol.* New York: Da Capo Press, 1970.

Brown, Jack D., et al. *Charles County Maryland: A History.* Hackensack, N.J.: Charles County Bicentennial Committee, Custombook, Inc., 1976.

Bryan, Wilhelmus Bogart. *A History of the National Capital.* Vol. 1 (1790–1814). New York: Macmillan, 1914.

Buchan, John. *The History of the Royal Scots Fusiliers, 1678–1918.* London: Nelson & Sons, 1925.

Buonaparte's Voyage to St. Helena; Comprising the Diary of Rear Admiral Sir George Cockburn. Boston: Lilly, Wait, Colman, & Holden, 1833.

Burnett, T. A. J. *The Rise and Fall of a Regency Dandy: The Life and Times of Scrope Berdmore Davies.* London: Murray, 1981.

Burrows, John W. *The Essex Regiment—1st Battalion (44th).* Southend-on-Sea: Published by arrangement with the Essex Territorial Army Association, Burrows & Sons, 1923.

Busey, Dr. Samuel C. *Personal Reminiscences and Recollections of Forty-Six Years' Membership in the Medical Society of the District of Columbia.* Washington, D.C.: Dornan, 1895.

Calvert, George H. *Autobiographic Study.* Boston: Lee & Shepard, n.d.

Carey, Mathew. *The Olive Branch: Or, Faults on Both Sides, Federal and Democratic.* 10th ed. 1818. Reprint, Freeport, N.Y.: Books for Libraries Press, 1969.

Cassell, Frank A. "The Great Baltimore Riot of 1812." *Maryland Historical Magazine* 70 (Fall 1975): 241–59.

Castiello, Kathleen Raben. "The Italian Sculptors of the United States Capitol: 1806–1834." Ph.D. diss., University of Michigan, 1975.

Clark, Allen C. *Greenleaf and Law in the Federal City.* Washington, D.C.: Roberts, 1901.

———. "James Heighe Blake, the Third Mayor of the Corporation of Washington, 1813–17." *Records of the Columbia Historical Society* 24 (1922): 136–63.

———. *Life and Letters of Dolly Madison.* Washington, D.C.: Roberts, 1914.

Coffin, William F. *1812; The War and Its Moral: A Canadian Chronicle.* Montreal: Lovell, 1864.

Compilation of the Messages and Papers of the Presidents, Prepared under the Direction of the Joint Committee on Printing, of the House and Senate. Vol. 2. New York: Bureau of National Literature, 1897.

Curtis, George Ticknor. *Life of James Buchanan, Fifteenth President of the United States.* Vol. 1. 1883. Reprint, Freeport, N.Y.: Books for Libraries Press, 1969.

Dictionary of American Biography. Vol. 9. New York: Scribner, 1935.

Dictionary of National Biography. Vol. 17. New York: Oxford University Press, 1921–22.

Documentary History of the Construction and Development of the United States Capitol Building and Grounds. Washington, D.C.: Government Printing Office, 1904.

Dutton, Charles J. *Oliver Hazard Perry.* New York: Longmans, Green, 1935.

Dyer, Oliver. *Great Senators of the United States Forty Years Ago.* New York: Bonner's Sons, 1889.

The 1812 Catalogue of the Library of Congress. Facsimile edition with an introduction by Robert A. Rutland. Washington, D.C.: Library of Congress, 1982.

Elting, Col. John R., ed. *Military Uniforms in America.* Vol. 2, *Years of Growth, 1796–1851.* San Rafael, Calif.: Presidio Press, 1977.

Ewell, James. *Planter's and Mariner's Medical Companion.* 3rd ed. Philadelphia: Anderson & Meehan, 1816.

Extract from a Diary of Rear-Admiral Sir George Cockburn with Particular Reference to Gen. Napoleon Buonaparte. London: Simpkin, Marshall, & Co., 1888.

Fearon, Henry Bradshaw. *Sketches of America: A Narrative of a Journey of Five Thousand Miles through the Eastern and Western States of America.* London: Longman, Hurst, Rees, Orme, & Brown, 1818.

Filby, P. W., and Edward G. Howard, comps. *Star-Spangled Books.* Baltimore: Maryland Historical Society, 1972.

Frary, I. T. *They Built the Capitol.* Richmond: Garrett & Massie, 1940.

Gerry, Elbridge, Jr. *The Diary of Elbridge Gerry, Jr.* New York: Brentano's, 1927.

Gerson, Noel B. *Light-Horse Harry: A Biography of Washington's Great Cavalryman, General Henry Lee.* New York: Doubleday, 1966.

Gleig, George Robert. *The Campaigns of the British Army at Washington and New Orleans.* 1847. Reprint, Totowa, N.J.: Rowman & Littlefield, 1972.

[Gleig, George Robert]. *A Subaltern in America: Comprising His Narrative of the Campaigns of the British Army at Baltimore, Washington, etc., during the Late War.* Baltimore: Carey, Hart, 1833.

Graves, Donald E. *Sir William Congreve and the Rocket's Red Glare.* Alexandria Bay, N.Y.: Museum Restoration Service, 1989.

Green, Constance Mclaughlin. *The Secret City: A History of Race Relations in the Nation's Capital.* Princeton, N.J.: Princeton University Press, 1967.

[Gubbins, R. R.]. *The 85th King's Light Infantry.* Ed. C. R. B. Barrett. London: Spottiswoode, 1913.

Hackett, F. W. "Capt. Thomas Tingey USN." Reprinted from *Proceedings of the U S Naval Institute* 33, no. 1 (1907): Whole No. 21.

Hamilton, Thomas. *Men and Manners in America.* 1833. Reprint, New York: Russell & Russell, 1968.

Hawkins, Rev. William. *Life of John H. W. Hawkins.* Boston: Dutton, 1863.

Hazelton, George C. *The National Capitol: Its Architecture, Art, and History.* New York: Taylor, 1902.

Hildt, John C. "Letters Relating to the Capture of Washington." *South Atlantic Quarterly* 6 (1907): 58–66.

Hines, Christian. *Early Recollections of Washington City.* 1866. Washington, D.C.: From the collection of the Columbia Historical Society, reprinted by the Junior League of Washington, 1981.

Historical Record of the Fourth, or the King's Own, Regiment of Foot. London: Longman, Orme, 1839.

Ingersoll, Charles, J. *Historical Sketch of the Second War between the United States of America and Great Britain.* Vol. 2. Philadelphia: Lea & Blanchard, 1849.

Jackson, Andrew. *The Papers of Andrew Jackson.* Ed. Harold Moser et al. Vol. 3. Knoxville: University of Tennessee Press, 1991.

James, William. *A Full and Correct Account of the Military Occurrences of the Late War between Great Britain and the United States of America.* Vol. 2. London: Black, Kingsbury, Parbury, & Allen, 1818.

———. *The Naval History of Great Britain.* Vols. 5–6. London: Bentley & Son, 1886.

Janson, Charles William. *The Stranger in America, 1793–1806.* 1807. Reprinted with introduction and notes by Dr. Carl S. Driver, New York: The Press of the Pioneers, 1935.

Jefferson, Thomas. *The Works of Thomas Jefferson.* Ed. Paul Leicester Ford. Vol. 9. New York: Putnam, 1905.

Jennings, Paul. *A Colored Man's Reminiscences of James Madison.* Brooklyn: Beadle, 1865.

Journal of the Executive Proceedings of the Senate. Vol. 2. Washington, D.C.: Duff Green, 1828.

Kimball, Marie G. "The Original Furnishings of the White House." *Antiques* 15 (June 1929): 481–86; 16 (July 1929): 33–37.

Klapthor, Margaret Brown. "Benjamin Latrobe and Dolley Madison Decorate the White House, 1809–1811." *Contributions from the Museum of History and Technology,* paper 49 (1966): 153–64.

Lamb, Martha J., ed. "Burning of Washington, 1814." *Magazine of American History* 27 (Jan.–June 1892): 465–68.

Latrobe, Benjamin Henry. *The Correspondence and Miscellaneous Papers of Benjamin Henry Latrobe.* Ed. John C. Van Horne. Vols. 2–3. New Haven: Yale University Press, 1986, 1988.

Lee, Cazenove Gardner, Jr. *Lee Chronicle: Studies of the Early Generations of the Lees of Virginia.* Ed. Dorothy Mills Parker. New York: New York University Press, 1957.

Lee, Gen. Henry. *Correct Account of the Conduct of the Baltimore Mob.* Winchester, Va.: CB, 1814.

Lee, Robert E., ed. *Memoirs of the War in the Southern Department of the United States.* New York: University Publishing, 1869.

Lord, Walter. *The Dawn's Early Light.* New York: Norton, 1972.

Lossing, Benson J. *The Pictorial Fieldbook of the War of 1812.* 1868. Reprint, Somersworth, N.H.: New Hampshire Publishing, 1976.

Machen, Arthur W., Jr., comp. *Letters of Arthur W. Machen with Biographical Sketch.* Baltimore: privately printed, 1917.

Madison, Dolley. *Memoirs and Letters of Dolly Madison.* Ed. Lucia Beverly Cutts. 1886. Reprint, Port Washington, N.Y.: Kennikat Press, 1971.

Madison, James. *The Writings of James Madison.* Ed. Gaillard Hunt. Vol. 8. New York: Putnam, 1908.

Marine, William M. *The British Invasion of Maryland, 1812–15.* Facsimile reprint of 1913 edition by Society of the War of 1812 in Maryland. Hatboro, Pa.: Tradition Press, 1965.

Martineau, Gilbert. *Napoleon's St. Helena.* Chicago: Rand McNally, 1968, translated from the French original, *La Vie Quotidienne à Sainte-Hélène au temps de Napoléon.* Paris: Librairie Hachette, 1966.

McClane, Allen. "Journal of the Campaign." In *Notices of the War of 1812* by John Armstrong, 2:232–36. New York: Wiley & Putnam, 1840.

McCormick, John H. "The First Master of Ceremonies of the White House." *Records of the Columbia Historical Society* 7 (1904): 170–94.

Mecklenburg, Marion F., and Justine S. Wimsatt. "The White House Full Length Portrait of George Washington by Gilbert Stuart, Conservation Treatment Report and Commentary." Kensington: Washington Conservation Studio, 1978.

"Memoir of Major-General Robert Ross." *United Service Journal and Naval and Military Magazine,* Part 1 (1829): 412–16.

Metcalf, Frank, J., and George H. Martin. *Marriages and Deaths, 1800–1820, from the "National Intelligencer," Washington, D.C.* Washington, D.C.: National Genealogical Society, 1968.

Monroe, James. *The Writings of James Monroe.* Ed. Stanislaus Murray Hamilton. Vol. 5. New York: Putnam, 1901.

Moore, Virginia Campbell. "Reminiscences of Washington as Recalled by a Descendant of the Ingle Family." *Records of the Columbia Historical Society* 3 (1900): 96–114.

Napier, Maj. Gen. Elers. *The Life and Correspondence of Admiral Sir Charles Napier, from Personal Recollections, Letters, and Official Documents.* Vol. 1. London: Hurst & Blackett, 1862.

A Narrative of the Battle of Bladensburg; In a letter to Henry Banning by an Officer of Gen. Smith's Staff. N.p., 1814.

The National Metropolitan Bank, 1814–1914, Washington, D.C. Washington, D.C.: Roberts, 1914.

Pack, James. *The Man Who Burned the White House: Admiral Sir George Cockburn, 1772–1853.* Annapolis, Md.: Naval Institute Press, 1987.

Parr, Marilyn Kay. "Augustus John Foster and the 'Washington Wilderness': Personal Letters of a British Diplomat." Ph.D. diss., George Washington University, 1987.

Paullin, Charles Oscar. *Commodore John Rodgers, Captain, Commodore, and Senior Officer of the American Navy, 1773–1838: A Biography.* Cleveland: Clark, 1910.

Peck, Taylor. *Round-Shot to Rockets: A History of the Washington Navy Yard and U.S. Naval Gun Factory.* Annapolis, Md.: Naval Institute, 1949.

Pitch, Anthony S. *Congressional Chronicles: Amusing and Amazing Anecdotes of the U.S. Congress and Its Members.* Potomac, Md.: Mino Publications, 1990.

Porter, Adm. David. *Memoir of Commodore David Porter.* Albany, N.Y.: Munsell, 1875.

Ralfe, James. *The Naval Biography of Great Britain.* Vol. 3. Boston: Gregg Press, 1972.

Report of the Commission on the Renovation of the Executive Mansion. Washington, D.C., 1952.

Report of the Committee of Grievances and Courts of Justice, House of Delegates, Maryland, on the Subject of the Recent Mobs and Riots in the City of Baltimore. Annapolis, Md.: n.p., 1813.

Rhees, William Jones, ed. *The Smithsonian Institution: Documents Relative to Its Origin and History.* Vol. 1. Washington, D.C.: Government Printing Office, 1901.

Robertson, Ignatius Loyola. *Sketches of Public Characters Drawn from the Living and the Dead.* New York: Bliss, 1830.

Robinson, Ralph. "New Light on Three Episodes of the British Invasion of Maryland in 1814." *Maryland Historical Magazine* 37 (September 1942): 273–90.

Roosevelt, Theodore. *The Naval War of 1812.* 1882. Reprint, Annapolis, Md.: Naval Institute Press, 1987.

Ross, Sir John, Baronet. "Ross of Bladensburg." *National Review* (London), May 1929, 443–50.

Royster, Charles. *Light-Horse Harry Lee and the Legacy of the American Revolution.* New York: Knopf, 1981.

Scharf, J. Thomas. *History of Maryland.* Vol. 3. Facsimile reprint of 1879 edition. Hatboro, Pa.: Tradition Press, 1967.

Schurz, Carl. *Life of Henry Clay.* 4th ed. Vol. 1. Boston: Houghton, Mifflin, 1888.

Scott, Capt. James. *Recollections of a Naval Life.* Vol. 3. London: Bentley, 1834.

Seale, William. *The President's House: A History.* Vol. 1. Washington, D.C.: White House Historical Association, 1986.

Seaton, Josephine. *William Winston Seaton of the "National Intelligencer."* 1871. Reprint, N.p.: Arno and *New York Times,* 1970.

The Senate Chamber, 1810–1859. Washington, D.C.: U.S. Senate Commission on Art and Antiquities, 1990.

Sheads, Scott S. *The Rockets' Red Glare: The Maritime Defense of Baltimore in 1814.* Centreville, Md.: Tidewater, 1986.

Shomette, Donald G. *Shipwrecks on the Chesapeake: Maritime Disasters on Chesapeake Bay and Its Tributaries, 1608–1978.* Centreville, Md.: Tidewater, 1982.

Smith, Sir Harry. *The Autobiography of Lt.-Gen. Sir Harry Smith.* London: Murray, 1903.

Smith, John Cotton. *The Correspondence and Miscellanies of the Hon. John Cotton Smith.* New York: Harper & Brothers, 1847.

"Some Unknown Foreigner." *Inchiquin, The Jesuit's Letters.* New York: Riley, 1810.

Steadman, Melvin Lee, Jr. *Falls Church by Fence and Fireside.* Falls Church, Va.: Falls Church Public Library, 1964.

Tayloe, Benjamin Ogle. *Our Neighbors on Lafayette Square.* 1872. Reprint, Washington, D.C.: Junior League of Washington, 1982.

Transactions and Proceedings of the 75th Anniversary of the Medical Society of the District of Columbia, Feb. 16, 1894. Washington, D.C.: Darby, 1894.

Tuckerman, Henry T. *The Life of John Pendleton Kennedy.* New York: Putnam, 1871.

Varnum, Joseph B. *Washington Sketch Book.* New York: Mohun, Ebbs, & Hough, 1864.

Wallace, Adam. *The Parson of the Islands: A Biography of the Rev. Joshua Thomas.* 1861. Reprint, Centreville, Md.: Tidewater, 1961.

Warden, D. B. *A Chorographical and Statistical Description of the District of Columbia.* Paris: Smith, 1816.

Washington, George. *The Writings of George Washington from the Original Manuscript Sources, 1745–1799.* Vols. 11, 35, 36. Washington, D.C.: Government Printing Office, 1934, 1940, 1941.

Watson, Winslow M. *In Memoriam: Benjamin Ogle Tayloe.* Philadelphia: Sherman, 1872.

Weller, M. I. "Unwelcome Visitors to Early Washington." *Records of the Columbia Historical Society* 1 (1897): 55–88.

Wharton, Anne Hollingsworth. *Social Life in the Early Republic.* 1902. Reissued, New York: Bloom, 1969.

White, Patrick C. T. *A Nation on Trial: America and the War of 1812.* New York: Wiley, 1965.

Williams, John S. *History of the Invasion and Capture of Washington and All the Events Which Preceded and Followed.* New York: Harper & Bros., 1857.

Wise, Henry A. *Seven Decades of the Union: The Humanities and Materialism, Illustrated by a Memoir of John Tyler, with Reminiscences of Some of His Great Contemporaries.* Philadelphia: Lippincott, 1881.

Wright, Sister Catherine. *Port O'Bladensburg: A Brief History of a 1742 Town.* Bladensburg, Md.: Town of Bladensburg Bicentennial Committee, 1977.

Index

About the Author

Anthony S. Pitch is the author of a number of books ranging from a biography to travel guides to anecdotes about Congress. His most recent book, *Chained Eagle*—a biography of the longest-held American prisoner of war in North Vietnam—was a main selection of the Military Book Club.

A former journalist in England, Africa, and Israel, Pitch was also Associated Press broadcast editor for Pennsylvania and a senior writer in the books division of *U.S. News and World Report* in Washington, D.C.

In addition to writing, he gives anecdotal history tours for, among others, the Smithsonian Institution Resident Associates, who invited him to design a tour based upon the manuscript of *The Burning of Washington: The British Invasion of 1814.*

Pitch lives in Potomac, Maryland, with his wife and their son and daughter.

The Naval Institute Press is the book-publishing arm of the U.S. Naval Institute, a private, nonprofit, membership society for sea service professionals and others who share an interest in naval and maritime affairs. Established in 1873 at the U.S. Naval Academy in Annapolis, Maryland, where its offices remain today, the Naval Institute has members worldwide.

Members of the Naval Institute support the education programs of the society and receive the influential monthly magazine *Proceedings* and discounts on fine nautical prints and on ship and aircraft photos. They also have access to the transcripts of the Institute's Oral History Program and get discounted admission to any of the Institute-sponsored seminars offered around the country.

The Naval Institute also publishes *Naval History* magazine. This colorful bimonthly is filled with entertaining and thought-provoking articles, first-person reminiscences, and dramatic art and photography. Members receive a discount on *Naval History* subscriptions.

The Naval Institute's book-publishing program, begun in 1898 with basic guides to naval practices, has broadened its scope in recent years to include books of more general interest. Now the Naval Institute Press publishes about one hundred titles each year, ranging from how-to books on boating and navigation to battle histories, biographies, ship and aircraft guides, and novels. Institute members receive discounts of 20 to 50 percent on the Press's more than eight hundred books in print.

Full-time students are eligible for special half-price membership rates. Life memberships are also available.

For a free catalog describing Naval Institute Press books currently available, and for further information about subscribing to *Naval History* magazine or about joining the U.S. Naval Institute, please write to:

Membership Department
U.S. Naval Institute
291 Wood Road
Annapolis, MD 21402-5034
Telephone: (800) 233-8764
Fax: (410) 269-7940
Web address: www.usni.org